Lecture Notes in Computer Science 3208

Commenced Publication in 1973
Founding and Former Series Editors:
Gerhard Goos, Juris Hartmanis, and Jan van Leeuwen

Hans Jürgen Ohlbach
Sebastian Schaffert (Eds.)

Principles and Practice of Semantic Web Reasoning

Second International Workshop, PPSWR 2004
St. Malo, France, September 6-10, 2004
Proceedings

 Springer

Volume Editors

Hans Jürgen Ohlbach
Sebastian Schaffert
Ludwig-Maximilians-Universität
Institut für Informatik
Oettingenstr. 67, 80538 München, Germany
E-mail: {ohlbach, schaffer}@pms.ifi.lmu.de

Library of Congress Control Number: 2004110896

CR Subject Classification (1998): H.4, H.3, I.2, F.4.1, D.2

ISSN 0302-9743
ISBN 3-540-22961-2 Springer Berlin Heidelberg New York

Springer is a part of Springer Science+Business Media

springeronline.com

© Springer-Verlag Berlin Heidelberg 2004
Printed in Germany

Typesetting: Camera-ready by author, data conversion by Scientific Publishing Services, Chennai, India
Printed on acid-free paper   SPIN: 11317241   06/3142   5 4 3 2 1 0

Preface

The best informal definition of the Semantic Web is maybe found in the May 2001 Scientific American article "The Semantic Web" (Berners-Lee et al.), which says "The Semantic Web is an extension of the current Web in which information is given well-defined meaning, better enabling computers and people to work in cooperation." People who work on the Semantic Web quite often base their work on the famous "semantic web tower", a product of Tim Berners-Lee's inspiring drawing on whiteboards. The lowest level is the level of character representation (Unicode) and the identification of resources on the Web (URIs). The highest level concerns the problem of trusting information on the Web. Somewhere in the middle of the tower is the logic level. It addresses the problem of representing information on the Web in a way so that inference rules can derive implicit information from explicitly stated information. The workshop "Principles and Practices of Semantic Web Reasoning" (PPSWR 2004) addressed problems on this level. It took place in September 2004 as a satellite event of the 20th International Conference on Logic Programming (ICLP) in St. Malo, France. After PPSWR 2003 in Mumbai, India, it was the second workshop in this series.

This book contains the articles presented at the workshop. The 11 papers were selected from 19 submissions by the program committee which consisted of

- François Bry, University of Munich, Germany
- François Fages, INRIA Rocquencourt, France
- Enrico Franconi, Free University of Bozen-Bolzano, Italy
- Georg Gottlob, University of Vienna, Austria
- Benjamin Grosof, MIT Sloan School of Management, USA
- Carsten Lutz, Dresden University of Technology, Germany
- Nicola Henze, University of Hannover, Germany
- Massimo Marchiori, W3C and University of Venice, Italy
- Hans Jürgen Ohlbach, University of Munich, Germany
- Sebastian Schaffert, University of Munich, Germany
- Michael Schröder, Dresden University of Technology, Germany
- Gerd Wagner, Eindhoven University of Technology, Netherlands
- Howard Williams, Heriot-Watt University, Edinburgh, UK
- Guizhen Yang, University at Buffalo, New York, USA

The main topics that were discussed in the workshop are:

- structures in XML documents:
  in the paper: *'On Subtyping of Tree-Structured Data – A Polynomial Approach'* by François Bry, Włodzimierz Drabent, and Jan Małuszyński;
- querying and updating XML documents:
  in the papers: *'Towards Generic Query, Update, and Event Languages for the Semantic Web'* by Wolfgang May, José Júlio Alferes, François Bry, and *'Data Retrieval and Evolution on the (Semantic) Web: A Deductive Approach'* by François Bry, Tim Furche, Paula-Lavinia Pătrânjan, and Sebastian Schaffert;

- invoking ontologies into the querying process:
  in the papers: *'Rules and Queries with Ontologies: A Unified Logical Framework'* by Enrico Franconi and Sergio Tessaris, *'Semantic Web Reasoning for Ontology-Based Integration of Resources'* by Liviu Badea, Doina Tilivea, and Anca Hotaran, and *'Static Typechecking of Datalog with Ontologies'* by Jakob Henriksson and Jan Małuszyński;
- manipulating and invoking temporal notions:
  in the papers: *'Reasoning About Temporal Context Using Ontology and Abductive Constraint Logic Programming'* by Hongwei Zhu, Stuart E. Madnick, and Michael D. Siegel, *'Towards a Multi-calendar Temporal Type System for (Semantic) Web Query Languages'* by François Bry and Stephanie Spranger, and *'Calendrical Calculations with Time Partitionings and Fuzzy Time Intervals'* by Hans Jürgen Ohlbach;
- non-monotonic reasoning:
  in the paper: *'DR-DEVICE: A Defeasible Logic System for the Semantic Web'* by Nick Bassiliades, Grigoris Antoniou, and Ioannis Vlahavas;
- Web services:
  in the paper: *'A PDDL Based Tool for Automatic Web Service Composition'* by Joachim Peer.

The PPSWR workshop was supported by the EU Network of Excellence CoLogNet (http://www.colognet.net) and the new EU Network of Excellence REWERSE (http://www.rewerse.net). The four-year program REWERSE (REasoning on the WEb with Rules and SEmantics) includes 27 European research and development organizations, and is supposed to bolster Europe's expertise in Web reasoning systems and applications, particularly Semantic Web systems. It consists of the main working groups: 'Rule Markup Languages', 'Policy Language, Enforcement, Composition', 'Composition and Typing', 'Reasoning-Aware Querying', 'Evolution', 'Time and Location', 'Adding Semantics to the Bioinformatics Web', and 'Personalized Information Systems'. The papers in this volume reflect most of the topics in REWERSE.

PPSWR 2005 is scheduled for September 12–16, 2005. It will take place as a 'Dagstuhl Seminar' in the Dagstuhl castle in Germany (http://www.dagstuhl.de/05371/).

September 2004   Hans Jürgen Ohlbach and Sebastian Schaffert

Table of Contents

On Subtyping of Tree-Structured Data: A Polynomial Approach

François Bry[1], Włodzimierz Drabent[2,3], and Jan Małuszyński[3]

[1] Institut für Informatik, Ludwig-Maximilians-Universität München, Germany
[2] Institute of Computer Science, Polish Academy of Sciences, Warszawa, Poland
[3] Department of Computer and Information Science, Linköping University, Sweden
francois.bry@ifi.lmu.de   drabent@ipipan.waw.pl   jmz@ida.liu.se

Abstract. This paper discusses subtyping of tree-structured data encountered on the Web, e.g. XML and HTML data. Our long range objective is to define a type system for Web and/or Semantic Web query languages amenable to static type checking. We propose a type formalism motivated by XML Schema and accommodating two concepts of subtyping: inclusion subtyping (corresponding to XML Schema notion of type restriction) and extension subtyping (motivated by XML Schema's type extension). We present algorithms for checking both kinds of subtyping. The algorithms are polynomial if certain conditions are imposed on the type definitions; the conditions seem natural and not too restrictive.

1   Introduction

This paper discusses subtyping of tree-structured data. With the Web, the Web page markup language HTML, and the emergence of XML as data specification formalism of choice for data on the Web, tree-structured data are receiving an increasing attention. Indeed, HTML and XML documents are tree-structured – cycles induced by ID and IDREF attributes and/or links being neglected as it is common with Web query languages.

The long range objective of the research reported about in this paper is to define a type system for Web and/or Semantic Web query languages amenable to static type checking, the query language Xcerpt [5, 2] being a premier candidate for such an extension. Such a type system should support subtyping so that the well-typed procedures/methods of the language could also be safely applied to subtypes. The question is thus about the suitable concept of type and subtype. We provide a formalism for specifying types motivated by XML Schema [13] and we show two relevant concepts of subtyping: *inclusion subtyping*, motivated by XML Schema notion of *type restriction*, and *extension subtyping*, motivated by XML Schema notion of *type extension*. We show conditions for type definitions under which subtyping can be checked in polynomial time.

As XML data are essentially tree-structured, a natural approach is to view types as sets of trees and subtyping as set inclusion. To specify such types a formalism of regular expression types is proposed in [8] and inclusion subtyping is discussed. Checking of the subtyping relations can then be reduced to checking

H.J. Ohlbach and S. Schaffert (Eds.): PPSWR 2004, LNCS 3208, pp. 1–18, 2004.

inclusion of sets specified by regular tree grammars [6]. Tree grammars are a formalism of choice for specifying types for XML documents because both DTD and XML schemas are derived from them. The inclusion problem for languages defined by tree grammars is decidable but EXPTIME-complete. It is argued in [8] that for the regular expression types needed *in practice* checking of inclusion is usually quite efficient. We propose a formalism which is a restricted variant of regular expression types. We argue that the restrictions reflect the usual requirements of the XML Schema, thus our formalism is sufficiently expressive for practical applications. On the other hand, it makes it possible to identify source of potential inefficiency. We formulate syntactic conditions on type definitions under which subtyping can be checked in polynomial time.

It seems that subtyping by inclusion is intuitively very close to the XML Schema concept of *type restriction*, and as argued in [3] replacement of the latter by the former would greatly simplify XML Schema.

In object-oriented processing, the methods of a class must be as well applicable to the subclasses of the class. Subtyping by inclusion is not sufficient to capture the notion of subclass. For example, given a type **person** of XML documents we may define a type **student** where the documents have the same elements as **person** augmented with the obligatory new element **university**, showing the affiliation of the student. This kind of definitions is supported by XML Schema mechanism of *type extension*. Notice that in our example none of the classes is the subset of the other. However, we would like to be able to apply all the methods of the class **person** to the objects of the class **student**. This can be done by ignoring the additional element of the input document. As the objective is static typing of the methods, we need yet another notion of subtyping, in addition to subtyping by inclusion. For our type formalism we define a formal notion of *extension subtype* that formalizes such situations. In this paper we outline an algorithm for checking extension subtyping and we give sufficient condition for type definitions under which the check is polynomial.

Detailed comparison of our formalism with those of XML Schema and of other schema languages is outside of the scope of this paper and is a subject of future work. Also we do not deal here with relation of these formalisms with ontologies; roughly speaking the former deal with the syntax of documents and the latter with semantics [9].

The paper is organized as follows. Section 2 discusses the kind of tree-structured data we want to deal with, and introduces a formalism of *type definitions* for specifying sets of such data. The next section gives an algorithm for validation of tree-structured data w.r.t. type definitions. Sections 4, 5 discuss, respectively, inclusion and extension subtyping. Section 6 presents conclusions.

2   Tree-Structured Data

2.1   Data Terms

This section formalizes our view of tree-structured data. The next one introduces a formalism for specifying decidable sets of such data.

We define a formal language of *data terms* to model tree-structured data such as XML documents. This definition does not explicitly capture the XML mechanism for defining and using references. We note that two basic concepts of XML are *tags* indicating nodes of an ordered tree corresponding to a document and *attributes*[1] used to attach attribute-value mappings to the nodes of a tree. Such a finite mapping can be represented as an unordered tree (see Example 2 below). It should also be noticed that *all* group of XML Schema [13] allows specifying elements that may appear in the document in any order. These observations bring us to the conclusion that we want to deal with labelled trees where the children of a node are either linearly ordered or are unordered. We will call them *mixed trees* to indicate their distinction from both ordered trees, and unordered trees.

We assume two disjoint alphabets: a countably infinite alphabet $\mathcal{L}$ of **labels**, and an alphabet $\mathcal{B}$ of **basic constants**. Basic constants represent some basic values, such as numbers or strings, while labels are tree constructors.

We now define a formal language of *data terms* for representing mixed trees. The linear ordering of children will be indicated by the brackets [,], while unordered children are placed in the braces {,}.

Definition 1.   A **data term** is an expression defined inductively as follows:

- Any basic constant is a data term,
- If l is a label and $t_1, \ldots, t_n$ are $n \geq 0$ data terms, then $l[t_1 \cdots t_n]$ and $l\{t_1 \cdots t_n\}$ are data terms.

Data terms not containing {,} will be called **ordered**.

The data terms $l[\,]$ or $l\{\}$ are different. One may consider it more natural not to distinguish between the empty sequence and the empty set of arguments. This however would result in some extra special cases in our definitions and algorithms further on.

Notice that the component terms are not separated by commas. This notation is intended to stress the fact that the label l in a data term $l[t_1 \cdots t_n]$ is not an n-argument function symbol. It has rather a single argument which is a sequence (string) of data terms $t_1, \ldots, t_n$ (where $n \geq 0$). Similarly the argument of l in $l\{t_1 \cdots t_n\}$ is a set of data terms.

Example 2. Consider the following XML document

```
<person friend="yes" coauthor="yes">
    <first-name>Francois</first-name>
    <last-name>Bry</last-name>
    <notes/>
</person>
```

It can be represented as a data term

$$person[\, attributes\{\, friend[\text{yes}]\ coauthor[\text{yes}]\, \}$$
$$first\text{-}name[\text{Francois}]\ \ last\text{-}name[\text{Bry}]\ \ notes[\,]\ \ ]$$

---

[1] However, there is no syntactic difference between tag names and attribute names.

where yes, Francois, Bry are basic constants and *attributes, friend, coauthor, first-name, last-name, notes* are labels.

The **root** of a data term t, denoted $root(t)$, is defined as follows. If t is a constant then $root(t) = t$. Otherwise t is of the form $l[t_1 \cdots t_n]$ or $l\{t_1 \cdots t_n\}$ and $root(t) = l$.

2.2   Specifying Sets of Data Terms

We now present a metalanguage for specifying decidable sets of data terms, which will be used as types in processing of tree-structured data. The idea is similar to that of [8] (see the discussion at the end of this section) and is motivated by DTD's and by XML Schema.

We define the sets of data terms by means of grammatical rules. We assume existence of *base types*, denoted by **type constants** from the alphabet $\mathcal{C}$ and a countably infinite alphabet $\mathcal{V}$ of **type variables**, disjoint with $\mathcal{C}$. Type constants and type variables will be called **type names**.

The intention is that base types correspond to XML primitive types. We assume that each type constant $C \in \mathcal{C}$ is associated with a set $[\![C]\!] \subseteq \mathcal{B}$ of basic constants. We assume that for every pair $C_1, C_2 \in \mathcal{C}$ of type constants we are able to decide whether or not $[\![C_1]\!] \subseteq [\![C_2]\!]$ and whether or not $[\![C_1]\!] \cap [\![C_2]\!] = \emptyset$. Additionally we assume that for each $C \in \mathcal{C}$ and a finite tuple $C_1, \ldots, C_n \in \mathcal{C}$ we are able to decide whether $[\![C]\!] \subseteq [\![C_1]\!] \cup \cdots \cup [\![C_n]\!]$.

We first introduce an auxiliary syntactic concept of a *regular type expression*. As usually, we use ϵ to denote the empty sequence.

Definition 3.   A **regular type expression** is a regular expression (see e.g. [7]) over the alphabet $\mathcal{V} \cup \mathcal{C}$.

Thus ϵ, ϕ and any type constant or type variable T are regular type expressions, and if τ, τ_1, τ_2, are type expressions then $(\tau_1 \tau_2)$, $(\tau_1 | \tau_2)$ and (τ^*) are regular type expressions. As usually, every regular type expression r denotes a (possibly infinite) *regular language* $L(r)$ over the alphabet $\mathcal{V} \cup \mathcal{C}$: $L(\epsilon) = \{\epsilon\}$, $L(\phi) = \emptyset$, $L(T) = \{T\}$, $L((\tau_1 \tau_2)) = L(\tau_1)L(\tau_2)$, $L((\tau_1 | \tau_2)) = L(\tau_1) \cup L(\tau_2)$, and $L((\tau^*)) = L(\tau)^*$. We adopt the usual notational conventions [7], where the parentheses are suppressed by assuming the following priorities of operators: $*$, concatenation, $|$.

It is well known that any language specified by a regular expression can also be defined by a *finite automaton*, deterministic (DFA) or non-deterministic (NFA). There exist algorithms that transform any regular expression of length n into an equivalent NFAϵ with $O(n)$ states, and any NFAϵ into an equivalent DFA (see e.g. [7]). In the worst case the latter transformation may exponentially increase the number of states. Brüggemann-Klein and Wood [4] introduced a class of 1-unambiguous regular expressions, for which this transformation is linear. For such regular expression, a natural transformation from NFAϵ to NFA results in an DFA.

Notice that the XML definition [12] requires (Section 3.2.1) that content models specified by regular expressions in element type declarations of a DTD are *deterministic* in the sense of Appendix E of [12]. This condition ensures existence of a DFA acceptor with number of states linear w.r.t. the size of the regular expression. It seems that this informal condition is equivalent with that of [4]. We do not put specific restrictions on our regular type expressions, but we expect that those used in practice would not cause exponential blow-up of the number of states of the constructed DFA acceptors.

As syntactic sugar for regular expressions we will also use the following notation:

- $\tau(n:m)$, where $m \geq n$ as a shorthand for $\tau^n |\tau^{n+1}| \cdots |\tau^m$,
  notice that τ^* can be seen as $\tau(0:\infty)$
- τ^+ as a shorthand for $\tau\tau^*$,
- $\tau^?$ as a shorthand $\tau(0:1)$,

where τ is a regular expression and n is a natural number and m is a natural number or ∞.

Definition 4. A **multiplicity list** is a regular type expression of the form

$$s_1(n_1:m_1) \cdots s_k(n_k:m_k)$$

where $k \geq 0$ and $s_1, \ldots, s_k$ are distinct type names.

It can be easily seen that for the language defined by a multiplicity list there exists a DFA acceptor with the number of states linear w.r.t. to the number of the type names in the list.

We now introduce a grammatical formalism for defining sets of data terms. Such a grammar will define a finite family of sets, indexed by a finite number of type variables $T_1, \ldots, T_m$. Each variable T_i will be associated with a set of data terms, all of which have identical root label l_i. This is motivated by XML, where the documents defined by a DTD have identical main tags. It is not required that $l_i \neq l_j$ for $i \neq j$. Our grammatical rules can be seen as content definitions for classes of data terms. So they play a similar role for data terms as DTD's (or XML Schemas) play for XML documents.

Definition 5. A **type definition** D for (distinct) type variables $T_1, \ldots, T_n$, for $n \geq 1$ is a set of **rules** $\{R_1, \ldots, R_n\}$ where each rule R_i is of the form

$$T_i \to E_i$$

and E_i is an expression of the form $l_i[r_i]$ or of the form $l_i\{q_i\}$, $i = 1, \ldots, n$, where every l_i is a label, r_i is a regular type expression over $\{T_1, \ldots, T_n\} \cup \mathcal{C}$ and every q_i is a multiplicity list over $\{T_1, \ldots, T_n\} \cup \mathcal{C}$.

Thus, we use two kinds of rules, which describe construction of ordered or unordered trees (data terms). As formally explained below, rules of the form $T \to l[r]$ describe a family T of trees where the children of the root are ordered and their allowed sequence is described by a general regular expression r. The rules of the form $T \to l\{q\}$ describe a family T of trees where the children of the root are unordered. The ordering of the children is thus irrelevant and the full power of regular expressions is not needed. We use instead the multiplicity list q which specifies allowed number of children of each type. A type definition not including the rules of the form $T \rightarrow l\{r\}$ (where $L(r)$ contains a non-empty string) will be called an **ordered** type definition.

We illustrate the definition by the following example. In our type definitions the type names start with capital letters, labels with lower case letters, and type constants with symbol #.

Example 6. We want to represent genealogical information of people by means of data terms. A person would be represented by the name, sex and a similar information about his/her parents. The latter may be unknown, in which case it will be missing in the data term. This intuition is reflected by the following grammar.

$$Person \rightarrow person[\,Name\ (M|F)\ Mother?\ Father?\,]$$
$$Name \rightarrow name[\#name]$$
$$M \rightarrow m[\,]$$
$$F \rightarrow f[\,]$$
$$Mother \rightarrow person[Name\ F\ Mother?\ Father?\,]$$
$$Father \rightarrow person[Name\ M\ Mother?\ Father?\,]$$

In the sequel we give a formal semantics of type definitions, which will correspond to this intuition.

Definition 5 requires that each type name maps to a label, but the mapping may not be one-one, as illustrated by the above example, where the types $Person, Father$ and $Mother$ map to the same label $person$. This is more general than XML, where there is a one-one correspondence between element types defined by a DTD and tags (see Section 3.1 in [12]).

Such a restriction facilitates validation of documents but excludes subtyping understood as document set inclusion. It turns out that we can facilitate validation and still have inclusion subtyping if the one-one correspondence between types and labels is enforced only locally for type symbols occurring in the regular expression of each rule of the grammar. This is reflected by the following definition.

Definition 7. The type definition D of Definition 5 is said to be **proper** if for each E_i $(i = 1, \ldots, n)$

- for any distinct type variables T_{i_1}, T_{i_2} occurring in E_i, $l_{i_1} \neq l_{i_2}$, and
- for any distinct type constants C_1, C_2 occurring in E_i, $[\![C_1]\!] \cap [\![C_2]\!] = \emptyset$.

Notice that the type definition of Example 6 is not proper. The regular expression of the first rule includes different types $Mother$ and $Father$ with the same label $person$. Replacing (in three rules) each of them by the type $Person$ would make the definition proper.

A type definition D associates with each type variable T_i a set of data terms, as explained below.

Definition 8. A **data pattern** is inductively defined as follows

- a type variable, a type constant, and a basic constant are data patterns,
- if $d_1, \ldots, d_n$ for $n \geq 0$ are data patterns and l is a label then $l[d_1 \cdots d_n]$ and $l\{d_1 \cdots d_n\}$ are data patterns.

Thus, data terms are data patterns, but not necessarily vice versa, since a data pattern may include type variables and type constants in place of data terms. Given a type definition D we use it to define a rewrite relation $\rightarrow_D$ on data patterns.

Definition 9 (of $\rightarrow_D$). Let d, d' be data patterns. $d \rightarrow_D d'$ iff one of the following holds:

1. For some type variable T
   - there exists a rule $T \rightarrow l[r]$ in D and a string $s \in L(r)$, or
   - there exists a rule $T \rightarrow l\{r\}$ in D and a string $s_0 \in L(r)$ and a permutation s of s_0

   such that d' is obtained from d by replacing an occurrence of T in d, respectively, by $l[s]$, or by $l\{s\}$.
2. d' is obtained from d by replacing an occurrence of a type constant S by a basic constant in $[\![S]\!]$.

Iterating the rewriting steps we may eventually arrive at a data term. This gives a semantics for type definitions.

Definition 10. Let D be a type definition for $T_1, \ldots, T_n$. A **type** $[\![T_i]\!]_D$ associated with T_i by D is defined as the set of all data terms t that can be obtained from T_i:

$$[\![T_i]\!]_D = \{\, t \mid T_i \rightarrow_D^* t \text{ and } t \text{ is a data term} \,\}$$

Additionally we define the set of data terms specified by a given data pattern d, and by a given regular expression r:

$$[\![d]\!]_D = \{\, t \mid d \rightarrow_D^* t \text{ and } t \text{ is a data term} \,\},$$
$$[\![r]\!]_D = \{\, t_1 \cdots t_k \mid t_1 \in [\![T_1]\!]_D, \ldots, t_k \in [\![T_k]\!]_D \text{ for some } T_1 \cdots T_k \in L(r) \,\}.$$

Definition 11 (of $label_D(T)$ and $type_D(t, r)$). Notice that:

- Every type variable T in D has only one rule defining it, the label of this rule will be denoted $label_D(T)$.
- Assume that D is proper. Thus given a term $l[t_1 \cdots t_n]$ and a rule $T \rightarrow l[r] \in D$, or a term $l\{t_1 \cdots t_n\}$ and a rule $T \rightarrow l\{r\} \in D$, for each t_i the root of t_i determines at most one type name S occurring in r such that
  - S is a type variable and $label_D(S) = root(t_i)$, or
  - S is a type constant and $t_i \in [\![S]\!]$.

  (In the first case t_i is not a basic constant, in the second it is.) Such type name S will be denoted $type_D(t_i, r)$. If such S does not exist, we assume that $type_D(t_i, r) = S_0$, where S_0 is some fixed type name not occurring in D.

If it is clear from the context which type definition is considered, we can omit the subscript in the notation $[\![\ ]\!]_D$, $label_D(\ )$ and $type_D(\ , \ )$.

Example 12. Consider the following type definition D (which is proper):

$$Person \rightarrow person[Name\,(M|F)\,Person(0:2)]$$
$$Name \rightarrow name[\#name]$$
$$M \rightarrow m[\,]$$
$$F \rightarrow f[\,]$$

Let $john, mary, bob \in [\![\#name]\!]$. Extending the derivation

$$Person \rightarrow person[Name\,M\,Person] \rightarrow^* person[name[\#name]\,m[\,]\,Person]$$

one can check that the following data term is in $[\![Person]\!]$

$$person[name[john]\,m[\,]\,person[name[mary]\,f[\,]\,person[name[bob]m[\,]]]].$$

Our type definitions are similar to those of [8]. The main differences are: 1. Our data are mixed trees instead of ordered trees. 2. Our types are sets of trees; sequences of trees described by regular expressions play only an auxiliary role. In addition, all elements of any type defined in our formalism have the same root label. In contrast to that, types of [8] are sets of sequences of trees. Allowing mixed trees creates better data modelling possibilities and we expect it to be useful in applications.

Apart of the use of mixed trees, our formalism is a restriction of that of [8] since a set of trees can be seen as a set of one-element sequences of trees. Our restriction seems not to be essential since we can also specify sets of sequences of trees by means of regular type expressions, even though such sets are not considered types. It reflects the intuition that type definitions are used for describing tree-structured data with explicitly labelled roots, and that data of the same type have identical root labels. This conforms to the practice of XML and makes it possible to design new validation and type inclusion algorithms with a potential for better complexity than the algorithms of [8].

In the rest of the paper we consider only proper data definitions, unless stated otherwise. This results in simpler algorithms. The class of ordered (i.e. without $\{\}$) proper type definitions is essentially the same as single-type tree grammars of [10]. Restriction to proper definitions seems reasonable, as the sets defined by main XML schema languages (DTD and XML Schema) can be expressed by such definitions [10].

3   Validating Data Terms

A data definition D describes expected structure of data and we will use it to validate given data items d, i.e. to check whether or not $d \in [\![T]\!]$, for a given type defined by D. This section gives a general algorithm for validating data terms against proper data definitions and examines its complexity.

Validating Ordered Data Terms. We first consider proper type definitions which are ordered (i.e. include no rules of the form $T \rightarrow \{r\}$). In that case each $[\![T]\!]$ is the set of ordered data terms derivable by the rules. We show an algorithm that for a given proper ordered type definition D, type name T, and data term $d = c[d_1 \cdots d_k]$ $(k \geq 0)$ decides whether or not $d \in [\![T]\!]_D$.

The algorithm depends on the fact that D is proper. This implies that for each distinct type names S, S' occurring in a regular expression r from D, $[\![S]\!]_D \cap [\![S']\!]_D = \emptyset$. Thus when checking whether a sequence $d_1 \cdots d_k$ of data terms is in $[\![r]\!]_D$ we need, for a given i, to check $d_i \in [\![S]\!]_D$ for at most one type name S, namely $S = type(d_i, r)$.

The algorithm employs checking whether $x \in L(r)$ for a string x and a regular expression r. This can be done in time $O(|r| \cdot |x|)$ [1]. Alternatively, one can construct a DFA for $L(r)$ for each regular expression in D; this is to be done once. Then the checking requires $|x|$ steps.

The validation algorithm is described as follows.

$validate(d, T)$:
    IF T is a type constant THEN
        check whether d is a basic constant in $[\![T]\!]$ and return the result
    ELSE (T is a type variable)
    IF d is a basic constant then return *false*
    ELSE
    IF the rule for T in D is $T \to c[r]$ THEN
      IF $root(d) \neq c$ THEN return *false*
      ELSE
        let $d = c[d_1 \cdots d_k]$ $(k \geq 0)$,
        let $T_i = type(d_i, r)$ for $i = 1, \ldots k$,
        IF $T_1 \cdots T_k \notin L(r)$
          THEN return *false*
        ELSE
          return $\bigwedge_{i=1}^{k} validate(d_i, T_i)$
    ELSE (no rule for T) return *false*.

This algorithm traverses the tree d. It checks if $x \in L(r)$, for some strings and regular expressions. The sum of the lengths of all the strings subjected to these checks is not greater than the number of nodes in the tree. Some nodes of d may require validation against base types. The time complexity of the algorithm is thus linear w.r.t. the size of d provided that the validation against base types is also linear.

Dealing with Mixed Trees. We now generalize the validation algorithm of the previous section to the case of mixed terms. So a type definition may contain rules of the form $T \to l\{r\}$, where r is a multiplicity list. The validation algorithm is similar, just the order of $d_1, \ldots, d_k$ within $l\{d_1 \cdots d_k\}$ does not matter.

$validate(d, T)$:
    IF T is a type constant THEN
        check whether d is a basic constant in $[\![T]\!]$ and return the result
    ELSE (T is a type variable)
    IF d is a basic constant THEN return *false*
    ELSE IF there is no rule for T in D THEN return *false*

ELSE IF $root(d) \neq label(T)$ THEN return *false*
ELSE IF the rule for T in D is of the form $T \rightarrow l\{r\}$ THEN
    IF d is of the form $l[d_1 \cdots d_k]$ $(k > 0)$ THEN return *false*
    ELSE
        let $d = d\{d_1 \cdots d_k\}$ $(k \geq 0)$,
        let $T_i = type(d_i, r)$ for $i = 1, \ldots k$,
        let N be the set of the type names occurring in r
            (notice that according to the definition of $type(d_i, r)$
            each $T_i \in N \cup \{S_0\}$, where $S_0 \notin N$),
        for each $S \in N \cup \{S_0\}$ count the number n_S of the occurrences of S
            in $T_1 \cdots T_n$,
        IF $n_{S_0} = 0$ and for each $S(i : j)$ occurring in the multiplicity list r
        $i \leq n_S \leq j$
            THEN return $\bigwedge_{i=1}^{k} validate(d_i, T_i)$
        ELSE return *false*
ELSE
IF the rule for T in D is of the form $T \rightarrow l[r]$ THEN
    IF d is of the form $l\{d_1 \cdots d_k\}$ $(k > 0)$ THEN return *false*,
    ELSE (now as in the previous algorithm)
        let $d = c[d_1 \cdots d_k]$ $(k \geq 0)$,
        let $T_i = type(d_i, r)$ for $i = 1, \ldots k$,
        IF $T_1 \cdots T_k \notin L(r)$
            THEN return *false*
        ELSE
            return $\bigwedge_{i=1}^{k} validate(d_i, T_i)$,
ELSE (no rule for T in D)
    return *false*.

As in the previous case, the algorithm is linear.

4 Checking Type Inclusion

The main subject of this section is an algorithm for checking type inclusion.
Before presenting the algorithm, we introduce some auxiliary notions. A simpler
algorithm for a more restricted class of type definitions was presented in [11].

A natural concept of subtyping is based on set inclusion.

Definition 13. *A type S (with a definition D) is an **inclusion subtype** of
type T (with a definition D') iff $[\![S]\!]_D \subseteq [\![T]\!]_{D'}$.*
We will denote this as $S \subseteq T$, provided D, D' are clear from the context.

In this section we show an algorithm for checking type inclusion. Assume
that we want to check $S \subseteq T$ for some types defined by proper type definitions
D, D' respectively. We assume that for each type constants C, C' from these
definitions we know whether $[\![C]\!] \subseteq [\![C']\!]$ and $[\![C]\!] \cap [\![C']\!] = \emptyset$. We also assume
that for each tuple of type constants $C, C_1, \ldots, C_n$ (where $[\![C_1]\!], \ldots, [\![C_n]\!]$ are

pairwise disjoint) we know whether $[\![C]\!] \subseteq [\![C_1]\!] \cup \cdots \cup [\![C_n]\!]$. These facts can be recorded in tables. Notice that in the latter case it is sufficient to consider only such $C_1, \ldots, C_n$ for which $[\![C]\!] \cap [\![C_i]\!] \neq \emptyset$ for $i = 1, \ldots, n$. (If some formalism is used to define the sets corresponding to (some) type constants then we require that algorithms for the checks above are given.)

By a **useless symbol** in a regular expression r over an alphabet Σ we mean a symbol $a \in \Sigma$ not occurring in any string $x \in L(r)$. Notice that if r does not contain the regular expression ϕ then r does not contain useless symbols. A type name T is **nullable** in a type definition D if $[\![T]\!]_D = \emptyset$.

To introduce our inclusion checking algorithm we need some auxiliary notions. For a pair of type variables S, T let us define a set $C(S, T)$ as the smallest (under $\subseteq$) set of pairs of type variables such that

- if $label_D(S) = label_{D'}(T)$ then $(S, T) \in C(S, T)$,
- if
    - $(S', T') \in C(S, T)$,
    - D, D' contain, respectively, rules $S' \to l[r_1]$ and $T' \to l[r_2]$, or $S' \to l\{r_1\}$ and $T' \to l\{r_2\}$ (with the same l),
    - type variables S'', T'' occur respectively in r_1, r_2, and $label_D(S'') = label_{D'}(T'')$

    then $(S'', T'') \in C(S, T)$. If D, D' are proper then for every S'' in r_1, there exists at most one T'' in r_2 satisfying this condition, and vice versa.

$C(S, T)$ is the set of pairs of types which should be compared in order to find out whether $S \subseteq T$.

$C(S, T)$ can be computed in time $O(kn^2 \log(kn))$, where n is the number of rules in the definitions and k is the maximal size of a regular expression in the definitions. There are examples of D, D' where $C(S, T)$ contains all the pairs of type variables form D, D' respectively.

Consider a type variable T in a type definition D. The unique rule $T \to l\alpha_{T,D} r_{T,D} \beta_{T,D}$ in D for T (where $\alpha_{T,D}\beta_{T,D}$ is $[]$ or $\{\}$) determines the regular expression $r_{T,D}$ and the parentheses $\alpha_{T,D}\beta_{T,D}$. When the parentheses are $[]$ then we are interested in the sequences of root labels in all children of the root l of the data terms in $[\![T]\!]_D$. This *label language* is defined as follows. For a given regular expression r

$$LL_D(r) = \left\{ l_1, \ldots, l_n \,\middle|\, \begin{array}{l} T_1 \cdots T_n \in L(r) \text{ and for } i = 1, \ldots, n \\ l_i = label_D(T_i) \text{ if } T_i \text{ is a type variable} \\ l_i \in [\![T_i]\!] \text{ if } T_i \text{ is a type constant} \end{array} \right\}$$

We often skip the subscript in LL_D when it is clear from the context.

For rules with parentheses $\{\}$ we will deal with permutations of the strings from label languages. For any language L we define

$$perm(L) = \{ x \mid x \text{ is a permutation of some } y \in L \}.$$

Now we discuss some necessary conditions for type inclusion and show that they are also sufficient. Assume that D does not contain nullable symbols, the regular expressions in D do not contain useless symbols and D' is proper. Let

$S, T \in \mathcal{V}$ and $[\![S]\!]_D \subseteq [\![T]\!]_{D'}$. Then $1. label_D(S) = label_{D'}(T)$ and $2. \alpha_{S,D} = \alpha_{T,D'}$. $3.$ If $\alpha_{S,D}\beta_{S,D} = [\,]$ then $LL_D(r_{S,D}) \subseteq LL_{D'}(r_{T,D'})$. $4.$ If $\alpha_{S,D}\beta_{S,D} = \{\}$ then $perm(LL_D(r_{S,D})) \subseteq perm(LL_{D'}(r_{T,D'}))$ (equivalently $LL_D(r_{S,D}) \subseteq perm(LL_{D'}(r_{T,D'}))$).

These inclusions (and the fact that D' is proper and $r_{S,D}$ does not contain useless symbols) imply that for every type variable X in $r_{S,D}$ there exists a unique type variable Y in $r_{T,D'}$, such that $(X, Y) \in C(S, T)$ (i.e. such that $label_D(X) = label_{D'}(Y)$). This holds for both kinds of parentheses in the rules for S, T. Moreover, $[\![X]\!]_D \subseteq [\![Y]\!]_{D'}$, as $[\![r_{S,D}]\!]_D \subseteq [\![r_{T,D'}]\!]_{D'}$. Thus, by induction, conditions $2, 3, 4$ hold for each pair of type variables from $C(S, T)$. (Condition 1 follows from the definition of $C(S, T)$).

On the other hand, assume that $2, 3, 4$ hold for each pair from $C(S, T)$. Take an $(X, Y) \in C(S, T)$ and assume that $X \rightarrow_D l[X_1 \cdots X_n] \rightarrow_D^* l[X_1' \cdots X_n']$, where $X_1' \cdots X_n'$ is obtained from $X_1 \cdots X_n$ by replacing the type constants occurring in $X_1 \cdots X_n$ by basic constants. Then there exist $Y_1, \ldots, Y_n, Y_1', \ldots, Y_n'$ such that $Y \rightarrow_D l[Y_1 \cdots Y_n] \rightarrow_D^* l[Y_1' \cdots Y_n']$, and for each $i = 1, \ldots, n$, $(X_i, Y_i) \in C(S, T)$ and $(X_i, Y_i) = (X_i', Y_i')$, or X_i, Y_i are type constants and $X_i' = Y_i' \in [\![Y_i]\!]$. An analogical property holds when $[\,]$ is replaced by $\{\}$. By induction we obtain that whenever a data term is derived from X in D then it is derived from Y in D'. Thus $[\![X]\!]_D \subseteq [\![Y]\!]_{D'}$.

These considerations result in the following algorithm for checking type inclusion and the proposition expressing its correctness and completeness.

$inclsubtype(S, T)$:

IF S, T are type constants THEN return $[\![S]\!] \subseteq [\![T]\!]$

IF one of the symbols S, T is a type constant and the other type variable THEN return *false*

ELSE IF $label_D(S) \neq label_{D'}(T)$ THEN return *false*

ELSE For each pair $(X, Y) \in C(S, T)$ do the following:

Let $X \rightarrow l\alpha r_{X,D}\beta \in D$ and $Y \rightarrow l\alpha' r_{Y,D'}\beta' \in D'$ (where $\alpha, \beta, \alpha', \beta'$ are parentheses) be the rules for X and Y in D, D'.

IF $\alpha\beta \neq \alpha'\beta'$ THEN return *false*

ELSE IF $\alpha\beta = \alpha'\beta' = [\,]$ THEN check whether

$$LL_D(r_{X,D}) \subseteq LL_{D'}(r_{Y,D'})$$

ELSE $(\alpha\beta = \alpha'\beta' = \{\})$ check whether

$$LL_D(r_{X,D}) \subseteq perm(LL_{D'}(r_{Y,D'})).$$

IF the checks for all the pairs from $C(S, T)$ succeed THEN return *true* ELSE return *false*.

Proposition 14. *Let D, D' be type definitions and S, T type names.*

If $inclsubtype(S, T)$ returns true then $[\![S]\!]_D \subseteq [\![T]\!]_{D'}$.

Assume that D has no nullable symbols, the regular expressions in D have no useless symbols and D' is proper. If $[\![S]\!]_D \subseteq [\![T]\!]_{D'}$ then $inclsubtype(S, T)$ returns true.

What remains is to check inclusion for label languages. An algorithm for $LL(r) \subseteq LL(r')$ follows directly from the proposition below.

Proposition 15. *Let r, r' be regular expressions occurring respectively in type definitions D, D'. Let D' be proper and r do not contain useless symbols. For each type constant C from r consider those type constants $C_{C,1}, \ldots, C_{C,k_C}$ from r' for which $[\![C]\!] \cap [\![C_{C,i}]\!] \neq \emptyset$. Let r_C be the regular expression $C_{C,1}|\cdots|C_{C,k_C}$.*

Let s be r with each type constant C replaced by r_C and each type variable T replaced by $label_D(T)$. Let s' be r' with each type variable T replaced by $label_{D'}(T)$. Then

$$LL_D(r) \subseteq LL_{D'}(r') \quad \text{iff} \quad L(s) \subseteq L(s'), \text{ and}$$
$$[\![C]\!] \subseteq \bigcup_{i=1}^{k_C} [\![C_{C,i}]\!] \text{ for each } C \in \mathcal{C} \text{ occurring in } r.$$

Proof. We skip the easy "if" part of the proof. Assume that $LL_D(r) \subseteq LL_{D'}(r')$. This means that for each $w \in L(r)$, $LL_D(w) \subseteq LL_{D'}(r')$. Hence for each type variable T occurring in w there occurs a type variable U in r' such that $label_D(T) = label_{D'}(U)$. Also, for each type constant C in w and each $c \in [\![C]\!]$ there is a type constant C' in r' (thus $C' \in \{C_{C,1}, \ldots, C_{C,k_C}\}$) such that $c \in [\![C']\!]$. Hence $[\![C]\!] \subseteq \bigcup_{i=1}^{k_C} [\![C_{C,i}]\!]$. Moreover, each $c \in [\![C]\!]$ is a member of at most one $[\![C_{C,i}]\!]$ (due to D' being proper). This holds for each type constant C from r, as each such C occurs in some $w \in L(r)$ (because r has no useless symbols).

Take an $x \in L(s)$. The string x can be obtained from some string $w \in L(r)$ by replacing each type variable T by $label_D(T)$ and each occurrence of any constant C by some $C_{C,j}$. From $LL_D(r) \subseteq LL_{D'}(r')$ it follows that if $w = T_1 \cdots T_n \in L(r)$ then $U_1 \cdots U_n \in L(r')$, where, for $i = 1, \ldots, n$, either both T_i, U_i are variables and $label_D(T_i) = label_{D'}(U_i)$ or both are type constants and $U_i = C_{T_i, j}$, for some j. Hence each $x \in L(s)$ can be obtained from a string $U_1 \cdots U_n \in L(r')$ by replacing each type variable U_i by $label_{D'}(U_i)$. Thus $L(s) \subseteq L(s')$. □

For the inclusion checking algorithm we also need a method for checking whether

$$LL_D(r) \subseteq perm(LL_{D'}(r')) \tag{1}$$

for given multiplicity lists r, r'. Inclusion (1) implies the following conditions.

1. For each $T(m:n)$ occurring in r, where T is a type variable and $n > 0$, r' contains $U(m':n')$ such that $label_D(T) = label_{D'}(U)$ and $m' \leq m, n \leq n'$.
2. For each $U(m':n')$ occurring in r', where U is a type variable and $m' > 0$, r contains $T(m:n)$ such that $label_D(T) = label_{D'}(U)$ and $m' \leq m, n \leq n'$.
3. For each $C(m:n)$, $C \in \mathcal{C}$, occurring in r, if $n > 0$ then $[\![C]\!] \subseteq \bigcup_{i=1}^{k_C} [\![C_{C,i}]\!]$, where $C_{C,1}, \ldots, C_{C,k_C}$ are as in Proposition 15.
4. For each $C'(m':n')$, $C' \in \mathcal{C}$, occurring in r', let $B_{C',1}, \ldots, B_{C',l_{C'}}$ ($l_{C'} \geq 0$) be those type constants of r for which $[\![B_{C',j}]\!] \cap [\![C']\!] \neq \emptyset$. Let $B_{C',1}(g_1:h_1), \ldots, B_{C',l_{C'}}(g_{l_{C'}}:h_{l_{C'}})$ be (the corresponding) subexpressions of r. Let $g'_j = g_j$ if $[\![B_j]\!] \subseteq [\![C']\!]$ and $g'_j = 0$ otherwise. Then

$$m' \leq \sum_{i=1}^{l_{C'}} g'_i \quad \text{and} \quad \sum_{i=1}^{l_{C'}} h_i \leq n'$$

To justify the last condition, notice that an $x \in LL(B_{C',j}(g_j : h_j))$ contains at most h_j and at least g'_j constants from $[\![C']\!]$.

Conversely, notice that the conditions $1, 2, 3, 4$ imply (1). Thus checking (1) boils down to checking $1, 2, 3, 4$ This completes the description of our inclusion checking algorithm.

Now we discuss the complexity of the inclusion checking algorithm. All the facts concerning the sets corresponding to type constants are recorded in tables, and can be checked in constant time. Checking inclusion of label languages is invoked by *inclsubtype* at most $|C(S, T)|$ times. The latter number is polynomial w.r.t. the size of the definitions D, D'. Checking condition (1) is polynomial. Inclusion checking for languages represented by DFA's is also polynomial.[2] However when the languages are represented by regular expressions it may be exponential. If however the regular expressions satisfy the condition of 1-unambiguity [4] (cf. the discussion in Sect. 2.2) then they can be in linear time transformed into DFA's. This makes checking whether $L(s) \subseteq L(s')$ polynomial. We obtain:

Proposition 16. *The presented algorithm for checking type inclusion is polynomial for type definitions in which the regular expressions are 1-unambiguous. In a general case it is exponential (w.r.t. the maximal size of a regular expression).*

5   Extension Subtyping

We introduce in this section a different kind of subtyping, which is motivated by the *extension* mechanism of XML Schema. We give a definition and an algorithm for checking whether two given types are in this relation.

In our approach a type T (defined by a proper type definition) is a set of trees of the form $l(t_1 \cdots t_n)$ where l is a label, each t_i is in some specific type T_i, and $label(t_i) = label(t_j)$ iff $T_i = T_j$. It may be desirable to consider another set of trees, obtained by adding children to the trees of T. We assume that the labels of the added children are different from the labels of already existing children. This restriction seems to be in conformance with the extension mechanism of XML Schema.

We will use the standard notion of a (language) homomorphism. By an *erasing homomorphism* we mean a homomorphism h such that $h(a) = a$ or $h(a) = \epsilon$, for any symbol a (from the domain of h).

The concept of extension subtype is formalized by

Definition 17. A set S_1 of data terms is an **extension subtype** of a set S_2 of data terms, denoted $S_1 \preceq S_2$, if $S_1 = S_2$ or there exist proper type definitions D_1, D_2 and a type variable T such that $S_1 = [\![T]\!]_{D_1}$ and $S_2 = [\![T]\!]_{D_2}$ and for each rule $U \to l[r_2]$ or $U \to l\{r_2\}$ of D_2, D_1 contains a rule $U \to l[r_1]$ or, respectively, $U \to l\{r_1\}$ such that $r_2 = h_U(r_1)$ for some erasing homomorphism h_U.

---

[2] In order to check whether $L(M) \subseteq L(M')$ for DFA's M, M', construct a product automaton $M \times M'$ and check whether no its reachable state is a pair of a final state of M and a non-final state of M'.

So for each $d_2 \in S_2$ there exists a $d_1 \in S_1$ obtained from d_2 by removing some subtrees, and each $d_1 \in S_1$ can be obtained in this way from some $d_2 \in S_2$.

Example 18. The following data type definitions define types A and A' such that $[\![A']\!]_{D'} \preceq [\![A]\!]_D$, as it is easy to rename type variables in D' so that the conditions of the definition above are satisfied. (# is a type constant; we may assume that $[\![\#]\!]$ is the set of character strings.)

$$
\begin{aligned}
D = \{\, & A \rightarrow address[NSC], \\
& N \rightarrow name[(FL)|I], \\
& I \rightarrow inst[\#], \\
& S \rightarrow street[\#], \\
& C \rightarrow city[\#]\}, \\
& F \rightarrow first[\#], \\
& L \rightarrow last[\#] \quad \}
\end{aligned}
\qquad
\begin{aligned}
D' = \{\, & A' \rightarrow address[N'S'C'P'], \\
& N' \rightarrow name[(F'M'L')|I'], \\
& I' \rightarrow inst[\#], \\
& S' \rightarrow street[\#], \\
& C' \rightarrow city[\#]\}, \\
& F' \rightarrow first[\#], \\
& M' \rightarrow middle[\#], \\
& L' \rightarrow last[\#], \\
& P' \rightarrow pcode[T'Z'], \\
& Z' \rightarrow zip[\#], \\
& T' \rightarrow country[\#] \quad \}
\end{aligned}
$$

If T_1, T_2 are both type constants then $[\![T_1]\!]_{D_1} \preceq [\![T_2]\!]_{D_2}$ iff $[\![T_1]\!] = [\![T_2]\!]$. If one of T_1, T_2 is a constant and the other a variable, then $[\![T_1]\!]_{D_1} \npreceq [\![T_2]\!]_{D_2}$. Otherwise T_1, T_2 are type variables and the following algorithm can be used to check whether $[\![T_1]\!]_{D_1} \preceq [\![T_2]\!]_{D_2}$. The algorithm first constructs the set $C(T_1, T_2)$ of pairs of type variables, as described in Section 4. Then it checks if type T_1 is an extension subtype of type T_2 in the following way.

extsubtype(T_1, T_2) :   .
    IF $C(T_1, T_2) = \emptyset$ THEN return *false*
    ELSE IF $C(T_1, T_2)$ contains a pair (T, U) such that one of the variables T, U
           is nullable (in, respectively, D_1 or D_2) and the other is not
           THEN return *false*
    ELSE IF $C(T_1, T_2)$ contains a pair (T, U) such that the rules $T \rightarrow l\alpha_1 r_1 \beta_1$
           and $U \rightarrow l\alpha_2 r_2 \beta_2$ (where $\alpha_i \beta_i$ is [ ] or {}, for $i = 1, 2$) for T, U
           from D_1, D_2, respectively, contain different kind of parentheses
           (i.e. $\alpha_1 \beta_1 \neq \alpha_2 \beta_2$)
           THEN return *false*
    ELSE for each $(T_1', T_2') \in C(T_1, T_2)$ do the following:
        IF both T_1', T_2' are not nullable THEN
           Let $T_1' \rightarrow l\alpha r_1 \beta$ and $T_2' \rightarrow l\alpha r_2 \beta$ be rules of D_1, D_2, respectively
           Let $h \colon \mathcal{V} \cup \mathcal{C} \rightarrow \mathcal{V} \cup \mathcal{C} \cup \{\epsilon\}$ be the erasing homomorphism that erases
              1. each type variable T (occurring in D_1) such that
                 $label_{D_1}(T) \notin \{\, label_{D_2}(U) \mid U$ occurs in $r_2, U \in \mathcal{V}\,\}$, and
              2. each type constant T (occurring in D_1) such that
                 $[\![T]\!] \neq [\![U]\!]$ for each $U \in \mathcal{C}$ occurring in r_2
           (so for all other type names $h(T) = T$).
           Now connect the non-erased type names from r_1 to the corresponding
           ones from r_2. Formally:

Construct a homomorphism $f : \mathcal{V} \cup \mathcal{C} \to \mathcal{V} \cup \mathcal{C}$ such that
1. for any type variable T occurring in $h(r_1)$, $f(T) = U$ where U is the type variable occurring in r_2 such that $label_{D_1}(T)$ $= label_{D_2}(U)$, (hence $(T, U) \in C(T_1, T_2)$),
2. for any type constant T occurring in $h(r_1)$, $f(T) = U$ where U is the type constant occurring in r_2 such that $[\![T]\!] = [\![U]\!]$.
(The previous step assures that $f(T)$ is defined for any type name T occurring in $h(r_1)$. As D_2 is proper, $f(T)$ is unique.)
IF the rules for T_1', T_2' contain $[\,]$ THEN
 check whether $L(f(h(r_1))) = L(r_2)$
ELSE (the rules for T_1', T_2' contain $\{\}$)
 check whether the multiplicity lists $f(h(r_1))$, r_2 are permutations of each other.
IF all the checks succeed THEN return *true* ELSE return *false*

Proposition 19. *Let D_1, D_2 be proper type definitions and T_1, T_2 type variables. If $extsubtype(T_1, T_2)$ returns true then $[\![T_1]\!]_{D_1} \preceq [\![T_2]\!]_{D_2}$.*

Proof. Assume that the algorithm returns *true*. Without lack of generality we can assume that the sets of type variables occurring in D_1 and D_2 are disjoint.

For each $(T_1', T_2') \in C(T_1, T_2)$ we create a pair of new rules. Consider the rule $T_1' \to l\alpha r_1 \beta$ of D_1 (where $\alpha\beta$ is $[\,]$ or $\{\}$), the rule $T_2' \to l\alpha r_2 \beta$ of D_2, and the homomorphisms h, f used for (T_1', T_2') by the algorithm. We can assume that $f(T) = T$ for any T not occurring in $h(r_1)$. The new rules are: $A_{T_1', T_2'} = T_2' \to l\alpha f(r_1)\beta$ and $B_{T_1', T_2'} = T_2' \to l\alpha f(h(r_1))\beta$. So the first rule is a renamed rule from D_1; type names from D_1 are replaced by the corresponding ones from D_2, whenever such corresponding name exists. The second one is the rule from D_2 with the regular expression replaced by an equivalent one.

Notice that $f(h(r_1)) = h(f(r_1))$. (If $h(U) = \epsilon$ then $f(U) = U$ and $h(f(U)) = \epsilon = f(h(U))$; otherwise $h(U) = U$, $f(U)$ is a symbol from D_2 and thus $h(f(U)) = f(U) = f(h(U))$.) Hence the rules $A_{T_1', T_2'}, B_{T_1', T_2'}$ satisfy the condition from Def. 17.

We construct two definitions

$$D_1' = \{ A_{T_1', T_2'} \mid (T_1', T_2') \in C(T_1, T_2) \} \cup D_1$$
$$D_2' = \{ B_{T_1', T_2'} \mid (T_1', T_2') \in C(T_1, T_2) \}$$

By Def. 17, $[\![T_2]\!]_{D_1'} \preceq [\![T_2]\!]_{D_2'}$. For each $(T_1', T_2') \in C(T_1, T_2)$, $[\![T_2']\!]_{D_1'} = [\![T_1']\!]_{D_1}$ and $[\![T_2']\!]_{D_2'} = [\![T_2']\!]_{D_2}$. Thus $[\![T_2]\!]_{D_1} \preceq [\![T_2]\!]_{D_2}$. $\square$

The algorithm performs checks for equality of languages defined by regular expressions. Such a check can be done by converting the regular expressions into DFA's, minimizing them and comparing. The latter two steps are polynomial and the first, as discussed previously, is polynomial for 1-unambiguous regular expressions. From this fact, and from inspection of *extsubtype*, we conclude:

Proposition 20. *The presented algorithm for checking extension subtyping is polynomial (w.r.t. the size of the type definitions involved) provided the regular* *expressions in the definitions are 1-unambiguous. Otherwise it is exponential (w.r.t. to the maximal size of a non 1-unambiguous regular expression).*

The notion of extention subtyping introduced here seems interesting and useful, because it is close to the extension mechanism of XML Schema and an efficient checking algorithm for it exists. What is missing, is a completeness proof of the algorithm, i.e. that whenever it returns *false* then indeed the first type is not an extension subtype of the other. We conjecture that the algorithm is complete. The future work is to prove this. In case it turns out to be false, we intend to modify the algorithm (and/or the definition of extension subtyping), in order to develop an efficient sound and complete algorithm for checking extension subtyping.

6   Conclusions

We discussed subtyping of tree-structured data, such as XML and HTML documents. We proposed a type formalism motivated by XML Schema and accommodating two concepts of subtyping: inclusion subtyping (corresponding to XML Schema notion of type restriction) and extension subtyping (motivated by XML Schema's type extension). We provided algorithms for checking both kinds of subtyping. Two restrictions on the type definitions are imposed. To simplify the algorithms, we require that type definitions are proper (cf. Def. 7). For the algorithms to be polynomial, the regular expressions in type definitions should be 1-unambiguous (in the sense of [4]). The restrictions seem acceptable; this opinion needs however practical verification.

Acknowledgements.   This research has been partially funded by the European Commission and by the Swiss Federal Office for Education and Science within the 6th Framework Programme project REWERSE number 506779 (cf. {http://rewerse.net}). The authors thank an anonymous referee for remarks concerning relations to ontology reasoning.

References

1. A. V. Aho, R. Sethi, and J. D. Ullman. *Compilers: Principles, Techniques and Tools.* Addison-Wesley, 1986.
2. Sacha Berger, François Bry, Sebastian Schaffert, and Christoph Wieser. Xcerpt and visXcerpt: From Pattern-Based to Visual Querying of XML and Semistructured Data. In *Proceedings of 29th Intl. Conference on Very Large Databases, Berlin, Germany (9th–12th September 2003)*, 2003.
3. A. Brown, M. Fuchs, J. Robie, and P. Wadler. MSL: A model for W3C XML Schema. In *Proc. of WWW10*, 2001.
4. A. Brüggemann-Klein and D. Wood. One-unambiguous regular languages. *Information and Computation*, 142(2):182–206, May 1998.

5. François Bry and Sebastian Schaffert. Towards a Declarative Query and Transformation Language for XML and Semistructured Data: Simulation Unification. In *Proceedings of International Conference on Logic Programming, Copenhagen, Denmark (29th July–1st August 2002)*, volume 2401 of *LNCS*, 2002.

6. H. Common, M. Dauchet, R. Gilleron, F. Jacquemard, D. Lugiez, S. Tison, and M. Tommasi. Tree automata techniques and applications. http://www.grappa.univ-lille3.fr/tata/, 1999.

7. J. E. Hopcroft, R. Motwani, and J. D. Ullman. *Introduction to Automata Theory, Languages and Computation*. Addison-Wesley, 2nd edition, 2001.

8. H. Hosoya, J. Vouillon, and B. C. Pierce. Regular expression types for XML. In *Proc. of the International Conference on Functional Programming*, pages 11–22. ACM Press, 2000.

9. M. Klein, D. Fensel, F. van Harmelen, and I. Horrocks. The relation between ontologies and XML schemas. *Electronic Trans. on Artificial Intelligence*, 2001. Special Issue on the 1st International Workshop "Semantic Web: Models, Architectures and Management", http://www.ep.liu.se/ea/cis/2001/004/.

10. M. Murata, D. Lee, M. Mani, and K. Kawaguchi. Taxonomy of XML schema languages using formal language theory. Submitted, 2003.

11. A. Wilk and W. Drabent. On types for XML query language Xcerpt. In *International Workshop, PPSWR 2003, Mumbai, India, December 8, 2003, Proceedings*, number 2901 in LNCS, pages 128–145. Springer Verlag, 2003.

12. Extensible markup language (XML) 1.0 (second edition), W3C recommendation. http://www.w3.org/TR/REC-xml, 2000.

13. XML Schema Part 0: Primer. http://www.w3.org/TR/xmlschema-0/, 2001.

Towards Generic Query, Update, and Event Languages for the Semantic Web

Wolfgang May, José Júlio Alferes, and François Bry

Institut für Informatik, Universität Göttingen, Germany
`may@informatik.uni-goettingen.de`
CENTRIA, Universidade Nova de Lisboa, Portugal
`jja@di.fct.unl.pt`
Institut für Informatik, Ludwig-Maximilians-Universität München, Germany
`francois.bry@ifi.lmu.de`

Abstract. We outline aspects of querying and updating resources on the Web and on the Semantic Web, including the development of query and update languages in course of the REWERSE project. When considering updates and communication of updates between autonomous sources, reactive behavior plays an important role such that an event language is required. This article provides a systematic outline of the intended research steps towards handling reactivity and evolution on the Web.

1 Introduction

Use of the *Web* today –commonly known as the "World Wide Web"– mostly focuses on the page-oriented perspective: most of the Web consists of browsable HTML pages only. From this point of view, the Web can be seen as a graph that consists of the resources as nodes, and the *hyperlinks* form the edges. Here, queries are stated against individual nodes, or against several nodes, e.g., with formalisms like F-Logic [16] or Lixto [3]; or in case that the sources are provided in XHTML, they can be queried by XQuery, XPathLog [17], or Xcerpt [5]. As such, the Web is mainly seen from its static perspective of autonomous *sources*, whereas the *behavior* of the sources, including active interaction of resources does not play any important role here.

But there is more on the Web of today than HTML pages. Leaving the superficial point of view of HTML pages, the Web can be seen as a set of *data sources*, some of which are still browsing-oriented, but there are also database-like resources that can actually be queried. In fact, besides HTML documents that are accessed as a whole, and in which (query) processing has then to be done separately, there are XML (including XHTML) data sources, described by DTDs or XML Schemas, that in general can be queried (e.g., by XPath/XQuery, XPathLog or Xcerpt). Moreover, specialized information sources (that we call, abstractly, *Web services*) exist that provide answers only to a restricted set of queries that are given abstractly as a set of name-value pairs.

With these representations, the perspective may shift more to the idea of a Web consisting of (a graph of) *information systems*. In these information systems, data extraction may be thought not only in terms of local queries, but also

H.J. Ohlbach and S. Schaffert (Eds.): PPSWR 2004, LNCS 3208, pp. 19–33, 2004.

in terms of global queries that are stated against the Web, or against a group (or community) of nodes on the Web. Given the highly heterogeneous and autonomous characteristics of the Web, this requires appropriate query languages, and a way to deal with the integration of data from the various sources. The aspects of query languages for this Web are discussed below, in Section 2.

But such an infrastructure of autonomous sources should allow for more than querying. Consider a set of sources of travel agencies and airline companies. It is important to be capable of querying such a set for, e.g. timetables of flights, availability of flight tickets, etc. But a Web consisting of information systems should allow for more. For example: it should allow for drawing conclusions based on knowledge (e.g. in the form of derivation rules) available on each node; it should allow for making reservations via a travel agency, and automatically make the corresponding airline company (and also other travel agencies) aware of that; it should allow airline companies to change their selling policies, and have travel agencies automatically aware of those changes; etc. The Web, as we see it, with such capabilities can be seen as forming an active, "living" infrastructure of autonomous systems, where reactivity, evolution and its propagation plays a central role. Given these requirements, the knowledge of one such system could be classified into three conceptual levels: facts (e.g. in XML or wrapped in XML); a knowledge base, given by derivation rules (e.g. marked up in RuleML); and behavior/reaction rules, specifying which actions are to be taken upon which event and given what conditions. In this context events may either be internal events (e.g., updates), or external events (e.g., messages), and actions may include (local) updates of the knowledge, remote actions (potentially structured by transactions), synchronization actions, and possibly "blackbox" actions. Since, for being autonomous, sources may rely on different data models with different modelling assumptions and languages, an external description of the interface is also needed.

This view of the Web raises new issues, and requires new languages, the aspects of which will be outlined in the remainder of the paper. Moreover, we provide a systematic outline of the intended research steps towards handling reactivity and evolution on the Web. For reaching this goal, our approach will be to start from existing technologies and extend them step by step, just as demanded by the specific needs encountered. In Section 2 we discuss query languages for the Web. Then, in Sections 3 to 6 we discuss languages for reactivity, evolution and communication on the (non-semantic) Web. Evolution and Reasoning on the Semantic Web are then discussed in Section 7.

2   Web Query Languages

2.1   Today's Web Query Languages

Query languages similar to (but different from) those used and developed for databases are needed on the Web for easing the retrieval of data on the Web, or easing the specification of (materialized or non-materialized) views (in the database sense) and for expressing complex updates, especially intensional updates (i.e., updates of intensional predicates expressed in terms of queries) that must then be translated into updates of the actual sources.

In addition to user-defined queries, queries play an important role also for the Web itself: dynamic Web pages (i.e., whose content is generated at query time) are non-materialized views (i.e., views that are computed at data retrieval time). Here, closedness of the language is obviously necessary: it is defined over Web contents, and its output must be valid Web contents.

Design of Web Query Languages. Early Web query languages developed from query languages for semistructured data, most of them have then been migrated to XML. The design decisions and experiences of these languages have to be considered when designing query and manipulation languages for the Web as a whole. An overview of these can be found in [19]:

Logic programming-style rule-based languages (immediately including an up-date language) have been presented with e.g. *WSL/MSL (Wrapper/Mediator Specification Language)* [12], and F-Logic [16]. *Lorel* [20] and StruQL [11] fol-lowed the SQL/OQL-style clause-based design; StruQL was then developed into XML-QL [10]. Other languages developed from the area of tree matching and transformations, e.g., *UnQL* [7], *XDuce* [13], or *YATL* [9].

The standard XML languages developed from the experience with the above-mentioned languages and from the SGML area. XPath has been established as an addressing language. It is based on path expressions for navigation, ex-tended with filters. It serves as the base for many other W3C languages in the XML world. XQuery extends XPath with SQL-like clause-based constructs FLWOR: FOR ... LET ... WHERE ... ORDER BY ... RETURN to a full-fledged query language. Variables are bound in the FOR and LET clauses to the answer sets of XPath expressions. The WHERE clause expresses further conditions, and the RETURN clause creates an XML structure as a result. While the selection parts in the FOR and LET clauses are XPath-based, an XML pattern in XML-QL style is used in the RETURN clause where the variables are embedded into literal XML and constructors. Proposals for extending XQuery with update constructs (XUp-date) have been published, e.g., in [22]. As a *transformation* language, XSLT fol-lows a completely different idea for providing information from the Web: Here, transformation rules specify how information is extracted from a data source.

Recent Non-standard XML Query Languages. The Lixto system [3] also uses a graphical interface for querying HTML, where a query is developed by in-teractively selecting nodes from a browser presentation. Internally, Lixto uses a logic programming language for XML called *Elog*, based on flattening XML data into Datalog. XPathLog [17] combines first-order logic, and XPath expressions extended with variable bindings. It is completely XPath-based both in the rule body (query part) and in the rule read (update part), thereby defining an update semantics for XPath expressions.

Xcerpt [5] is a *pattern-based* language for querying and transforming XML data. Its basic form follows a clean, rule-based design where the query (matching) part in the body is separated from the generation part in the rule head. XML instances are regarded as terms that are matched by a term pattern in the rule body, generating variable bindings. An extension with updates, called *XChange*, is currently designed as a clause-based language.

Comparison of Design Concepts. The existing languages for handling semi-structured data and XML differ in several facets in terms of the concepts they use, e.g., access mechanisms and homogeneity of the query and generation part (patterns, path expressions), underlying data model (graph vs. tree), nature of the underlying theoretical framework (logic-based or denotational semantics), and last but not least clause-based or logic-programming-style syntax and semantics. All languages discussed above are *rule-based* and *declarative*, generating variable bindings by a matching/selection part in the "rule body" and then using these bindings in the "rule head" for generating output or updating the database. This rule-based nature is more or less explicit: F-Logic, MSL/WSL (Tsimmis), XPathLog, and Elog use the ":-" Prolog syntax, whereas UnQL, Lorel, StruQL, XML-QL, XQuery/XUpdate, and Xcerpt cover their rule-like structure in an SQL-like clause syntax. These clausal languages allow for a straightforward extension with update constructs.

2.2   Requirements on Query Languages for the Web

Obviously, a Web query language must allow to include explicitly multiple data sources. For this, queries should also be robust against certain changes in a data source, e.g., splitting a data source over several ones that are linked by XLink/XPointer. The execution model must be modular in the sense that it combines answers contributed by multiple data sources. It must consider that data sources provide different, possibly restricted, functionality (answering arbitrary queries, providing access to bulk data, answering a fixed set of data). Thus, closedness is also an important property: query languages are used to define views that act themselves as virtual data sources, and that must be in the same format as the other sources.

In the context of the Web, end even more of the Semantic Web, querying goes much further can "only" accessing the base data, as can e.g. be done by SQL or XML query languages. Query answering on the Semantic Web in general also requires to use meta-data, e.g., expressed using RDF or OWL, but maybe also thesauri (as used in information retrieval and computational linguistics), and thus must support *reasoning* about the query, data, and metadata. The actual forms of reasoning to be applied with RDF, OWL, thesauri, etc., and in general on the forthcoming Semantic Web are rather unclear today – this is one of the goals of current research.

For providing a base for such research, flexible, and extensible query languages including "lightweight reasoning facilities" appear to be a good choice for a first step towards generic tools for the Semantic Web. For several reasons, we propose to use rule-based languages for querying:

Rules provide a natural modularization, and the rule-based paradigm covers a lot of sub-paradigms for designing a wide range of language types as described above: SQL and XQuery are actually a form of simple rules (for defining views),

XSLT is rule-based, and languages like Datalog provide a multitude of semantics for any kinds of reasoning. Coming back to the modularization issue, a simple form of non-monotonic negation in presence of recursion (such as restriction to stratified programs) seems to be sufficient for a deductive query language for the Semantic Web. Additional expressive power can be restricted and extended by choosing suitable semantics – e.g. recursion is needed for computing closure relations (as those of RDF and OWL) and can be easily "bought" with using a fixpoint semantics. In [6] it is shown how the rule-based language Xcerpt can be used for reasoning on Web meta-data such as RDF and OWL data. In it, recursive rules are a convenient way to express common forms of reasoning on the Semantic Web e.g. for traversing several edges relating remote concepts. Such complex semantics of rule languages are well investigated in logic programming.

Additionally, rule-based languages can easily be extended to updates and in general to the specification of dynamics on the Web. Here, research on ECA rules and active databases can be applied and extended.

As another consequence of their modularity, rule-based languages are relatively easy to understand and program.

Modular Design of Language Processors. The use of rule-based languages allows also for a modular design of language processors. These consist then of two components: one for the interpretation of rule heads and bodies, and one for implementing the global semantics for suitably evaluating a set of rules.

The language base will most probably be provided by XML, where the individual languages are distinguished by their syntax, i.e., the namespaces and their element names and attribute names. Thus, a generic rule processor will be able to handle arbitrary rules (not only query rules, but also updates and general reaction rules) and to apply appropriate processing to each type of rules. This way, also new languages can be integrated at any time.

3   Local Behavior: Answering Queries and Being Reactive

The simplest activity on the Web is query answering. From the point of view of the user, querying is a static issue: there is no actual temporal aspect in it (except possibly a delay). Nevertheless, from the point of view of the resources, there comes reactivity into play: when answering queries, the resources must answer in reaction to a query message, and in case that the query is answered in cooperation of several sources, they must also send messages to other resources.

Such cooperation is in general required when considering communities of resources on the Web. Even more, cooperation and communication is already necessary when a resource contains references in any form to another resources. Two types of cooperation for query answering can be distinguished:

Distributed Query Answering of Explicit Queries. Explicit queries in any XML query language can be stated against XML resources that are specified by a

DTD or an XML Schema. Such resources can contain references to other XML resources by XLink elements with XPointers. A model for answering queries in the presence of XLink references has been investigated in [18]. The actual evaluation of a query in this model results in (re)active communication of result sets and/or subqueries between resources. This behavior is a simple form of reactivity.

Query Answering by Web Services. Web services can also be used for answering (often only a specific set of) queries. For this, they can either use their local knowledge (e.g., facts and derivation rules), or they can also contact other resources for answering a query (e.g., a travel agency service that uses the schedules of trains and flights from several autonomous sources). In this case, the behavior of the Web service is actually not simply query-answering, but can be seen as a general (re)active behavior, given by an external interface description (e.g., in WSDL) that can provide much more functionality than only query answering. Such Web services are instances of general *reactivity*: there is a message, and the resource performs some actions. Moreover, Web services may have an internal state (e.g., reservation systems) that they update.

For including general reactivity of Web services into the intended reasoning on the Semantic Web, a formal specification of their behavior is required. Here, we distinguish two types of Web services, according to the possibilities of reasoning about their behavior (and updating it): Web services where a formal specification of their behavoir exists –either directly rule-based or by any formal method– can be subject to reasoning, whereas other Web services will be considered as black boxes.

Note that, so far, we have described a mainly non-changing, but *active* Web consisting of nearly isolated passive and locally active Web resources. In this setting, evolution on the Web takes place by: either local changes in data sources via updates (e.g. changing a flight schedule); or local evolution of Web services by reaction to events due to their own, specified, behavior. However, this scenario already raises a number of issues deserving investigation, and will serve as our base case for *reactivity*. From this base case, independent, different dimensions can be derived. Namely: the definition of a global model theory and reasoning about global constraints and consistency aspects based on computing answers to queries; testcases for basic communication of resources via *messages* and *reaction rules*; expressing and reasoning about general non-state-changing reactivity on the Web; extension from queries to updates (where updates require the evaluation of a query e.g. for addressing the actual item to be updated). Such updates on the XML level will provide our simplest case of *dynamics*.

4   Updates and Evolution of the Web

Evolution of the Web is a twofold aspect: on today's Web, evolution means mainly evolution of individual Web sites that are updated locally. In contrast, considering the Web as a "living organism" that *consists* of autonomous data sources, but that will *show* a global "behavior" (as already investigated above for query answering) leads to a notion of evolution of the Web as *cooperative evolution* of its individual resources.

In this context, update languages are needed for several tasks, besides simply updating of the contents of a Web site by its owner, or as a reaction on actions of some user (e.g. when a user books a flight, the reservation of a seat must be stored in the underlying database). The updated site can be either the local database of the respective Web site, but most likely, this is an update to a remote database (e.g. in the above example when the booking is done via a travel agency, and the reservation must be forwarded to an update of the carrier company) – seen as a *view update*. But update languages must also allow for modifying the data and *behavior* of a Web site, e.g. in adaptive Web systems (the user modelling data must be updated, and the behavior of the system will change).

Thus, when "updating the Web", two aspects must be taken into account: there are "local" updates that apply to a given Web site only; and there are updates in a "distributed" scenario, that must be propagated from one Web site to another.

In the first case, an update language according to the data model of the respective Web site is required. In the second, there must be a declarative, semantic framework for generically specifying the update, and additionally, a framework how to *communicate* the update (e.g. to Web sites that provide a materialized view on others' data) is required.

As already mentioned above, local update languages are in general extensions of query languages: the query language is used (i) for determining what data is updated, and (ii) for determining the new value. Note that in both cases, the respective answer is in general not a single data record or a single value, but can be a set or – in the XML case – a substructure. Moreover, the value of (ii) can be dependent on the current item of the answer computed in (i).

Example 1. *Consider a Web site of an online shop, where for all articles the prices without and with VAT are given. An update of the VAT rate to this page would require to update the prices for* all *items of an answer set with an individually computed new price. (obviously, a good design in reality would only store the net price and compute the gross price by multiplying it with the current percentage for the VAT.)*

So, the local update languages will be directly based on the local query languages – in most cases, languages for operating on XML data such as XQuery/XUpdate or Xcerpt/Xchange.

Update languages for the *Web* are to be based on query languages for the Web. Using XML as the common date model, these and local languages can most likely be the same. So, the problem in general (distributed) updates is not the update language itself, but lays in the communication and propagation of updates between resources.

Update propagation consists of (i) propagating an update, and (ii) processing/materializing the update at another Web resource. The latter, we have just seen, is solved by local update languages, so the remaining problem turns out how to communicate updates on the (Semantic) Web. This problem again is twofold: (i) infrastructure and organization, and (ii) language. The former will be dealt with later in Section 6 since it is not directly a language-related issue. Next, we investigate language aspects of this communication.

5   Languages for Reactive Behavior on the Web

Following a well-known and successful paradigm, we propose to use rules, more specifically, *reactive rules* according to the *Event-Condition-Action* (ECA) paradigm for the specification of reactivity. An important advantage of them is that the *content* of the communication can be separated from the *generic semantics* of the rules themselves. Cooperative and reactive behavior is then based on events (e.g., an update at a data source where possibly others depend on). The depending resources detect events (either they are delivered explicitly to them, or they poll them via the communication means of the Web; see next section) Then, conditions are checked (either simple data conditions, or e.g. tests if the event is relevant, trustable etc.), which are queries to one or several nodes and are to be expressed in the proposed query language. Finally, an appropriate action is taken (e.g., updating own information accordingly). This action can also be formulated as a transactions whose ACID properties qensure that either all actions in a transaction are performed, or nothing of is done.

Thus, the language for the ECA rules must comprise a language for describing events (in the "Event" part), the language for queries (in the "Condition" part), and a language for actions (including updates) and transactions (in the "Action" part). An important requirement here is, that specification and event detection is as much declarative and application-level as possible. The design of event languages should be based on the experiences in the area of *active database systems.*

Events. An (atomic) event is in general any detectable occurrence on the Web, i.e., (local) system events, incoming messages including queries and answers, transactional events (commit, confirmations etc), updates of data anywhere in the Web, or any occurrences somewhere in an application, that are (possibly) represented in explicit data, or signalled as the event itself. For these *atomic events*, it must also be distinguished between the event itself (carrying application-specific information), and its metadata, like the type of event (update, temporal event, receipt of message, ...), time of occurrence, the time of detection/receipt (e.g., to refuse it, when it had been received too late), the event origin or its generator (if applicable; e.g. in terms of its URI).

Reactive rules often do not specify reactions on atomic events, but use the notion of *complex events*, e.g., "when E_1 happened and the E_2 and E_3, but not E_4 after at least 10 minutes, then do A". Complex events are usually defined in terms of an *event algebra* [8, 21]. Thus, a declarative language for describing complex events is required, together with algorithms for handling complex events. This language should not be concerned with what the information contained in the event might be, but only with types of events.

So, several integrated languages have to be defined: the surrounding language for complex events, a language for atomic events and their metadata, and languages for expressing the contents of different types of events.

This point, again, calls for modular design – an event processor must be able to process all kinds of atomic events and to cooperate with the complex event module (which can be rule-driven by itself), and to forward the event *contents* to suitable processors.

A main difference wrt. active database systems is here that on the Web with its autonomous, often a priori unknown nodes, more information about time points and identity of event generatoring instances must be present since there is no centralized, common synchronization.

An aspect here that will become important and has to be tackled, is integrability of the event meta language, the event contents languages, and the query language. It is desirable that the specification of complex events can be combined with requirements on the state of resources at given intermediate timepoints, e.g. "when at timepoint t_1, a cancellation comes in and somewhere in the past, a reservation request came in in a timepoint when all seats were booked, then, the cancellation is charged with an additional fee". In this case, the complex event handler has to state a query at the moment when a given event arrives. For being capable of describing these situations, a logic (and system) that deals with sequences of events and queries is required. Such approaches have e.g. been presented in *Transaction Logic* [4] and in *Statelog* [15]; we will also investigate the use of Evolving Logic Programs [1] for this purpose.

The view described up to this point is to result in a rule-based infrastructure for implementing and reasoning about evolution on the Web. This infrastructure relies on the detection of (complex) events and the communication of messages (represented in XML), and on reaction rules that define the behavior of resources upon detection of events. Local knowledge is defined by facts, derivation rules, and reaction rules. All of this local knowledge is encoded in XML, and is updatable, in the sense that the update language to be developed must be capable of changing both fact, derivation rules and reactive rules. Here we may rely on the studies done in the context of logic programming about updating derivation and reactive rules (e.g. in [2]).

Several research steps must be taken in order to reach these results, besides the definition and implementation of a global language of rules, events, and messages covering evolutionary and reactive behavior (in the lines described above). Namely, one further needs to find and investigate suitable formalizations for describing the autonomous, distributed nature of this knowledge, and its change in time, and to express a global semantics and reasoning principles about the *Web Evolution and Reactivity* rule language in these formalisms.

For using the resulting infrastructure, possible communication structures inside groups of nodes on the Web must be identified and classified. These structures are essential for having global strategies of propagating the knowledge among the various nodes, and will be the subject of the next section.

6   Communication Structure and Knowledge Propagation

Communication on the Web as a living organism consisting of autonomous sources and groups or communities of sources requires knowledge about capabilities and behavior of participating resources. Thus, every resource must be distinguished by its capabilities, both from the point of view as a knowledge base, and from a directly functional point (i.e. its interface, e.g. considered as a Web service). In general, for establishing and maintaining communities, metadata about available resources must be communicated, before actual data can be handled. This general case requires the definition of semantic properties of nodes (as on the Semantic Web), and is discussed in Section 7. However, several aspects of the structure for communication and propagation of data can be discussed, and deserve investigation, even on a non-Semantic Web infrastructure as the one described up to now.

Without metadata about resources, communication concerning the *evolution* of the Web is bound to definite links between resources. In this setting, evolution takes place if a resource (or its knowledge) evolves locally, and another resource that depends upon it also evolves (as a reaction).

Example 2. *Consider the Website of a vendor of computer parts, where for each article some technical data and the price is given, and another resource that compares the offers of several vendors and shows e.g., the cheapest vendor for all parts etc. In case that a vendor page changes, the comparison page must also change.*

For this to be possible without the recourse to a Semantic Web, the roles of resources must be predefined. Here resources can be classified according to their role as information providers/consumers: Some resources only provide information: these are data "sources" that are updated locally by their maintainers (e.g., the flight schedule database of the *Lufthansa*). We call such resources *information sources*. Other resources *combine* information from other resources according to their own application logic, and that in course provide this information (e.g. travel agencies providing packages of flights and train connections). We call such resources *information transformers*. A third kind of resources only uses information from others but are not (or only in small scale) used as information providers (e.g., statistics about the average load of flights).

Moreover there must exist knowledge about other resources and their roles, for evolution to take place. The above roles of resources induce different handlings of the *communication paths*. One possibility is to have a *registered communication path*, where the "provider" knows about the "client" who uses its data. In another possibility the user of the information knows his "provider", but not vice versa.

Additionally, information transformers can be classified according to their way how their knowledge is represented, and how it is maintained. An information transformer may not materialize its knowledge but, rather, answer queries only by transforming them into queries against sources/transformers via its application logic. Alternatively, an information transformer may maintain an own (materialized) database that is populated with data that is derived from information from other sources/transformers.

The application logic of non-materializing transformers is in general specified Datalog-like where their *knowledge base* is represented via *derivation rules*. There is no internal knowledge except the rule base, thus, answers are always computed from the current state of the used transformers or sources. There is no knowledge maintenance problem; on the other hand, such resources totally depend on the 24/7 availability of their information providers.

The application logic of materializing transformers can either be specified in a Datalog-style, or by *reactive rules* that say how to update their information according to incoming messages (or a combination of both). In the latter case, the resource is more independent from its providers, but the *view maintenance problem* comes up.

Using peer-to-peer-communication, the propagation of knowledge between sources –which is obviously desirable to keep resources up-to-date– can then be done in two distinct ways:

- Push: an information source/transformer informs registered users of the updates. A directed, targeted propagation of changes by the *push* strategy is only possible along registered communication paths. It takes place by explicit *messages*, that can be update messages, or just information about what happened.
- Pull: resources that obtain information from a fixed informer can *pull* updates by either explicitly asking the infor mer whether he executed some updates recently, or can regularly update themselves based on queries against their providers. Communication is based on queries and answers (that are in fact again sent as messages). Here, *continuous query* services can be helpful.

For putting to work this form of propagation of knowledge on the Web, even at a non-semantic level, much work remains to be done. Firstly we have to extend the basic approach (queries) described in Section 3 to updates: updates of XML data (using XQuery/XUpdate, XPathLog, or XChange). Here, we have to deal also with updates "along" XLink references, extending the querying approach described in [18]. In a next research step, the communication of changes due to evolution of a resource to other resources by the *push* strategy will be studied and implemented. Here, especially the representation of messages in combination with appropriate reaction rules of the "receiving" source has to be designed. Also, *active* rules that implement the *pull* strategy will be investigated, together with suitable strategies (e.g. change-log in XML) of information providers.

Note that both in the case of push and pull strategies, the actual reactivity, i.e., how the instance that is informed reacts on an *event*, is expressed by ECA rules as described in the previous section.

7   Evolution and Reasoning on the Semantic Web

The aim of the Semantic Web endeavor is to provide a *unified, integrated* view on the Web on a conceptual level by enriching today's Web data with meta-data. This meta-data attaches explanations or formalizations of the base data meaning and thus allows for an automatic retrieval of data or of services offered on the Web in terms of the data or service descriptions provided by the meta-data.

In our research we assume that the Semantic Web will consist of sets of resources (or *communities*) that can be accessed by using a common semantic level (i.e., conceptual model, ontology, and access mechanisms). For an application area, there can be several such communities. Queries are then stated against the semantic level that forwards them towards the individual sources (via a mapping), and that combines the results also according to the semantic level. Communities can have different intra-community structure, which in course has implications to the interface towards the user. In a centralized community, there exists a central resource that does the mapping tasks, and that serves as user interface for querying. In a non-centralized community, each source performs the mapping task by itself when it is queried, and (sub)queries are forwarded to relevant nodes in the community to be answered. The mapping between the communities must be done by special *bridge* resources that belong to two or more communities and that *mediate* between the ontologies. These bridge resources will use GLAV-like [14] bidirectional ontology mappings between participating communities for mapping queries, answers, and also communication messages between the communities.

The issue of query languages for the Semantic Web, and the research steps we intend to take in this direction, have already been briefly discussed in Section 2. But the Semantics Web also raises new issues, and opens new possibilities for studying and building an infrastructure for evolution in the Web:

Example 3 (Update on the Semantic Web). *Consider an update in the timetable of Lufthansa that adds a daily flght from Berlin to Timbuktu at 12:00, arriving at 20:00. There will be several other resources for whom this information is relevant. First there are german travel agencies etc. who use the Lufthansa schedule for their offers. For these, it is probably the case that they are directly informed, or that they query the LH timetable regularly. There will also be other resources that have no immediate connection to the LH resource. E.g., a taxi service at Timbuktu can have the rule "when a european airline provides a flght to Timbuktu, we should provide a car at the airport with a driver who speaks the language of the country where the plane comes from". Here, the resource should somehow be able to detect updates somewhere on the Semantic Web that are relevant for itself.*

For this, it is clear that we need a "global" language for updating and communicating updates, and communication strategies how to propagate pieces of information through the Semantic Web. For languages, we will investigate possibilities of lifting the above sketched ones in order to be able to work on the ontological level. For studying communication strategies, i.e. how to propagate pieces of information through the Semantic Web, we focus on two scenarios: Firstly, in "controlled" communities, the participating resources are known a priori and contribute to a common task (e.g. in a tourist information system, which is one of the prospective testbed scenarios in REWERSE). Second, in "dynamic" communities the participating resources are not completely known a priori, but the whole Semantic Web is considered as a potential information source. In this case, peers that provide a given information must be searched and then queried to answer a message. Here, search for a given "service" must be organized in a CORBA-like way - but, in general without a central repository.

The latter case allows to use the union of *all* information throughout the Web. In it, the *Semantic*-property of the Web is crucial for automatically mediating between several actual schemata. Moreover, such communities provide a natural notion of community-global state, as the union of the knowledge in each community resource. For maintaining the consistency of the global state in this environment of autonomous resources, appropriate communication and reasoning mechanisms are needed. These must be able to foster communication of updates between the participating resources.

Reasoning on (and about) the Semantic Web is an area that deserves further research on various topics, among which the ones below that we will study in the course of the REWERSE project; especially the following issues:

Uncertainty and Incomplete Knowledge. The Semantic Web gives the user (and its resources) an "infinite" feeling (no instance can ever claim to collect all knowledge of the Web as a whole). Thus, "global" reasoning inside the Web must be based on a "as-far-as-I-know"-logic: all reasoning *on* the Web has to cope with uncertainty and incomplete knowledge, and, in case of derived facts in general also with nonmonotonic "belief" revisions (negation, aggregates).

Dealing with Quality of Information. Obviously, the Web (and also the Semantic Web) contains inconsistent information - both by simply erroneous or outdated information. Additionally, many information sources provide opinions, beliefs, conjectures and speculations. Often, these should also be handled (e.g., for answering questions like "what stocks in automobile industry are recommended to buy?"). Even, information *about* (here, we do not mean metadata, but e.g., evaluations of the trustworthyness and the quality, or comments about statements of other resources) resources is available. Thus, reasoning has to cope with inconsistencies, incompleteness, and with modal information.

Inconsistencies and Consistency Management. Inconsistencies can occur inside the information of a resource (to be avoided), between resources of a "community" (in most cases, also to be avoided), and across the whole Web (immanent). The latter ones cannot be avoided, but must be *handled* by each resource.

For consistency management, in addition to simply "importing" updates, resources must be able to apply additional reasoning. There may be the case that the receiver of an update does not want to implement an update because he does not believe it. Then, the community-global knowledge becomes either inconsistent (when dealing with facts), or there are different "opinions" or "presentations" (e.g., when handling news from different news services). Additionally, a resource can come to the decision that one of its informers must be replaced by another one. So, the communities can be subject to internal restructuring (still sharing the same ontology, but with different communication paths).

The Semantic Web itself also has to act in a self-cleaning way: Resources that provide erroneous or outdated information can be notified, requested for update, and potentially sanctioned by others. For doing this, instances with powerful reasoning capabilities (and equipped with some authority!) are needed. Communities inside the Semantic Web will turn out to be useful for this kind of *quality management*.

Temporal Aspects. Mainly for reasoning *about* evolution and reactivity in the Web, a logic for reasoning about several states is needed. We need to be able to express evolution and reactivity of individual resources, and of the global state. Here again, two issues will be investigated:

For describing and reasoning about immediate reactions, e.g., for update propagation and consistency maintenance, only a low number of successive states is needed. Here, a detailed reasoning on the states is required, and a logic in the style of classical temporal logics, LTL or CTL with a Kripke semantics based on a given semantics for individual states, could be used.

On the other hand, reasoning about activities involving a higher number of states for describing *transaction*-like activities on the Web, mostly takes place on a higher level of abstraction. Here, the temporal aspect is dominating over the actual data, and a logic in the style of Transaction Logic [4] is useful.

8   Conclusions

This article has outlined aspects of querying and updating resources on the Web and on the Semantic Web and stressed approaches the authors are investigating in the framework of the REWERSE research project (cf. http://rewerse.net). Much remains to be done. Firstly, a querying framework has to be selected and enhanced into a formalism for specifying evolution and reactivity on the Web and Semantic Web. This has to be done considering conventional Web applications and query languages as well as the emerging Semantic Web query languages as well as Semantic Web use cases. Secondly, the approaches proposed have to be checked against these use cases as well as against other use cases developed in other contexts, possibly stressing other concerns.

Acknowledgement

This research has been funded by the European Commission and by the Swiss Federal Office for Education and Science within the 6th Framework Programme project REWERSE number 506779 (cf. http://rewerse.net).

References

1. J. J. Alferes, A. Brogi, J. A. Leite, and L. M. Pereira. Evolving logic programs. In S. Flesca et al, editor, *JELIA '02*, pages 50–61. Springer LNAI, 2002.
2. J. J. Alferes, J. A. Leite, L. M. Pereira, H. Przymusinska, and T. C. Przymusinski. Dynamic updates of non-monotonic knowledge bases. *The Journal of Logic Programming*, 45(1–3):43–70, 2000.
3. R. Baumgartner, S. Flesca, and G. Gottlob. Visual web information extraction with Lixto. In *Intl. Conference on Very Large Data Bases (VLDB)*, 2001.
4. A. J. Bonner and M. Kifer. An overview of transaction logic. *Theoretical Computer Science*, 133(2):205–265, 1994.
5. F. Bry and S. Schaffert. Towards a declarative query and transformation language for XML and semistructured data: Simulation unification. In *Intl. Conf. on Logic Programming (ICLP)*, pages 255–270, 2002.
6. F. Bry, T. Furche, P. Pătrânjan, and S. Schaffert. Data retrieval and evolution on the (semantic) web: A deductive approach. Technical Report PMS-FB-2004-13, University of Munich, May 2004.
7. P. Buneman, S. Davidson, G. Hillebrandt, and D. Suciu. A query language and optimization techniques for unstructured data. In *ACM Intl. Conference on Management of Data (SIGMOD)*, pages 505–516, Montreal, Canada, 1996.
8. S. Chakravarthy, V. Krishnaprasad, E. Anwar, and S.-K. Kim. Composite events for active databases: Semantics, contexts and detection. In VLDB, 1994.
9. S. Cluet, C. Delobel, J. Siméon, and K. Smaga. Your mediators need data conversion. In *ACM Intl. Conference on Management of Data (SIGMOD)*, 1999.
10. A. Deutsch, M. Fernandez, D. Florescu, A. Levy, and D. Suciu. XML-QL: A query language for XML. http://www.w3.org/TR/1998/NOTE-xml-ql, 1998.
11. M. Fernandez, D. Florescu, J. Kang, A. Levy, and D. Suciu. STRUDEL: A web-site management system. In *ACM SIGMOD*, pages 549–552, 1997.
12. H. Garcia-Molina, Y. Papakonstantinou, D. Quass, A. Rajaraman, Y. Sagiv, J. Ullman, V. Vassalos, and J. Widom. The TSIMMIS approach to mediation: Data models and languages. *Journal of Intelligent Information Systems*, 8(2), 1997.
13. H. Hosoya, B. Pierce. Xduce: A typed XML processing language. *WebDB 2000*.
14. M. Lenzerini. Information integration. In *International Joint Conference on Artificial Intelligence (IJCAI)*, 2003.
15. Bertram Ludäscher. *Integration of Active and Deductive Database Rules*. DISDBIS 45, infix-Verlag, Sankt Augustin, 1998. PhD thesis, Universität Freiburg.
16. B. Ludäscher, R. Himmeröder, G. Lausen, W. May, and C. Schlepphorst. Managing semistructured data with FLORID: A deductive object-oriented perspective. *Information Systems*, 23(8):589–612, 1998.
17. W. May. A rule-based querying and updating language for XML. In *Workshop on Databases and Programming Languages (DBPL 2001)*, Springer LNCS 2397, 2001.
18. W. May. Querying linked XML document networks in the web. In *11th. WWW Conference*, 2002. Available at http://www2002.org/CDROM/alternate/166/.
19. W. May. Xpath-logic and xpathlog: A logic-programming style XML data manipulation language. *Theory and Practice of Logic Programming*, 4(3), 2004.
20. J. McHugh, S. Abiteboul, R. Goldman, D. Quass, and J. Widom. Lore: A database management system for semistructured data. *SIGMOD Record*, 26(3):54–66, 1997.
21. M. P. Singh. Semantical considerations on workflows: An algebra for intertask dependencies. In *Proc. DBPL-5*, volume 5, 1995.
22. I. Tatarinov, Z. Ives, A. Halevy, and D. Weld. Updating XML. In *ACM Intl. Conference on Management of Data (SIGMOD)*, pages 133–154, 2001.

Data Retrieval and Evolution on the (Semantic) Web: A Deductive Approach

François Bry, Tim Furche, Paula-Lavinia Pătrânjan, and Sebastian Schaffert

Institut für Informatik, Ludwig-Maximilians-Universität München
Oettingenstr. 67, D-80538 München, Germany

Abstract. To make use of data represented on the Semantic Web, it is necessary to provide languages for Web data retrieval and evolution. This article introduces into the (conventional and Semantic) Web query language *Xcerpt* and the event and update language *XChange*, and shows how their deductive capabilities make them well suited for querying, changing and reasoning with data on both the conventional and the Semantic Web. To this aim, small application scenarios are introduced.

1 Introduction

The *Semantic Web* is an endeavour aiming at enriching the existing Web with meta-data and data and meta-data processing to allow computer systems to actually *reason* with the data instead of merely *rendering* it. To this aim, it is necessary to be able to *query* and *update* data *and* meta-data. Existing Semantic Web query languages (like DQL[1] or TRIPLE[2]) are special purpose, i.e. they are designed for querying and reasoning with special representations like OWL[3] or RDF[4], but are not capable of processing generic Web data, and are furthermore restricted to a specific reasoning algorithm like a certain description logic (e.g. $\mathcal{SHIQ}$). In contrast, the language *Xcerpt* presented in this article (and more extensively in e.g. [1]) is a general purpose language that can query any kind of XML data, i.e. "conventional" Web as well as Semantic Web data, and at the same time provides advanced reasoning capabilities. It could thus serve to implement a wide range of different reasoning formalisms.

Likewise, the maintenance and evolution of data on the (Semantic) Web is necessary: the Web is a "living organism" whose dynamic character requires languages for specifying its evolution. This requirement regards not only updating data from Web resources, but also the propagation of changes on the Web. These issues have not received much attention so far, existing update languages (like XML-RL Update Language [2]) and reactive languages [3] developed for XML data offer the possibility to execute just simple update operations while important features needed for propagation of updates on the Web are still missing. The

---

[1] DAML Query Language, http://www.daml.org/dql.
[2] TRIPLE Language, http://triple.semanticweb.org.
[3] Web Ontology Language, http://www.w3.org/TR/owl-ref/
[4] Resource Description Framework, http://www.w3.org/TR/rdf-primer/

H.J. Ohlbach and S. Schaffert (Eds.): PPSWR 2004, LNCS 3208, pp. 34–49, 2004.

language *XChange* also presented in this article builds upon the query language Xcerpt and provides advanced, Web-specific capabilities, such as propagation of changes on the Web (*change*) and event-based communication between Web sites (*exchange*), as needed for agent communication and Web services.

This article is structured as follows: Section 2 summarises the design principles underlying the languages Xcerpt and XChange. Section 3 gives a brief introduction into the Web query language Xcerpt, and illustrates the use of recursion as a first step towards Semantic Web querying. Section 4 subsequently introduces the event language XChange that builds upon Xcerpt. Section 5 introduces a simple Semantic Web scenario and uses it to illustrate how Xcerpt and XChange can be used for querying and evolution on the Semantic Web. Finally, Section 6 concludes with a summary and perspectives for future research.

2 Design Principles of Xcerpt and XChange

2.1 Principles of Xcerpt

Pattern-Based Queries. Most query languages for the Web, like XQuery or XSLT, use a path-based or *navigational* selection of data items, i.e. a selection is specified in terms of path expressions (usually expressed in the language XPath) consisting of a sequence of location steps that specify how to reach nodes in the data tree in a stepwise manner. In contrast, Xcerpt uses a *positional* or *pattern-based* selection of data items. A query pattern is like a *form* that gives an *example* of the data that is to be selected, like the forms of the language QBE or query atoms in logic programming. As in logic programming, a query pattern can furthermore be augmented by zero or more variables, which serve to retrieve data items from the queried data.

Incomplete Patterns. As data on the Web (e.g. XML) often differs much in structure and does not necessarily conform to an (accessible) schema, query patterns in a Web query language like Xcerpt need to be much more flexible than in logic programming or relational databases. Therefore, Xcerpt allows to specify incompleteness in *breadth* (i.e. within the same parent in the data tree) as well as in *depth* (i.e. on paths in the data tree), and it is possible to consider *ordered* and *unordered* content.

Rules. Xcerpt programs consist of deduction rules (*if ... then ...* rules) that may interact via (possibly recursive) rule chaining. Rules are advantageous as they are easy to comprehend even for novice users and can serve to structure a program into logical components. They are also well-suited for *deduction*, i.e. they allow to give meaning to data very much like rules in logic programming.

Backward Chaining. Rule-based query languages for traditional database systems (like *Datalog*) mainly use *forward chaining*, where rules are applied to the current database until saturation is achieved (it is thus *data driven*). On the Web, forward chaining is not always possible, for the database is the whole Web, which is not feasible as an initial point for forward chaining. As a consequence, a *backward chaining* approach is sought for. Backward chaining is *goal driven*, i.e. only such resources are retrieved that are necessary to answer the query.

Separation of Querying and Construction. Most XML query languages (e.g. XQuery and XSLT, but also pattern-based approaches such as XML-QL) mix querying and construction by embedding data selection in construction patterns and by using subqueries inside construction patterns. In this way, however, the structure of the queried data is no longer apparent from the query. Therefore, a strict separation of querying and construction is favourable.

Reasoning Capabilities. A query language for the Web should be capable of querying both, XML data (on the standard Web) and meta-data (on the Semantic Web). Most currently available query languages are specific to a certain task, i.e. they are either capable of querying XML data, or capable of querying and reasoning with meta-data in a specific formalism. However, meta-data might be given in different formalisms (like OWL Light/DL/Full or RDF), wherefore it is desirable that a query language is generic enough to work with any kind of meta-data, and provides generic reasoning capabilities (e.g. like Prolog) that allow to implement a wide range of different formalisms.

2.2   Principles of XChange

Communication Between Web Sites. XChange uses *events* to communicate between Web Sites. An event is an XML document with a root element with label `event` and the four parameters (represented as child elements as they may contain complex content) `raising-time` (i.e. the time of the raising machine when the event is raised), `reception-time` (i.e. the time of the receiving machine when the event is received), `sender` (i.e. the URI of the site where the event has been raised), and `recipient` (i.e. the URI of the site where the event has been received). An `event` is an envelope for arbitrary XML content, and multiple `events` can be nested (e.g. to create trace histories).

Peer-to-peer communication. XChange events are directly communicated between Web sites without a centralised processing or management of events. All parties have the ability to initiate a communication. Since communication on the Web might be unreliable, synchronisation is supported by XChange.

No broadcasting. The approach taken in XChange excludes broadcasting of events on the Web, as sending events to *all* sites is not adequate for the framework which XChange has been designed for (i.e. the Web). Hence, before an event is sent, its recipient Web sites are determined.

Transactions as Updating Units. Since it is sometimes necessary to execute *complex updates* in an *all-or-nothing manner* (e.g. when booking a trip on the Web, a hotel reservation without a flight reservation is useless), the concept of transactions is supported by the language XChange. More precisely, XChange transactions are composed of events posted on the Web and updates to be performed on one or more Web sites.

Complex applications specifying evolution of data and meta-data on the (Semantic) Web require a number of features that cannot always be specified by simple programs. In XChange transactions can also be used as *means for structuring* complex XChange programs.

Rule-Based Language. The language XChange aims at establishing reactivity, expressed by *reaction rules*, as communication paradigm on the Web. Reaction rules (also called *Event-Condition-Action* rules or active rules) are rules of the form `on` `event` `if` `condition` `do` `action`. At every occurrence of the event, the rule is triggered and the corresponding action is executed if the specified condition is satisfied. The components of an XChange Event-Condition-Action rule are:

- *Event* is an Xcerpt query against events received by the Web sites,
- *Condition* is an Xcerpt query against (local or remote) Web resources, and
- *Action* might be raising events and/or executing updates. These actions may be compound and considered as transactions. XChange considers *transactions* instead of isolated actions as active rules heads.

Pattern-Oriented Update Specifications. A metaphor for XChange (and at the same time one of the novelties of the update language) is to see XChange update specifications (i.e. Xcerpt queries against data terms, augmented with update operations) as forms, answers as form fillings yielding the data terms after update execution.

3 Xcerpt: Querying the Web

An Xcerpt program consists of at least one *goal* and some (possibly zero) *rules*. Rules and goals contain query and construction patterns, called *terms*. Terms represent tree-like (or graph-like) structures. The children of a node may either be *ordered*, i.e. the order of occurrence is relevant (e.g. in an XML document representing a book), or *unordered*, i.e. the order of occurrence is irrelevant and may be chosen by the storage system (as is common in database systems). In the term syntax, an *ordered term specification* is denoted by square brackets [ ], an *unordered term specification* by curly braces { }.

Likewise, terms may use *partial term specifications* for representing incomplete query patterns and *total term specifications* for representing complete query patterns (or data items). A term t using a partial term specification for its subterms matches with all such terms that (1) contain matching subterms for all subterms of t and that (2) might contain further subterms without corresponding subterms in t. Partial term specification is denoted by *double* square brackets [[ ]] or curly braces {{ }}. In contrast, a term t using a total term specification does not match with terms that contain additional subterms without corresponding subterms in t. Total term specification is expressed using *single* square brackets [ ] or curly braces { }.

Data Terms represent XML documents and the data items of a semistructured database, and may thus only contain total term specifications (i.e. single square brackets or curly braces). They are similar to *ground* functional programming expressions and logical atoms. A *database* is a (multi-)set of data terms (e.g. the Web). A non-XML syntax has been chosen for Xcerpt to improve readability, but there is a one-to-one correspondence between an XML document and a data term.

Example 1. The following two data terms represent a train timetable (from `http://railways.com`) and a hotel reservation offer (from `http://hotels.net`).

At site `http://railways.com`:	At site `http://hotels.net`:

```
travel {                              voyage {
  last-changes-on { "2004-04-30" },     currency { "EUR" },
  currency { "EUR" },                   hotels {
  train {                                 city { "Vienna" },
    departure {                           country { "Austria" },
      station { "Munich" },               hotel {
      date { "2004-05-03" },                name { "Comfort Blautal" },
      time { "15:25" }                      category { "3 stars" },
    },                                      price-per-room { "55" },
    arrival {                               phone { "+43 1 88 8219 213" },
      station { "Vienna" },                 no-pets {}
      date { "2004-05-03" },              },
      time { "19:50" }                    hotel {
    },                                      name { "InterCity" },
    price { "75" }                         category { "3 stars" },
  },                                        price-per-room { "57" },
  train {                                   phone { "+43 1 82 8156 135" }
    departure {                           },
      station { "Munich" },               hotel {
      date { "2004-05-03" },                name { "Opera" },
      time { "13:20" }                      category { "4 stars" },
    },                                      price-per-room { "106" },
    arrival {                               phone { "+43 1 77 8123 414" }
      station { "Salzburg" },             },
      date { "2004-05-03" },            ...
      time { "14:50" }                 },
    },                                ...
    price { "25" }                    }
  },
  train {
    departure {
      station { "Salzburg" },
      date { "2004-05-03" },
      time { "15:20" }
    },
    arrival {
      station { "Vienna" },
      date { "2004-05-03" },
      time { "18:10" }
    }
  }...
}
```

Query Terms are (possibly incomplete) patterns matched against Web resources represented by data terms. They are similar to the latter, but may contain *partial* as well as *total* term specifications, are augmented by *variables* for selecting data items, possibly with *variable restrictions* using the $\rightsquigarrow$ construct (read *as*), which restricts the admissible bindings to those subterms that are matched by the restriction pattern, and may contain additional query constructs like *position matching* (keyword `position`), *subterm negation* (keyword `without`), *optional subterm specification* (keyword `optional`), and *descendant* (keyword `desc`).

Query terms are "matched" with data or construct terms by a non-standard unification method called *simulation unification* that is based on a relation called *simulation.* In contrast to Robinson's unification (as e.g. used in Prolog), simulation unification is capable of determining substitutions also for incomplete and unordered query terms. Since incompleteness usually allows many different alternative bindings for the variables, the result of simulation unification is not only a single substitution, but a (finite) *set of substitutions*, each of which yielding ground instances of the unified terms such that the one ground term matches with the other.

Construct Terms serve to reassemble variables (the bindings of which are specified in query terms) so as to construct new data terms. Again, they are similar to the latter, but augmented by *variables* (acting as place holders for data selected in a query) and the *grouping construct* `all` (which serves to collect all instances that result from different variable bindings). Occurrences of `all` may be accompanied by an optional sorting specification.

Example 2. Left: A query term retrieving departure and arrival stations for a train in the train document. Partial term specifications (partial curly braces) are used since the train document might contain additional information irrelevant to the query. *Right:* A construct term creating a summarised representation of trains grouped inside a `trains` term. Note the use of the `all` construct to collect all instances of the `train` subterm that can be created from substitutions in the substitution set resulting from the query on the left.

```
travel {{                               trains {
  train {{                                all train {
    departure {{                            from { var From },
      station { var From } }},              to   { var To }
    arrival {{                            }
      station { var To }   }}           }
  }}
}}
```

Construct-Query Rules (short: rules) relate a construct term to a query consisting of AND and/or OR connected query terms. They have the form

CONSTRUCT *Construct Term* FROM *Query* END

Rules can be seen as "views" specifying how to obtain documents shaped in the form of the construct term by evaluating the query against Web resources (e.g. an XML document or a database). Queries or parts of a query may be further restricted by arithmetic constraints in a so-called condition box, beginning with the keyword `where`.

Example 3. The following Xcerpt rule is used to gather information about the hotels in Vienna where a single room costs less than 70 Euro per night and where pets are allowed (specified using the `without` construct).

```
CONSTRUCT
  answer [ all var H ordered by [ P ] ascending ]
FROM
  in {
    resource { "http://hotels.net"},
    voyage {{
      hotels {{
        city { "Vienna" },
        desc var H ⤳ hotel {{
          price-per-room { var P },
          without no-pets {}
        }}
      }}
    }}
  } where var P < 70
END
```

An Xcerpt query may contain one or several references to *resources*. Xcerpt rules may furthermore be *chained* like active or deductive database rules to form complex query programs, i.e. rules may query the results of other rules. Recursive chaining of rules is possible. In contrast to the inherent structural recursion used e.g. in XSLT, which is essentially limited to the tree structure of the input document, recursion in Xcerpt is always explicit and free in the sense that any kind of recursion can be implemented. Applications of recursion on the Web are manifold:

- structural recursion over the input tree (like in XSLT) is necessary to perform transformations that preserve the overall document structure and change only certain things in arbitrary documents (e.g. replacing all **em** elements in HTML documents by **strong** elements).
- recursion over the conceptual structure of the input data (e.g. over a sequence of elements) is used to iteratively compute data (e.g. create a hierarchical representation from flat structures with references).
- recursion over references to external resources (hyperlinks) is desirable in applications like a Web crawler that recursively visit Web pages.

Example 4. The following scenario illustrates the usage of a "conceptual" recursion to find train connections, including train changes, from Munich to Vienna.

The **train** relation (more precisely the XML element representing this relation) is defined as a "view" on the train database (more precisely on the XML document seen as a database on trains):

```
CONSTRUCT
  train [ from [ var From ], to [ var To ] ]
FROM
  in {
    resource { "file:travel.xml" },
    travel {{
      train {{
        departure {{ station { var From } }},
        arrival   {{ station { var To }   }}
      }}
    }}
  }
END
```

A recursive rule implements the transitive closure **train-connection** of the relation **train**. If the connection is not direct (recursive case), then all intermediate stations are collected in the subterm `via` of the result. Otherwise, `via` is empty (base case).

```
CONSTRUCT
  train-connection [
    from [ var From ],
    to   [ var To ],
    via  [ var Via, all optional var OtherVia ]
  ]
FROM
  and {
    train [ from [ var From ], to [ var Via ] ],
    train-connection [
      from [ var Via ],
      to   [ var To ],
      via  [[ optional var OtherVia ]]
    ]
  }
END
CONSTRUCT
  train-connection [
    from [ var From ],
    to   [ var To ],
    via  [ ]
  ]
FROM
  train [ from [ var From ], to [ var To ] ]
END
```

Based on the "generic" transitive closure defined above, the following rule retrieves only connections between Munich and Vienna.

```
GOAL
  connections {
    all var Conn
  }
FROM
  var Conn ⤳ train-connection [[ from { "Munich" } , to { "Vienna" } ]]
END
```

4   XChange: Evolution on the Web

XChange is a declarative language for specifying evolution of data and meta-data on the (Semantic) Web.

Events. As mentioned in section 2.2, XChange events are XML data, hence a generic data exchange between Web sites is supported by XChange, simplifying the transfer of parameters (e.g. raising time, recipient(s)) and thus the execution of actions in a user-defined synchronised manner.

Example 5. Assume that a train has 30 minutes delay. The control point that observes this raises the following event and sends it to `http://railways.com`:

```
event {
  recipient { "http://railways.com" },
  delay {
    train { departure { station { "Munich" }, date { "2004-09-23" },
                        time { "21:30" } },
            minutes-delay { "30" } }
  }
}
```

The recipient sites (e.g. `http://railways.com` in Example 5) process the incoming events in order to execute (trans)actions or to raise other events. Thus only the information of interest for these sites is used (e.g. the time stamps may be used to decide whether the events are too old or not). The processing of events is specified in XChange by means of *event-raising rules*, *event-driven update rules*, and *event-driven transaction rules*.

Event-Raising Rules. The body of an event-raising rule may contain Xcerpt queries to incoming events, Xcerpt queries to XML resources (local or remote), and conditions that variables (specified in the queries to incoming events or XML resources) should satisfy. The head of an event-raising rule contains resource specifications (i.e. the resources to which events shall be sent) and event specifications (used to construct event instances). In the following, an example of an XChange event-raising rule is given.

Example 6. Mrs. Smith uses a travel organiser that plans her trips and reacts to happenings that might influence her schedule. The site `http://railways.com` has been told to notify her travel organiser of delays of trains Mrs. Smith travels with:

```
RAISE
  event {
    recipient { "http://travelorganizer.com/Smith" },
    delay {
      train { departure { var M, estimated-time { var DT + var Min } },
              arrival { var U, estimated-time { var AT + var Min } }
      }
    }
  }
ON
  event {{
    delay {{
      train {{ departure { var M ↝ station { "Munich" },
                           var Date ↝ date { "2004-09-23" },
                           time { var DT ↝ "21:30" } },
               minutes-delay { var Min } }}
    }}
  }}
FROM
  in {
    resource { "http://railways.com" },
    travel {{ train {{ departure {{ var M, var Date, time { var DT } }},
                       arrival {{ var U ↝ station { "Vienna" }, time { var AT } }}
             }}
    }}
  }
END
```

Update Rules. The XChange update language uses rules to specify intensional updates, i.e. a description of updates in terms of queries. The notion of update rules is used to denote rules that specify (possibly complex) updates (i.e. insertion, deletion, and replacement). The body of an XChange update rule may (and generally does) contain Xcerpt queries (to XML resources and/or incoming events), which specify bindings for variables and conditions that variables should satisfy. The head of an XChange update rule contains resource specifications for the data that is to be updated, update specifications, and relations between the desired updates.

An XChange update specification is a (possibly incomplete) pattern for the data to be updated, augmented with the desired update operations. The notion of update terms is used to denote such patterns containing update operations for the data to be modified. An update term may contain different types of update operations. The head of an update rule may contain one or more update terms.

Example 7. At `http://railways.com` the train timetable needs to be updated as reaction to the event given in Example 5:

```
UPDATE
  in {
    resource { "http://railways.com" },
    travel {{
      last-changes-on { var L replaceby var RTime },
      train {{
        departure {{ station { var DS }, var Date, time { var DT },
                    insert estimated-time { var DT + var Min } }},
        arrival {{ time { var AT }, insert estimated-time { var AT + var Min } }}
      }}
    }}
  }
ON
  event {{
    raising-time { var RTime },
    delay {{
      train {{ departure { station { var DS }, var Date, time { var DT } },
              minutes-delay { var Min } }}
    }}
  }}
END
```

Synchronisation of Updates. XChange provides the capability to specify relations between complex updates and execute the updates synchronously (e.g. when booking a trip on the Web one might wish to book an early flight *and* of course the corresponding hotel reservation, *or* a late flight *and* a shorter hotel reservation). As the updates are to be executed on the Web, network communication problems could cause failures of update execution. To deal with such problems, an explicit specification of synchronisation of updates is possible with XChange, a kind of control which logic programming languages lack. Means to realise synchronisation of updates on the Web: dependent updates (specified by means of XChange synchronisation operations, which express ordered/unordered *conjunction* of updates, or ordered/unordered *disjunction* of updates), time specification for updates (expressing e.g. an explicit time reference, or a timeout for update execution), and user specified commitment (realised by supporting transactions in XChange).

Transaction Rules. Transaction rules are very similar to XChange update rules, with the important difference that transactions (consisting of event and/or update specifications that should be raised and/or executed in an all-or-nothing manner) are specified in the head of reaction rules. In case of transaction abort, a rollback mechanism that undoes partial effects of a transaction is to be used.

XChange transactions are transactions executed on user requests or as reactions to incoming XChange events. The latter transactions are specified in the head of XChange event-driven transaction rules. An example of an event-driven transaction rule is given next.

Example 8. The travel organiser of Mrs. Smith uses the following rule: if the train of Mrs. Smith is delayed such that her arrival will be after 23:00h then book a cheap hotel at the city of arrival and send the telephone number of the hotel to her husband's address book. The rule is specified in XChange as:

```
TRANSACTION
  and [
    update {
      in { resource { "http://hotels.net" },
        reservations {{
          insert reservation { var H, name { "Christina Smith" },
                               from { "2004-09-23" }, until { "2004-09-24" } }
        }}  }  },
    update {
      in { resource { "address-book://addresses/my-husband" },
        addresses {{
          insert my-hotel { phone { var Tel },
                            remark { "I'm staying in Vienna over night!" } }
        }}  }  }
  ]
ON
  event {{
    sender { "http://railways.com" },
      delay {{
        train {{ arrival { station { var City ⤳ "Vienna" }, estimated-time { var ETime } }
        }}
      }}
  }} where var ETime after 23:00
FROM
  in {
    resource { "http://hotels.net" },
    voyage {{
      hotels {{ city { var City },
                desc var H ⤳ hotel {{ price-per-room {var P}, phone { var Tel } }} }}
    }}
  } where var P < 70
END
```

5   Querying and Evolution on the Semantic Web

The vision of the Semantic Web is that of a Web where the semantics of data is available for processing by automated means. Based on standards for representing Semantic Web (meta-)data, such as RDF and OWL, the need for a expressive, yet easy-to-use query language to access the large amounts of data expected to be available in the Semantic Web is evident. However, in contrast to most current approaches for querying the Semantic Web, we believe that it is crucial to be able to access both conventional and Semantic Web data within the same query language. The following examples illustrate based on a small set of RDF data some of the peculiarities and pitfalls of a Semantic Web query language and how these can be handled in Xcerpt and XChange.

Example 9. The data term shows a small excerpt from a book database together with a sample ontology over novels and other literary works. Some of the concepts used are drawn from the "Friend of a Friend" (foaf) project[5]. The rest of this paper uses prefixes to abbreviate the URLs for RDF, RDFS and OWL properties.

---

[5] http://www.foaf-project.org/

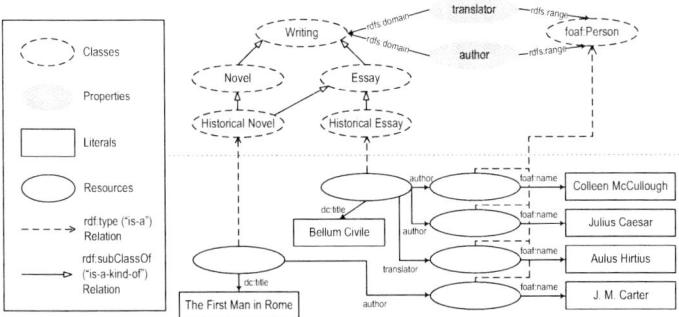

Fig. 1. RDF Graph for Example 9

At site `http://bookdealer.com`:

```
RDF {                                          &translator @ rdf:Property {
  Historical_Novel {                             rdfs:domain {
    author {                                       ^&writing
      foaf:Person {                              }
        foaf:name{"Colleen McCullough"}          rdfs:range {
      }                                            ^&foaf:Person
    },                                           }
    dc:title{"The First Man in Rome"}          }
  }                                            &historical_novel @ rdfs:Class {
  Historical_Essay {                             rdfs:label { "Historical_Novel" },
    author {                                     rdfs:subClassOf {
      foaf:Person {                                &novel @ rdfs:Class {
        foaf:name { "Julius Caesar" }              rdfs:label { "Novel" },
      },                                           rdfs:subClassOf {
      foaf:Person {                                  &writing @ rdfs:Class {
        foaf:name { "Aulus Hirtius" }                  rdfs:label { "Writing" }
      }                                            } } }
    },                                         }
    dc:title { "Bellum Civile" },              rdfs:subClassOf {
    translator {                                 &historical_essay @ rdfs:Class {
      foaf:Person {                                rdfs:label { "Historical_Essay" }
        foaf:name { "J. M. Carter" }             rdfs:subClassOf {
  } } }                                            &essay @ rdfs:Class {
  &author @ rdf:Property {                          rdfs:label { "Essay" }
    rdfs:domain {                                  rdfs:subClassOf {
      ^&writing                                      ^&writing
    }                                          } } } }
    rdfs:range {                               }
      ^&foaf:Person                          }
    }                                      }
  }
```

This data term represents the RDF graph shown in Figure 1: There are two books in the data, the first one is classified (via `rdf:type`) as a *Historical Novel*, a term defined in the sample ontology. Furthermore, it has an `author` that is a `foaf:Person` with `foaf:name` "Colleen McCullough". The second one also has a `translator` and several `authors`. The sample ontology is basically a conceptual hierarchy for a (small subset of) terms used to classify books and other literary works. The terms are related by `rdfs:subClassOf`, indicating that, e.g., a *Historical Novel* is a kind of *Novel* that, in turn, is a kind of *Writing*. Note the Xcerpt notation `id @ ... (^id`, resp.) for representing ID (`IDREF`, resp.) attributes.

For reasons of brevity and readability, a representation of the RDF graph as an Xcerpt data term is used that is very close to the syntactic representation of RDF graphs in XML. In this respect, our approach is similar to [4] for querying RDF data with XQuery. However, as is illustrated in the following, there are several peculiarities of Semantic Web data that most query languages for the conventional Web do not support easily.

Properties Are Optional and Multi-valued. In RDF, relations such as `author` or `rdf:type` between objects (also referred to as resources) are called properties. In contrast to traditional knowledge representation techniques, such as Frames, all properties in RDF are optional and multi-valued: it is not possible to formally restrict the number of properties of the same type between two resources. E.g., a `Writing` may have no translator, one translator, or any number of translators.

In Xcerpt, optional and multi-valued properties can easily be retrieved by using `all` and `optional`, as shown in Example 10.

Example 10. Retrieve all writings from `http://bookdealer.com` together with their title only if they have a title. Also return any authors or translators for each book, if there are any. `subClassOf[ var BookType, "Writing"]` expresses that the type of the resource must be a subclass of `Writing` (cf. Example 12).

```
CONSTRUCT
  RDF {
    var BookType {
      optional dc:title{ var Title },
      all optional author{ var Author },
      all optional translator{ var Translator }
    }
  }
FROM
  and {
    in {
      resource { "http://bookdealer.com" },
      RDF {{
        desc var BookType {
          optional author{ var Author },
          optional dc:title{ var Title },
          optional translator{ var Translator }
        }
      }}
    },
    subClassOf[ rdfs:Class {{ rdfs:label{var BookType} }},
               rdfs:Class {{ rdfs:label{"Writing"} }}      ]
  }
END
```

Inference. One of the most fundamental promises of the Semantic Web is that, given a machine-processable semantics for data, new data can be inferred from existing one automatically.

Example 11. All persons that have published together can be retrieved by the following program. The reflexivity of the co-author relation is expressed using unordered subterm specification (i.e. curly braces), as in `co-author{var X, var Y}`.

```
CONSTRUCT
  co-author{var X, var Y}
FROM
  and {
    in {
      resource { "http://bookdealer.com" },
      RDF {{
        var BookType {{
          author { var X },
          author { var Y },
        }}
      }}
    },
    subClassOf[ rdfs:Class {{ rdfs:label{var BookType} }},
               rdfs:Class {{ rdfs:label{"Writing"} }}    ]
  }
END
```

More interesting is the kind of inference that arises from traversing the structure of the RDF graph recursively, similar to the train connections in Example 4. This is required, e.g., to compute the closure of transitive relations. RDF Schema defines two such transitive relations `rdfs:subClassOf` and `rdfs:subPropertyOf`, OWL allows the definition of additional transitive properties by classifying them as subclasses of `owl:TransitiveProperty`.

Support for RDF Schema. RDF Schema extends RDF with a set of predefined properties and specifies a (partial) semantics for these properties. Most notably, means for defining a subsumption hierarchy for concepts and properties are provided by `rdfs:subClassOf` and `rdfs:subPropertyOf`. These properties are transitive. E.g., if a query asks for all `Writings`, also resources that are classified as `Novels` or `Historical_Essays` should be returned (under the sample ontology specified above).

Example 12. The semantics of, e.g., `rdf:subClassOf` can be easily implemented in Xcerpt as demonstrated by the following program. The transitive closure of `rdf:subClassOf` is computed using recursion (cf. Example 4).

```
CONSTRUCT
  subClassOf[ var Subclass, var Superclass ]
FROM
  or { RDF {{
         desc var Subclass ~> rdfs:Class {{
           rdfs:subClassOf {
             var Superclass ~> @ rdfs:Class {{ }}
           }
         }}
       }},
       and [ RDF {{
               desc var Subclass ~> rdfs:Class {{
                 rdfs:subClassOf {
                   var Z ~> rdfs:Class {{ }}
                 }
               }}
             }},
             subClassOf[ var Z, var Superclass ]    ]
  }
END
```

Other predefined relations from RDF (Schema) such as `rdf:type`, `rdfs:domain`, or `rdfs:range` can be implemented in a similar manner.

Evolution. Evolution and reactivity are at the core of the Semantic Web vision. It is crucial that relevant changes to data that has been used by a Semantic Web agent, e.g. in deciding which book to buy or what train to book, are consistently and rapidly propagated to all interested parties.

Example 13. Mrs. Smith is very interested in Essays and therefore wants to be notified about any new book that is classified as an Essay once it is added to the list of books managed by `http://bookdealer.com`. The following two XChange programs illustrate this scenario, the left hand shows the event specification, the right hand an update that triggers the event.

```
RAISE                                          UPDATE
  event {                                        in {
    recipient { "http://.../Smith" },              resource { "http://bookdealer.com" },
    new_book {                                     RDF {{
      type { var Type },                             insert Historical_Novel {
      all optional var Title                           dc:title { "Ein Kampf um Rom" }
    }                                                  author {
  }                                                      foaf:Person {
ON                                                         foaf:name { "Felix Dahn" }
  event {                                                }
    sender {"http://bookdealer.com"},                  }
    RDF {{                                           }
      insert var Type {{                           }}
        optional var Title ⤳ dc:title{{}}          }
      }}                                           END
    }}
  }
FROM
  subClassOf [
    rdfs:Class {{ rdfs:label{var Type} }},
    rdfs:Class {{ rdfs:label{"Essay"} }}
  ]
END
```

6   Perspectives and Conclusion

This article first introduced into the deductive query language Xcerpt and the event and update language XChange. It furthermore illustrated how the deductive capabilities of these languages make them well suited for querying and evolution on the *conventional* as well as the *Semantic* Web.

Xcerpt and XChange are ongoing research projects. Whereas the language Xcerpt is already in an advanced stage [1] (cf. also `http://www.xcerpt.org`), work on the language XChange has begun more recently, but first results are promising. Applying both languages to more complex Semantic Web applications is currently investigated and will likely result in the implementation of (partial) reasoners for certain ontologies. Also, including native support for certain reasoning constructs might increase usability and/or performance.

Acknowledgement. This research has been funded by the European Commission and by the Swiss Federal Office for Education and Science within the 6th Framework Programme project REWERSE number 506779 (cf. `http://rewerse.net`).

References

1. Schaffert, S., Bry, F., Querying the Web Reconsidered: A Practical Introduction to Xcerpt. In: Extreme Markup Languages 2004, Montreal, Canada (2004)

2. Liu, M., Lu, L., and Wang, G.: A Declarative XML-RL Update Language. In: Proc. Int. Conf. on Conceptual Modeling (ER2003). LNCS 2813, Springer-Verlag (2003)
3. Papamarkos, G., Poulovassilis, A., and Wood, P.T: Event-Condition-Action Rule Languages for the Semantic Web. In: Workshop on Semantic Web and Databases, VLDB'03, Berlin, VLDB'03 (2003)
4. Robie, J.: The Syntactic Web: Syntax and Semantics on the Web. In: XML Conference and Exposition 2001, Orlando, Florida (2001)

Rules and Queries with Ontologies: A Unified Logical Framework

Enrico Franconi and Sergio Tessaris

Faculty of Computer Science, Free University of Bozen-Bolzano, Italy
lastname@inf.unibz.it

Abstract. In this paper we present a common framework for investigating the problem of combining ontology and rule languages. The focus of this paper is in the context of Semantic Web (SW), but the approach can be applied in any Description Logics (DL) based system. In the last part, we will show how rules are strictly related to queries.

1 Introduction

The need for integrating rules within the Semantic Web framework was clear since the early developments. However, up to the last few years, the research community focused its efforts on the design of the so called *Ontology Layer*. Nowadays, this layer is fairly mature in the form of Description Logics based languages such as OWL-Lite and OWL-DL, which are now among W3C recommendations.

One of the key features of SW ontology languages development is the attention to the computational properties of the main reasoning tasks. In particular, decidability is seen as one of the characteristics which should be preserved by these languages. This constraint led to the restriction of the expressivity of ontology language which can be heavy for certain applications (e.g. Web Services, or integration of information systems). The problem increasing the expressivity of SW ontology languages over the established Ontology Layer, together with the need of providing powerful query languages, directed the research towards the investigation of the possibility of combining OWL languages with Rules based languages.

In recent years, more research has been devoted towards the integration of different sorts of rule based languages on top of the ontology layer provided by the OWL languages and in more general terms on top of a generic DL, and this work already produced some proposals for extending OWL languages. However, these proposals comes from different research communities, and often are difficult to compare because of the diverse underlying semantic assumptions.

With this work we provide an unifying framework in which the existing (and future) proposals can be compared. Moreover, we present a thorough analysis

This work has been partially supported by the EU projects Sewasie, KnowledgeWeb, and Interop.

H.J. Ohlbach and S. Schaffert (Eds.): PPSWR 2004, LNCS 3208, pp. 50–60, 2004.
© Springer-Verlag Berlin Heidelberg 2004

of the main contributions, with a particular attention to their expressive power and restrictions to guarantee the decidability of key inference problems. By using our framework, we show that – under the appropriate restrictions – there are strong correspondences among the proposals. This enable us to isolate interesting fragments of the proposed languages in which we can compare the reasoning abilities.

We reckon that, since the early 90s, the Description Logics community produced several important results w.r.t. the problem of integrating DL languages and rules. For this reason we do not restrict our analysis to proposals in the context of Semantic Web. On the contrary, we show that a careful analysis of this body of work provides a valuable reference to explore the borders of expressivity and tractability of the combination of the two kinds of language.

In this paper we identify three different approaches: the axiom-based approach, the logic programming approach, and the autoepistemic approach. We provide an exact characterisation of the three approaches, together with a correspondence among relevant fragments in the three cases.

Moreover, we turn our attention at the problem of querying knowledge represented by means of an ontology web language. We show that there is a strong connection between rules and queries, and that our framework is able to capture this fundamental aspect of reasoning in the Semantic Web.

Our work on a common framework is directed to provide the Semantic Web community a tool which can be the basis for the discussion towards a common rule language for the Semantic Web. To this purpose we emphasise which, according to our opinion, is the correct semantics for a rule language. On this track we are currently working on a proposal for the OWL-Log language, which combines OWL ontology languages and rules. Our proposal takes into account the existing works, as well as establishes standards as RuleML.

2   Rule-Extended Knowledge Bases

Let us consider a first-order function-free language with signature $\mathcal{A}$, and a description logic (DL) knowledge base Σ with signature subset of $\mathcal{A}$.

In this paper we do not introduce any particular DL formalism. In our context, DL individuals correspond to constant symbols, DL atomic concepts and roles (and features) are unary and binary predicates in the case of a classical DL or a OWL language, and DL atomic n-ary relations correspond to predicates of arity n in the case of a $\mathcal{DLR}$-like DL. Note that description logics with concrete data-types (such as OWL-Lite) are allowed as well.

A *term* is any constant in $\mathcal{A}$ or a variable symbol. If R is a predicate symbol of arity n and $t_1, \ldots, t_n$ are terms, $R(t_1, \ldots, t_n)$ is an *atom*, and an atom $R(t_1, \ldots, t_n)$ or a negated atom $\neg R(t_1, \ldots, t_n)$ are *literals*. A *ground* literal is a literal involving only constant terms. A set of ground literals is *consistent* if it does not contain an atom and its negation. If l is a literal, l or *not l* are *NAF-literals* (negation as failure literals). DL atoms, DL literals, and DL NAF-literals are atoms, literals, and NAF-literals whose predicates belong to the DL signature. A *rule r* may be of the forms:

$$h_1 \wedge \ldots \wedge h_\ell \leftarrow b_1 \wedge \ldots \wedge b_m \qquad \text{(classicalrule)}$$
$$h_1 :- b_1 \wedge \ldots \wedge b_m \wedge not\ b_{m+1} \wedge \ldots \wedge not\ b_n \qquad \text{(lp − rule)}$$
$$h_1 \wedge \ldots \wedge h_\ell \Leftarrow b_1 \wedge \ldots \wedge b_m \qquad \text{(autoepistemicrule)}$$

where $h_1, \ldots, h_\ell, b_1, \ldots, b_n$ are literals. Given a rule r, we denote by $H(r)$ the set $\{h_1, \ldots, h_\ell\}$ of *head* literals, by $B(r)$ the set of *body* literals $\{b_1, \ldots, b_n\}$, by $B^+(r)$ the set of *NAF-free* body literals $\{b_1, \ldots, b_m\}$, and by $B^-(r)$ the set of *NAF-negated* body literals $\{b_{m+1}, \ldots, b_n\}$. We denote by $\mathsf{vars}(\{l_1, \ldots, l_n\})$ the set of variables appearing in the literals $\{l_1, \ldots, l_n\}$. The *distinguished variables* of a rule r are the variables that appears both in the head and in the body of the rule, i.e., $D(r) = \mathsf{vars}(H(r)) \cap \mathsf{vars}(B(r))$. A *ground rule* is a rule involving only ground literals. A rule is *safe* if all the variables in the head of the rule are distinguished. A *DL rule* is a rule with only DL literals. A set of literals is *tree-shaped* if its co-reference graph is acyclic; a co-reference graph includes literals and variables as nodes, and labelled edges indicate the positional presence of a variable in a literal. An *atomic* rule is a rule having a single literal in the head. A set of rules is *acyclic* if they are atomic and no head literal transitively depends on itself; a head literal h directly depends on a literal l if there is an atomic rule r with head h and with l part of the body $B(r)$. A set of rules is a *view* set of rules if each rule is atomic and no head literal belongs to the DL signature. A *rule-extended knowledge base* $\langle \Sigma, \mathcal{R} \rangle$ consists of a DL knowledge base Σ and a finite set $\mathcal{R}$ of rules.

3   The Axiom-Based Approach

Let us consider a rule-extended knowledge base $\langle \Sigma, \mathcal{R} \rangle$ restricted to only classical rules.

Let I_Σ be a model of the description logics knowledge base Σ, i.e. $I_\Sigma \models \Sigma$. I is a model of $\langle \Sigma, \mathcal{R} \rangle$, written $I \models \langle \Sigma, \mathcal{R} \rangle$, if and only if I extends I_Σ with the interpretation of the non-DL predicates, and for each rule $r \in \mathcal{R}$ then

$$I \models \forall \mathbf{x}, \mathbf{y}. \exists \mathbf{z}. \left(\bigwedge B(r) \rightarrow \bigwedge H(r) \right)$$

where $\mathbf{x}$ are the distinguished variables of the rule $D(r)$, $\mathbf{y}$ are the non distinguished variables of the body $(\mathsf{vars}(B(r)) \setminus D(r))$, and $\mathbf{z}$ are the non distinguished variables of the head $(\mathsf{vars}(H(r)) \setminus D(r))$.

Let us define now the notion of logical implication of a ground literal l given a rule extended knowledge base: $\langle \Sigma, \mathcal{R} \rangle \models l$ if and only if $I \models l$ whenever $I \models \langle \Sigma, \mathcal{R} \rangle$. Note that the problems of DL concept subsumption and DL instance checking, and the problem of predicate inclusion (also called *query containment*) are all reducible to the problem of logical implication of a ground literal. Logical implication in this framework is undecidable, as it generalises the so-called *recursive CARIN* as presented in [Levy and Rousset, 1998]. Logical implication in an axiom-based rule extended knowledge base remains undecidable even in the case of atomic negation-free safe DL rules with a DL having just the universal role constructor $\forall R.\ C$. Note that logical implication in an axiom-based rule extended knowledge base even with an empty TBox in Σ is undecidable (see, e.g., [Baget and Mugnier, 2002]).

In order to recover decidability, we reduce the expressivity of the approach in several ways; all the following restrictions disallow non DL predicates in the rules.

Theorem 1.   *1. If we restrict the axiom-based approach to have only DL rules with tree shaped heads and bodies and without negated atomic roles, the problem of logical implication in the rule extended knowledge base is NEXPTIME-complete with $\mathcal{ALCQI}$, OWL-Lite and OWL-DL as the underlying description logics knowledge base language.*

   2. If in addition to the above conditions, constants are disallowed from the rules, the problem of logical implication in the rule extended knowledge base is EXPTIME-complete with any DL in EXPTIME (such as $\mathcal{ALCQI}$ or OWL-Lite) as the underlying description logics knowledge base language.

   3. [Levy and Rousset, 1998]: If we restrict the axiom-based approach to have only acyclic atomic negation-free safe DL rules with the $\mathcal{ALCNR}$ DL as the underlying description logics knowledge base language, the problem of logical implication is decidable in NEXPTIME.

The SWRL proposal [Horrocks and Patel-Schneider, 2004] can be considered as a special case of the axiom-based approach presented above. SWRL uses OWL-DL or OWL-Lite as the underlying description logics knowledge base language (which admits data types), but it restricts the rule language to safe rules and without negated atomic roles. From the point of view of the syntax, SWRL rules are an extension of the abstract syntax for OWL DL and OWL Lite; SWRL rules are given an XML syntax based on the OWL XML presentation syntax; and a mapping from SWRL rules to RDF graphs is given based on the OWL RDF/XML exchange syntax. Logical implication in SWRL is still undecidable. The complexity results listed in Theorem 1 are applicable to SWRL as well.

Another way to make the axiom-based approach decidable is to reduce the expressivity of the DL, in order to disallow universal-like statements, while keeping rules cyclic.

In [Levy and Rousset, 1998] it is shown that logical implication is decidable with atomic negation-free safe DL rules with the simple DL containing conjunction, disjunction, qualified existential, least cardinality and primitive negation.

In [Calvanese *et al.*, 2004] a proposal is made of a very simple knowledge representation language, which captures the fundamental features of frame-based formalisms and of ontology languages for the semantic web; the precise definition of the language can be found in [Calvanese *et al.*, 2004]. In this setting, it can be shown that the negation-free axiom-based approach is decidable, and the problem of logical implication of a ground literal is in EXPTIME, and it is polynomial in data complexity.

Conceptual graph rules [Baget and Mugnier, 2002] can be seen as a simple special case of an axiom-based rule extended knowledge base: CG-rules are negation-free, they do not have existential variables in the body, and Σ is TBox-free. Many decidable subclasses of CG-rules are special cases of the decidable cases presented above (but with Σ having a TBox); in particular, decidability of *range restricted CG-rules* is the TBox-free special case stated above [Levy and Rousset, 1998] of atomic negation-free safe DL rules.

4   The DL-Log Approach

Let us consider a rule-extended knowledge base $\langle \Sigma, \mathcal{R} \rangle$ where $\mathcal{R}$ is restricted to be a view set of lp-rules $\mathcal{P}$ (called *program*).

The *non-DL Herbrand base* of the program $\mathcal{P}$, denoted by $\mathcal{HB}_{\mathcal{P}^-}$, is the set of all ground literals obtained by considering all the non-DL predicates in $\mathcal{P}$ and all the constant symbols from $\mathcal{A}$. An *interpretation* I wrt $\mathcal{P}$ is a consistent subset of $\mathcal{HB}_{\mathcal{P}^-}$. We say I is a *model* of a ground literal l wrt the knowledge base Σ, denoted $I \models_{\Sigma} l$, if and only if

- $l \in I$, when $l \in \mathcal{HB}_{\mathcal{P}^-}$
- $\Sigma \models l$, when l is a DL literal

We say that I is a model of a ground rule r, written $I \models_{\Sigma} r$, if and only if $I \models_{\Sigma} H(r)$ whenever $I \models_{\Sigma} b$ for all $b \in B^+(r)$, and $I \not\models_{\Sigma} b$ for all $b \in B^-(r)$. We denote with $\mathsf{ground}(\mathcal{P})$ the set of rules corresponding to the grounding of $\mathcal{P}$ with the constant symbols from $\mathcal{A}$. We say that I is a model of a rule-extended knowledge base $\langle \Sigma, \mathcal{P} \rangle$ if and only if $I \models_{\Sigma} r$ for all rules $r \in \mathsf{ground}(\mathcal{P})$; this is written as $I \models \langle \Sigma, \mathcal{P} \rangle$.

Let us define now the notion of logical implication of a ground literal l given a rule extended knowledge base: $\langle \Sigma, \mathcal{P} \rangle \models l$ if and only if $I \models_{\Sigma} l$ whenever $I \models \langle \Sigma, \mathcal{P} \rangle$. In the case of a NAF-free program, as well in the case of a program with stratified NAF negation, it is possible to adapt the standard results of datalog, which say that in these cases the logical implication can be reduced to model checking in the (canonical) minimal model. So, if $I_m^{\mathcal{P}}$ is the minimal model of a NAF-free or stratified program $\mathcal{P}$, then $\langle \Sigma, \mathcal{P} \rangle \models l$ if and only if $I_m^{\mathcal{P}} \models_{\Sigma} l$.

In the case of an unrestricted program $\mathcal{P}$, an answer set semantics can be adopted to characterise logical implication. In this paper we do not define the semantics of unrestricted rule extended knowledge bases; for a precise account, please refer to [Rosati, 1999; Eiter *et al.*, 2004].

Theorem 2. *[Eiter et al., 2004]: The combined complexity of logical implication in a rule extended knowledge base with an EXPTIME-complete description logic (like, e.g., $\mathcal{ALCQI}$ or OWL-lite) is EXPTIME-complete in the case of NAF-free or stratified programs and it is NEXPTIME-complete in the unrestricted case. In a rule extended knowledge base with a NEXPTIME-complete description logic (like, e.g., $\mathcal{ALCQIO}$ or OWL-DL) the complexity is NEXPTIME-complete in the case of NAF-free programs and it is NP^{NEXP}-complete in the case of stratified programs and in the unrestricted case as well.*

In addition, it is possible to prove that the problem of logical implication of a DL literal in a rule extended knowledge base is independent on the presence of the program P. This means that the DL knowledge base is unaffected by the rule system, which can be seen as built on top of the DL knowledge base.

The DL-Log approach was first introduced with AL-Log. The AL-Log approach [Donini et al., 1998b] is as a restriction of DL-Log. In fact, in AL-Log only view negation-free safe rules, whose DL predicates are only unary, with the $\mathcal{ALC}$ DL, are allowed. The complexity of logical implication is shown to be in NEXPTIME. [Rosati, 1999] extended AL-Log by allowing any DL predicate in the body of the rules. [Eiter et al., 2004] introduced DL-Log in the way we are presenting here.

An extension of DL-Log is the one where the recursive program is given a fixpoint semantics, which involves all individuals in the model, not only the ones in the Herbrand universe. In this extension, logical implication is undecidable with any DL having the ability to state at least atomic inclusion axioms between concepts [Calvanese and Rosati, 2003]. It can be shown that, in the fixpoint based semantics, the DL-Log approach can be reconstructed by adding, for each rule, a special non-DL unary $top_{\mathcal{HB}}$ atom for each variable appearing in each DL literal of the rule, thus constraining the DL variables to be in the Herbrand universe anyway. Note also that in the case of acyclic rules, the fixpoint semantics coincide with the axiom-based semantics.

It is worthwhile mentioning at the end of this section three additional recent works that relate DLs with lp-rules: DLP [Grosof et al., 03] and [Motik et al., 04; Swift, 2004]. In these papers it is shown how to *encode* the reasoning problem of a DL into a pure logic programming setting, i.e., into a rule extended knowledge base with a Σ without TBox. In the case of DLP, this is accomplished by encoding a severely restricted DL into a NAF-free negation-free DL program. In the two latter approaches, the full power of disjunctive logic programming is needed to perform the encoding of quite expressive DLs, at the cost of an exponential blow-up in space of the encoding.

5   The Autoepistemic Approach

Let us consider a rule-extended knowledge base restricted to autoepistemic rules.

Let I_Σ be a model, over the non empty domain Δ, of the description logics knowledge base Σ, i.e. $I_\Sigma \models \Sigma$. Let's define a variable assignment α in the usual way as a function from variable symbols to elements of Δ. A model of $\langle \Sigma, \mathcal{R} \rangle$ is a non empty set M of interpretations I, each one extending a DL model I_Σ with some interpretation of the non-DL predicates, such that for each rule r and for each assignment α for the distinguished variables of r the following holds:

$$\left(\forall I \in M.\ I, \alpha \models \exists \mathbf{x}.\ \bigwedge B(r) \right) \rightarrow \left(\forall I \in M.\ I, \alpha \models \exists \mathbf{y}.\ \bigwedge H(r) \right)$$

where $\mathbf{x}$ are the non distinguished variables of the body $(\mathsf{vars}(B(r)) \setminus D(r))$, and $\mathbf{y}$ are the non distinguished variables of the head $(\mathsf{vars}(H(r)) \setminus D(r))$.

Let us define now the notion of logical implication of a ground literal l given a rule extended knowledge base: $\langle \Sigma, \mathcal{R} \rangle \models l$ if and only if

$$\forall M. \ (M \models \langle \Sigma, \mathcal{R} \rangle) \rightarrow \forall I \in M. \ (I \models l)$$

The autoepistemic approach was first introduced by [Donini *et al.*, 1998a], with the goal of formalising the *constraint rules* implemented in many practical DL systems. Such rules, in fact, are simple to implement since they influence the ABox reasoning, but leave the TBox reasoning unaffected. These rules are also the basis of the recent formalisations of peer-to-peer systems [Franconi *et al.*2003]. As shown in [Franconi *et al.*, 2003], the autoepistemic semantics as defined above is equivalent to the context-based semantics of [Ghidini and Serafini, 1998], and to the use of the autoepistemic operator, as defined, e.g., in [Reiter, 1992]. Using the results in [Marx, 1999; Gabbay *et al.*, 2003], we can show that logical implication is decidable in the case of a rule extended knowledge base with DL rules with tree shaped body and heads, with the $\mathcal{ALC}$ DL; the precise complexity bounds are still unknown.

6   Queries

We now introduce the notion of a query to a rule extended knowledge base, that includes a DL knowledge base, a set of rules, and some facts.

Definition 1. *A* query *to a rule extended knowledge base is a (possibly ground) literal* $q_{\mathbf{x}}$ *with variables* $\mathbf{x}$ *(possibly empty). The* answer set *of* $q_{\mathbf{x}}$ *is the set of all substitutions of* $\mathbf{x}$ *with constants* $\mathbf{c}$ *from* $\mathcal{A}$, *such that the for each substitution the grounded query is logically implied by the rule extended knowledge base, i.e.,*

$$\{ \mathbf{c} \ \text{in} \ \mathcal{A} \mid \langle \Sigma, P \rangle \models q_{[\mathbf{x}/\mathbf{c}]} \}.$$

This definition of query is based on the notion of *certain answer* in the literature and it is very general. Given a Σ, we define *query rule* over Σ as a set of view rules together with a query literal selected from some head. In this way we capture the notion of a complex query expressed by means of a set of rules on top of an ontology.

The definition of query given above encompasses the different proposals of querying a DL knowledge base appeared in the literature. An important special case of query rule is with view acyclic DL axiom-based rules, which is better known as *conjunctive query* if each head literal appears only in one head, or *positive query* otherwise. Quite importantly, this restriction includes the seminal body of work on query answering with conjunctive queries (or with positive queries) with the very expressive $\mathcal{DLR}$ description logic (which includes $\mathcal{ALCQI}$) summarised in [Calvanese *et al.*, 2000]. In this context, logical implication is EXPTIME-hard and in 2EXPTIME; in the case of a fixed finite domain (*closed domain assumption*) logical implication becomes coNP-complete in data complexity [Calvanese *et al.*, 2000]. Practical algorithms for query answering have been studied in [Tessaris *et al.*, 2002]. A proposal targeted towards the semantic web languages has been presented in [Horrocks and Tessaris, 2002].

Recently, the Joint US/EU ad hoc Agent Markup Language Committee has proposed an OWL query language called OWL-QL [Fikes *et al.*, 2003], as a candidate standard language, which is a direct successor of the DAML Query Language (DQL). The query language is not fully formally specified, however it can be easily understood as allowing for conjunctive queries with distinguished variables (called *must-bind* variables) and non distinguished variables (called *don't-bind* variables). In addition, *may-bind* variables apparently provide the notion of a *possible* answer as opposed to the *certain* answer which has been adopted in this paper. Query premises of OWL-QL allow to perform a simple form of local conditional query; this could be encoded as *assertions in DL queries* as introduced in [Eiter *et al.*, 2004].

7   Comparing the Three Approaches

We first show in this section the conditions under which the three approaches coincide. This corresponds essentially to the case of negation-free view rule-extended knowledge bases with empty TBoxes. Note that this is the case of pure Datalog without a background knowledge base, for which it is well known that the three different semantics give rise to the same answer set.

Theorem 3. *If we restrict a rule extended knowledge base with classical rules to view negation-free DL rules with TBox-free Σ, a rule extended knowledge base with lp-rules to NAF-free negation-free DL programs with TBox-free Σ, and a rule extended knowledge base with autoepistemic rules to view negation-free DL rules with TBox-free Σ, the semantics of the rule extended knowledge base with classical rules, with lp-rules, and with with autoepistemic rules coincide, i.e., the logical implication problem is equivalent in the three approaches.*

The above theorem is quite strict and it fails as soon as we release some assumption. We will show this by means of few examples. Consider the following knowledge base Σ, common to all the examples:

```
is-parent  ≐ ∃is-parent-of
my-thing  ≐ is-parent ⊔ ¬is-father
is-parent-of(john, mary)
is-parent(mary)
```

where we define, using standard DL notation, a TBox with the `is-parent` concept as anybody who is parent of at least some other person, and the concept `my-thing` as the union of `is-parent` and the negation of `is-father` (this should become equivalent to the top concept as soon as `is-father` becomes a subconcept of `is-parent`); and an ABox where we declare that John is a parent of Mary, and that Mary is parent of somebody.

Consider the following query rules, showing the effect of existentially quantified individuals coming from some TBox definition:

```
Q_ax(x)  ←  is-parent-of(x,y)
Q_lp(x)  :-  is-parent-of(x,y)
Q_ae(x)  ⇐  is-parent-of(x,y)
```

The query $Q_{ax}(x)$ returns {john, mary}; the query $Q_{lp}(x)$ returns {john}; the query $Q_{ae}(x)$ returns {john, mary}.

Consider now the query rules, which shows the impact of negation in the rules:

```
Q_ax(x,y)  ←  ¬is-parent-of(x,y)
Q_lp(x,y)  :-  ¬is-parent-of(x,y)
Q_ae(x,y)  ⇐  ¬is-parent-of(x,y)
```

The query Q_{ax}(mary, john) returns false; the query Q_{lp}(mary, john) returns true; the query Q_{ae}(mary, john) returns false.

Consider now the following alternative sets of rules, which show that autoepistemic rules, unlike the axiom-based ones, do not influence TBox reasoning:

```
is-parent(x)  ←  is-father(x)
Q_ax(x)  ←  my-thing(x)

is-parent(x)  ⇐  is-father(x)
Q_ae(x)  ⇐  my-thing(x)
```

In the first axiom-based case, the query Q_{ax}(paul) returns true; in the second autoepistemic case the query Q_{ae}(paul) returns false (we assume that paul is an individual in Σ).

8   Conclusions

In this paper we have shown the differences and the similarities among three different semantics for rules in a knowledge base. We have also seen how queries can actually be seen as special case of rules.

We are currently working on the specification of the OWL-Log rule-extended knowledge base language in the DL-Log approach. OWL-Log is based on the various dialects of OWL (OWL-Lite and OWL-DL), and a syntax based on the interoperation between OWL and RuleML is planned.

References

[Baget and Mugnier, 2002] Jean-Francois Baget and Marie-Laure Mugnier. Extensions of simple conceptual graphs: the complexity of rules and constraints. *Journal of Artificial Intelligence research (JAIR)*, 16:425–465, 2002.

[Calvanese and Rosati, 2003] Diego Calvanese and Riccardo Rosati. Answering recursive queries under keys and foreign keys is undecidable. In *Proc. of the 10th Int. Workshop on Knowledge Representation meets Databases (KRDB 2003)*, pages 3–14. CEUR Electronic Workshop Proceedings, http://ceur-ws.org/Vol-79/, 2003.

[Calvanese *et al.*, 2000] Diego Calvanese, Giuseppe De Giacomo, and Maurizio Lenz-erini. Answering queries using views over description logics knowledge bases. In *Proc. of the 16th Nat. Conf. on Artificial Intelligence (AAAI 2000)*, pages 386–391, 2000.

[Calvanese *et al.*, 2004] Diego Calvanese, Giuseppe De Giacomo, Domenico Lembo, Maurizio Lenzerini, and Riccardo Rosati. What to ask to a peer: ontology-based query reformulation. In *Proc. of the 9th Int. Conf. on the Principles of Knowledge Representation and Reasoning (KR 2004)*, 2004.

[Donini *et al.*, 1998a] F. M. Donini, M. Lenzerini, D. Nardi, W. Nutt, and A. Schaerf. An epistemic operator for description logics. *Artificial Intelligence*, 100(1-2): 225–274, April 1998.

[Donini *et al.*, 1998b] Francesco M. Donini, Maurizio Lenzerini, Daniele Nardi, and Andrea Schaerf. *AL*-log: integrating datalog and description logics. *Journal of Intelligent Information Systems*, 10(3): 227–252, 1998.

[Eiter *et al.*, 2004] Thomas Eiter, Thomas Lukasiewicz, Roman Schindlauer, and Hans Tompits. Combining answer set programming with description logics for the se-mantic web. In *Proc. of the International Conference of Knowledge Representation and Reasoning (KR'04)*, 2004.

[Fikes *et al.*, 2003] Richard Fikes, Patrick Hayes, and Ian Horrocks. OWL-QL - A Language for Deductive Query Answering on the Semantic Web. Technical report, Knowledge Systems Laboratory, Stanford University, Stanford, CA, KSL-03-14, 2003.

[Franconi *et al.*, 2003] Enrico Franconi, Gabriel Kuper, A. Lopatenko, and L. Serafini. A robust logical and computational characterisation of peer-to-peer database sys-tems. In *International VLDB Workshop On Databases, Information Systems and Peer-to-Peer Computing (DBISP2P'03)*, 2003.

[Gabbay *et al.*, 2003] D.M. Gabbay, A. Kurucz, F. Wolter, and M. Zakharyaschev. *many-Dimensional Modal Logics: Theory and Applications*. Elsevier, 2003.

[Ghidini and Serafini, 1998] Chiara Ghidini and Luciano Serafini. Distributed first order logics. In Franz Baader and Klaus Ulrich Schulz, editors, *Frontiers of Com-bining Systems 2*, Berlin, 1998. Research Studies Press.

[Grosof *et al.*, 2003] Benjamin N. Grosof, Ian Horrocks, Raphael Volz, and Stefan Decker. Description logic programs: combining logic programs with description logic. In *Proc. of the Twelfth International World Wide Web Conference (WWW 2003)*, pages 48–57. ACM, 2003.

[Horrocks and Patel-Schneider, 2004] Ian Horrocks and Peter F. Patel-Schneider. A proposal for an owl rules language. In *Proc. of the Thirteenth International World Wide Web Conference (WWW 2004)*, 2004.

[Horrocks and Tessaris, 2002] Ian Horrocks and Sergio Tessaris. Querying the semantic web: a formal approach. In *Proc. International Semantic Web Conference 2002 (ISWC-02)*, pages 177–191, 2002.

[Levy and Rousset, 1998] Alon Y. Levy and Marie-Christine Rousset. Combining Horn rules and description logics in CARIN. *Artificial Intelligence*, 104(1–2):165–209, 1998.

[Marx, 1999] Maarten Marx. Complexity of products of modal logics. *J. Log. Comput.*, 9(2):197–214, 1999.

[Motik *et al.*, 2004] Boris Motik, Ulrike Stattler, and Ullrich Hustadt. Reducing SHIQ description logic to disjunctive datalog programs. In *Proc. of the International Conference of Knowledge Representation and Reasoning (KR'04)*, 2004.

[Reiter, 1992] Raymond Reiter. What should a database know? *Journal of Logic Programming*, 14(2,3), 1992.

[Rosati, 1999] Riccardo Rosati. Towards expressive KR systems integrating datalog and description logics: a preliminary report. In *Proc. of the 1999 International Description Logics workshop (DL'99)*, pages 160–164, 1999.

[Swift, 2004] Terrance Swift. Deduction in ontologies via ASP. In *Proc. of LPNMR 2004*, pages 275–288, 2004.

[Tessaris *et al.*, 2002] Sergio Tessaris, Ian Horrocks, and Graham Gough. Evaluating a modular abox algorithm. In *Proc. of the International Conference of Knowledge Representation and Reasoning (KR'02)*, pages 227–238, 2002.

Semantic Web Reasoning for Ontology-Based Integration of Resources

Liviu Badea, Doina Tilivea, and Anca Hotaran

AI Lab, National Institute for Research and Development in Informatics
8-10 Averescu Blvd., Bucharest, Romania
{badea,doina,ahotaran}@ici.ro

Abstract. The Semantic Web should enhance the current World Wide Web with reasoning capabilities for enabling automated processing of possibly distributed information. In this paper we describe an architecture for Semantic Web reasoning and query answering in a very general setting involving several heterogeneous information sources, as well as domain ontologies needed for offering a uniform and source-independent view on the data. Since querying a Web source is very costly in terms of response time, we focus mainly on the query planner of such a system, as it may allow avoiding the access to query-irrelevant sources or combinations of sources based on knowledge about the domain and the sources.

Taking advantage of the huge amount of knowledge implicit and distributed on the Web is a significant challenge. The main obstacle is due to the fact that most Web pages were designed for human-centred browsing rather than being machine-processable. In addition to static HTML pages the Web currently offers online access to a large number information resources, such as databases with a Web interface. But real-life applications frequently require combining the information from several such resources, which may not have been developed with this interoperability requirement in mind. Thus, a large amount of knowledge is implicit, heterogeneously distributed among various resources and thus hard to process automatically.

The recent developments towards a "Semantic Web" should help address these problems. Being able to explicitly represent domain-specific knowledge in the form of ontologies, should allow reasoning about such machine-processable Web pages.

The emergence of standards for data markup and interchange such as XML and for representing information about resources and their semantics (such as RDF and RDF Schema) can be seen as a first step in the transition towards a Semantic Web. However, the vast majority of Web pages still conform to the HTML standard, which only controls their visual aspects rather than their informational content. Extracting the informational content from such pages which essentially contain free text is a difficult practical problem. The Resource Description Framework (RDF) has been designed to complement such human-oriented text with machine-processable annotations. A large number of prototype systems able to read and reason about such annotations have been developed (TRIPLE [7], Metalog [20], SiLRI [8], Ontobroker [9]). However, currently only a very small minority of Web pages have RDF annotations. Moreover,

H.J. Ohlbach and S. Schaffert (Eds.): PPSWR 2004, LNCS 3208, pp. 61–75, 2004.

existing annotations tend to refer to basic features such as document author, creation date, etc., but do not duplicate the information content of the page.

On the other hand, a large number of information sources have a Web interface and could be the building blocks of complex applications, were it not for the unavoidable semantic mismatch between such resources developed by different people. Such Web interfaces produce pages with a partially stable structure, so that their content can be automatically extracted using wrappers, thus replacing human annotation (which is a significant bottleneck in practice).

Dealing with information sources rather than a fixed set of Web pages may pose additional problems. For example, systems like TRIPLE read *all* the relevant (RDF) annotations *before* reasoning about them. In the case of large data sources however, it is obviously impossible to retrieve the *entire* content of such sources before starting reasoning. Also, if additional knowledge is available about the sources, some source accesses may be avoided altogether. Therefore, dealing with information sources requires a certain form of *query planning*, i.e. the ability of constructing and reasoning about alternative sequences of source accesses (plans) before actually querying these sources. Also, *streaming the query responses* may allow starting processing before the entire content of the information source is retrieved.

In this paper we present an approach to such more complex Semantic Web scenarios, involving the integration of heterogeneous resources using rules and ontologies.

The most significant problem faced when trying to combine several resources is related to their heterogeneity. This heterogeneity can be either *structural* (different schemas), or *semantic* (the same entity can be represented using different terms from different vocabularies). Integrating such resources can be achieved by mapping them (both their schemas and their content) to a *common* "knowledge" level, at which their interoperation is straight-forward. This common level involves not just a common (domain-specific) vocabulary, but also formal (machine processable) descriptions of the terms of this vocabulary, as well as the relationships between them, which form a so-called *ontology*. A *mediator architecture* [22] can be used for query answering.

A researcher specialized in Knowledge Representation and Reasoning (KRR) might be very disappointed by current Web technology, which:

- involves to a large extent HTML pages in mostly free text (not machine processable)
- the knowledge is not well structured
- there is virtually no support for reasoning.

Thus, since current state of the art in Natural Language Processing does not allow extracting the deep semantics of free text, the temptation may be very high to change everything. However, as it isn't easy to impose a radically new (even if better) Web standard, we adopt an *evolutionary* rather than revolutionary approach and conform as much as possible to current and emerging Web standards.

In the following we concentrate mainly on the query planning component of a mediator-based Semantic Web architecture – other important issues such as wrappers and especially ontologies deserve a more detailed discussion, but which is outside the scope of this paper.

1   The Architecture: Public and Private Levels

The distinctive feature of the Semantic Web is reasoning. However, the various W3C standards related to the (Semantic) Web are not easy to use by a reasoner, especially due to their heterogeneity (XML, RDF, RuleML, etc.). A *uniform* internal level would be much more appropriate for supporting inference and reasoning. The architecture of our system therefore separates a so-called *"public" level* from the *internal level*. The public level refers to the data, knowledge and models exchanged on the Web and between applications and must conform to the current and emerging Web standards such as XML, RDF(S), RuleML, etc.

1.1   The Internal Representation

We use *F-logic* [12] for describing the content of information sources as well as the domain ontology for several important reasons. First, a logic-based language is not only declarative, but also offers support for reasoning. However, a Prolog-like syntax using predicates with a fixed number of arguments and a position-oriented argument access is not well suited for dealing with the semi-structured data available on the Web. On the other hand, F-logic combines the logical features of Prolog with the frame-oriented features of object-oriented languages, while offering a more powerful query language (allowing e.g. aggregation and meta-level reasoning about the schema). Last but not least, F-logic is widely used in the Semantic Web community [7,18,8,9].

In the following (and throughout the whole paper) we use the term *"predicate"* to denote an F-logic molecule, such as $X{:}c[a1{-}{>}Y1, \ldots]$.

While the data content of an information source can be represented by a number of so-called *source predicates s*, the user might prefer to have a *uniform* interface to *all* the sources instead of directly querying the sources *s*. In fact, she may not even *want* to be aware of the structure of the information sources. Therefore, the mediator uses a uniform knowledge representation language in terms of so-called *"model predicates"*, which represent the user's perspective on the given domain and refer to concepts and terms of an associated domain ontology.

There are two main viewpoints on representing sources and their interactions: *"Global as View"* (GAV) and *"Local as View"* (LAV) [16]. The query planner presented in this paper can deal with both GAV and LAV approaches. However, we encourage the use of LAV, since it spares the knowledge engineer the effort of explicitly determining and representing the source interactions.

1.2   Source Predicates, Model Predicates and Description Rules

The content of the various Web information sources is represented by so-called *source predicates*. For a uniform and integrated access to the various sources these are described (at the mediator level) in terms of so-called *model predicates*.

More precisely, we distinguish between *content* predicates and *constraint* predicates.

Content predicates (denoted in the following with *p*, *q*) are predicates which directly or indirectly represent the *content* of information sources. They can be either *source* predicates or *model predicates*.

Source predicates (denoted with *s*) directly represent the content of (part of) an information source (for example, the content of a Web page or the answer returned by a Web service).

Model predicates (denoted with *b*) are used to describe the "global model", including the domain ontology and the information content of the sources in terms of this ontology.

As opposed to content predicates, *constraint predicates* (denoted by *c*) are used to express specific constraints on the content predicate descriptions.

For example, a source *s* containing information about underpaid employees (with a salary below 1000), would be described as:

E:s[name–>N, salary–>S] —> *E:employee[name–>N, salary–>S], S<1000.*

Constraint predicates can be either *internal* (treatable internally by the query engine of the source), or *external* (constraints that can only be verified at the mediator level, for example by the built-in constraint solvers of the host CLP environment). Constraints treatable *internally* by the sources can be *verified* at the source level (by the query engines of the sources), but they are also *propagated* at the mediator (CLP) level. Constraints treatable only *externally* need to be both verified and propagated at the mediator level.

A *complete* description of the source predicates in terms of model predicates is neither possible nor useful, since in general there are too many details of the functioning of the application. Thus, instead of *complete* (iff) descriptions, we shall specify only approximate (necessary) definitions of the source predicates in terms of model predicates (thus, only the relevant features of the sources will be encoded).

In the following, we use a *uniform* notation for the domain and source ***description rules***:

$$Antec, Constr_a \rightarrow Conseq, Constr_c \qquad\qquad (dr)$$

where *Antec* and *Conseq* are conjunctions of content predicates, while $Constr_a$ and $Constr_c$ are conjunctions of constraints. Variables occurring in the consequent but not in the antecedent are implicitly existentially quantified. As in Prolog and F-logic, all other variables are implicitly universally quantified.

Description rules are necessary definitions of (combinations of) source or model predicates in terms of model predicates and constraints. (*Source descriptions* are special cases of description rules where the antecedent contains only source predicates. *Integrity constraints* are description rules with only constraints – typically '*fail*' – in the consequent.)

1.3 Querying the Sources: Wrappers

While the traditional Web was designed mainly for browsing, the Semantic Web should enable automated processing of Web sources. A Semantic Web system should therefore be able to deal not just with *static* Web pages (in various formats such as HTML, XML), but also with *dynamically generated* pages as well as Web services.

While the semantics of static Web pages is encoded using static annotations (e.g. in RDF) the information content of dynamically generated Web pages needs to be extracted by automatic *wrappers*. These have to be quite flexible, i.e. able to deal with XML files, or even possible non-well-formed HTML. Due to its wide spread use worldwide, we currently employ *XQuery* for implementing our wrappers (we also use *tidy*[1] to preprocess non-well-formed HTML sources).

2   Ontologies and Mapping Rules

A key component in a SW application is a *domain ontology*, used by a certain community to enable sharing and exchange of knowledge in a particular domain. Due to the heterogeneous nature of the sources, mapping rules from the various sources to the common ontology are needed for obtaining a unified view of these sources (see Section 4 below for examples).

OWL (http://www.w3.org/2004/OWL/) has recently emerged as a de-facto standard for Web ontologies. Since OWL is a description logic-based extension to RDF(S), it provides useful inference services, mainly for checking the consistency of a schema as well as for subsumption testing. However, description logics (DL) with tractable inference services tend to have limited expressiveness, so that they are closer to a dynamic type checker rather than to a more expressive reasoner. A large part of the semantics encoded in such an OWL ontology thus resides "in the names" rather than in the formulas themselves, thereby making the usefulness of the reasoning services questionable w.r.t. the limited expressiveness and the computational overhead (dealing with instances in current DL implementations is especially inefficient). Also, most real-life ontologies require the use of rules and domain-specific constraints for supplementing the limited expressiveness of description logics. However, combining DLs with rules is highly non-trivial, both theoretically and from the point of view of tractability [18]. A pragmatic approach would avoid the computational complexities of a *complete* DL reasoner by implementing a fast, albeit incomplete set of DL propagation rules.

We currently employ Protégé[2], a widely used Ontology development tool. Ontologies are exported in RDF(S) format and automatically converted to the internal (F-logic) format. As discussed above, additional rules may be needed to extend the expressiveness of RDF(S).

3   Reasoning and Query Planning

Since querying a Web source is extremely costly in terms of response time, every possible optimization that might avoid accessing irrelevant sources should be attempted. The knowledge available about a particular source or combination of sources may imply the inconsistency of some potential query plan even *before* access-

---

[1] http://tidy.sourceforge.net/
[2] http://protege.stanford.edu

ing the sources. The purpose of the query planner is to avoid executing such inconsistent plans and possibly to use additional cost measures for ranking plans.

The majority of Semantic Web implementations using F-logic [7,18,8,9] retrieve the content of *all* the sources before query answering. However, in applications in which there are alternative plans for a given query, some of these plans may be inconsistent and - for efficiency - the associated sources should not be accessed. This cannot be achieved simply by the normal F-logic query answering mechanism and requires some form of meta-interpretation.

Query planning amounts to unfolding the query in terms of sources and propagating the relevant constraints to eliminate the inconsistent plans. Since this type of reasoning is performed *before* accessing the sources, it can be viewed as an *abductive procedure* [14] in which the source predicates play the role of abducibles.

Due to their flexibility and declarative nature, Constraint Handling Rules (CHRs) [10] represent an ideal framework for implementing the reasoning mechanism of the query planner.

Constraint Handling Rules (see [10] for more details) represent a flexible approach to developing user-defined constraint solvers in a declarative language. As opposed to typical constraint solvers, which are black boxes, CHRs represent a 'no-box' approach to CLP.

CHRs can be either *simplification* or *propagation* rules.

A *simplification* rule *Head <=> Guard | Body* replaces the head constraints by the body provided the guard is true (the *Head* may contain multiple CHR constraint atoms).

Propagation rules Head ==> Guard | Body add the body constraints to the constraint store without deleting the head constraints (whenever the guard is true). A third, hybrid type of rules, *simpagation rules Head₁ \ Head₂ <=> Guard | Body* replace *Head₂* by *Body* (while preserving *Head₁*) if *Guard* is true. (Guards are optional in all types of rules.)

CHRs allow us to combine in an elegant manner the backward reasoning necessary for implementing query unfolding with the forward propagation of abducibles and constraints.

A description rule of the form (dr) will be encoded in CHR using

- *goal regression rules*: for reducing queries given in terms of model predicates to queries in terms of source predicates,

$$\mathbf{G} \; Conseq :\text{-} \; \mathbf{G} \; Antec, \; Constr_a \qquad\qquad (b)$$

- *propagation rules*: for completing (intermediate) descriptions in order to allow the discovery of potential inconsistencies.

$$\mathbf{H} \; Antec \; ==> \; Constr_a \; | \; \mathbf{H} \; Conseq, \; Constr_c \qquad\qquad (f)$$

In our CHR embedding of the *abductive procedure* we use two types of constraints, $\mathbf{G}p$ and $\mathbf{H}p$, for each predicate p. While $\mathbf{H}p$ represents facts explicitly propagated (abduced), $\mathbf{G}p$ refers to the *current closure* of the predicate p (i.e. the explicit definition of p *together* with the explicitly abduced literals $\mathbf{H}p$).

While propagating $\boldsymbol{H}p$ amounts to simply assuming p to hold (abduction), propagating $\boldsymbol{G}p$ amounts to trying to prove p either by using its definition $def(p)$, or by reusing an already abduced fact $\boldsymbol{H}p$. In fact, our description rules can be viewed as a generalization of abductive logic programs with integrity constraints interpreted w.r.t. the 'propertyhood view'[3].

A set of subgoals in terms of source predicates (induced by backward chaining from the user query using the goal regression rules) may not necessarily be consistent. Applying forward propagation rules ensures the completion ("saturation") of the (partial) query plan and enables detecting potential conflicts *before* actually accessing the sources.

$Constr_a$ and $Constr_c$ in (f) represent constraint predicate calls, for which the associated constraints solvers are assumed to be available. The occurrence of $Constr_a$ in the guard ensures that the consequent is propagated only if $Constr_a$ hold.

Source and domain models are described using rules of the form (dr), which are then automatically translated by the system into CHR goal regression and propagation rules (b) and (f). The following *additional problem-independent rules* (gh) and (re) are used for obtaining the complete CHR encoding of a model.

- a CHR simpagation rule[4] for matching a goal $\boldsymbol{G}p$ with any existing abduced facts $\boldsymbol{H}p$:

$$\boldsymbol{H}p(X_1) \setminus \boldsymbol{G}p(X_2) \;\text{<=>}\; X_1 = X_2 \;;\; X_1 \neq X_2, \boldsymbol{G}p(X_2). \tag{re}$$

  This rule should have a higher priority than the unfolding rule in order to avoid re-achieving an already achieved goal. Note that, for completeness, we are leaving open the possibility of achieving $\boldsymbol{G}p(X_2)$ using its definition or reusing other abduced facts.

- a rule taking care of the consistency between goals and facts that simply hold (since goals will be achieved eventually, they also have to hold):

$$\boldsymbol{G}p \;\text{==>}\; \boldsymbol{H}p \tag{gh}$$

We have already mentioned the fact that we have to distinguish between goals involving a given predicate p (which will be treated by a mechanism similar to the normal Prolog backward chaining mechanism) and the instances $\boldsymbol{H}p$ of p, which trigger forward propagation rules. Operationally speaking, while goals $\boldsymbol{G}p$ are "consumed" during goal regression, the fact that p holds should persist even after the goal has been achieved, to enable the activation of the forward propagation rules of p. Note that rule (gh) should have a higher priority than (b) to allow goals p to propagate $\boldsymbol{H}p$ before applying the goal regression rules for p.

Certain forward propagation rules (f) may propagate facts that may never be involved (directly or indirectly) in conflicts. These facts may be very useful to the end

---

[3] The detailed presentation of the semantics is outside the scope of this paper and will be pursued elsewhere. Briefly, the goal regression rules make up the program P, the sources are regarded as (temporary) abducibles A, while the forward propagation rules play the role of the ALP integrity constraints I. Our notion of integrity constraints is however more general than that used in ALP.

[4] The rule is more complicated in practice, due to implementation details.

user in certain applications, especially whenever the user would like to see all the known facts about the instances returned by the query. However, in other applications, we may wish to refrain from propagating such facts that may never lead to an inconsistency (detected by an integrity constraint). In this case, we perform a static dependency analysis of the rules, and generate forward propagation rules (f) only for predicates that may propagate an inconsistency.

4 An Example

In this paper, we consider a hardware configuration problem as a typical example. A component integrator selling customized computer configurations may use components from several component providers, while trying to satisfy a set of compatibility and user constraints. This problem has many typical features of the Semantic Web:

- it involves distributed and dynamically changing information sources (the component catalogs of the different providers available via Web interfaces)
- the information is semantically heterogeneous, requiring a domain ontology for a uniform access
- the domain involves complex compatibility constraints between components, requiring constraint propagation during query planning
- there are several alternative sources for some given component, which makes query planning necessary.

Here we consider just a fragment of this hardware configuration domain, in order to emphasize the main features of our architecture. Assume we have two main component providers, or vendors, *flamingo* and *oktal*. (Since their catalogs are accessible via the Web in HTML format, a wrapper is used for extracting the relevant information from these Web pages.) A user query may ask for a system with an upper bound on the total price. Here we just concentrate on a "simple system" containing just a motherboard and a processor. Of course, the two components must satisfy a compatibility constraint (e.g. one should not attempt to use an AMD processor on an Intel-Pentium compatible motherboard).

Since the sources are heterogeneous, we first use so-called "mapping rules" to describe their content in terms of the ontology. For example, motherboards sold by *flamingo* are mapped onto the ontology concept *motherboard* (note that here we have a trivial mapping of all slots, with an additional *m_vendor* slot recording the name of the vendor):[5]

$Mb{:}fl\_motherboard[A{-}{>}X] \longrightarrow Mb{:}motherboard[A{-}{>}X, m\_vendor{-}{>}flamingo]$ (r1)

Any additional knowledge about the content of the sources may be very useful during query planning for discarding inconsistent plans even before accessing the sources. For example, we may know a lower bound for the price of a *flamingo*

---

[5] In the following, we use the more concise F-logic syntax for rules. As already discussed above, the actual syntax will involve an XML encoding of a rule markup language, such as *RuleML* (http://www.ruleml.org) or *Xcerpt* [4].

motherboard. We may also know that *flamingo* distributes only *intel* and *msi* boards. This is specified using the following source description rules:

$Mb:fl\_motherboard[m\_price->P] \longrightarrow P \geq 70.$ (ic1)

$Mb:fl\_motherboard[brand->Br] \longrightarrow member(Br, [intel, msi]).$ (ic2)

We have similar rules for *oktal* motherboards, as well as for processors (available also from both *flamingo* and *oktal*):

$Mb:okt\_motherboard[A->X] \longrightarrow Mb:motherboard[A->X, m\_vendor->oktal].$ (r2)

$Mb:okt\_motherboard[m\_price->P] \longrightarrow P \geq 70.$ (ic3)

$Mb:okt\_motherboard[brand->Br] \longrightarrow member(Br, [gigabyte, msi]).$ (ic4)

$Pr:fl\_processor[A->X] \longrightarrow Pr:processor [A->X, p\_vendor->flamingo].$ (r3)

$Pr:fl\_processor[p\_price->P] \longrightarrow P \geq 150.$ (ic5)

$Pr:okt\_processor[A->X] \longrightarrow Pr:processor[A->X, p\_vendor->oktal].$ (r4)

$Pr:okt\_processor[p\_price->P] \longrightarrow P \geq 150.$ (ic6)

Note that the source descriptions (ic1), (ic2), (ic3), (ic4), (ic5) and (ic6) express knowledge about the content of the sources. (These descriptions could either be provided by the knowledge engineer or could be automatically retrieved from previous source accesses.)

However, answering queries frequently requires knowledge about the sources that cannot be inferred from their content alone. For example, *oktal* offers discounts for purchases over a given threshold, while *flamingo* does not:

$oktal:vendor[name->oktal, discount-> 0.1, discount\_threshold->200].$ (r5)

$flamingo:vendor[name->flamingo, discount-> 0, discount\_threshold->0].$ (r6)

The domain ontology encodes our knowledge about this particular domain, such as the concept hierarchy, descriptions of slots/attributes (type, cardinality constraints, etc.), and any additional description rules involving these concepts. For example, *motherboard*s and *processor*s are sub-concepts of *component*:

motherboard :: *component*.

processor :: *component*.

For an example of an ontology description rule, we may describe a simple *system* as a set of matching components, such as a *motherboard* and a *processor*. (Note the compatibility constraint between *motherboard* and *processor*: '$Pr.id = Mb.supported\_CPU$'.)

$Mb:motherboard, Pr:processor, Pr.id = Mb.supported\_CPU \longrightarrow$ (r7)

$X:system[motherboard->Mb, processor->Pr].$

To show the functioning of the query planner, we consider the following user query which asks for a system with an upper bound of *210* on the (possibly discounted) price:

$?- S:system[motherboard->Mb[brand = gigabyte], processor->Pr],$ (q1)

$compute\_discounted\_price(S, S\_price), S\_price \leq 210.$

For simplicity, the computation of the discounted price is performed by *compute_discounted_price(S, S_price)*.

The query is answered by first invoking the query planner, and subsequently executing the resulting plans. As discussed previously, query planning *unfolds* the query in terms of source calls while *propagating constraints* with the purpose of discarding the inconsistent plans before the actual source accesses. Note that constraint propagation is interleaved with query unfolding, so that inconsistencies are detected as early as possible.

In our example, query planning starts by unfolding the query (q1) to the following subgoals and constraint (as discussed previously, **G** stands for '*goal*', while **H** stands for '*holds*'):

$$GS:system[motherboard{\to}Mb[brand = gigabyte], processor{\to}Pr] \qquad (g1)$$
$$Gcompute\_discounted\_price(S, P) \qquad (g2)$$
$$S\_price \leq 210 \qquad (c1)$$

Then (g1) will be unfolded with (r7-B)[6] to:

$$GMb:motherboard[brand = gigabyte] \qquad (g3)$$
$$GPr:processor \qquad (g4)$$

Since motherboards can be acquired either from *flamingo* or from *oktal*, (g3) will be unfolded first with (r1-B) to the following (we first try to acquire the motherboard from *flamingo*):

$$GMb:fl\_motherboard[brand{\to}gigabyte, m\_price{\to}MP, ...] \qquad (g5)$$

This will propagate (with rule (gh)) **HMb:fl_motherboard[brand→gigabyte, m_price→MP,...]** which in turn will activate (r1-F) and propagate

$$HMb:motherboard[m\_vendor{\to}flamingo, brand{\to}gigabyte, ...]. \qquad (h1)$$

But now, (h1) will trigger the (ic2) integrity constraint, which fails because the required brand for the motherboard (*gigabyte*) is not included in the list of distributed brands of the vendor *flamingo*.

Alternatively, we could obtain a motherboard from *oktal*, i.e. unfold **GMb:motherboard** (g3) with (r2-B) to:

$$GMb:okt\_motherboard[brand{\to}gigabyte, m\_price{\to}MP, ...] \qquad (g5)$$
$$HMb:okt\_motherboard[brand{\to}gigabyte, m\_price{\to}MP, ...] \qquad (h2)$$

is propagated with rule (gh). In this case, (r2-F) will propagate

$$HMb:motherboard[m\_vendor{\to}oktal, brand{\to} gigabyte, ...]. \qquad (h3)$$

(h2) will trigger (ic2), which will be consistent because the brands known to be distributed by *oktal* are *gigabyte* and *msi*. (h3) will also trigger (ic3) and propagate the price constraint *Mb.m_price ≥ 70* (c2).

---

[6] (ri-B) is the goal reduction rule (*backward* version) of the rule (ri), while (ri-F) is the associated *forward* propagation rule.

Having selected a consistent source for the motherboard, we now consider selecting a processor. The goal (g2) *GPr:processor* will be first unfolded using (r3-B) to:

$$GPr:fl\_processor[p\_price->PP,\ldots] \tag{g6}$$

and will propagate with (gh) and (r3-F):

$$HPr:fl\_processor[p\_price->PP] \tag{h4}$$

which will trigger (ic5) and propagate the price constraint $Pr.p\_price \geq 150.$ (c3)

Then the next goal, *Gcompute_discounted_price*(S, S_Price) (g2), is unfolded and partially evaluated. For the simplicity of the presentation, we do not present here all the intermediate steps. Briefly, although at query planning time the prices of the components are not yet known, we can nevertheless propagate the constraints (c2) and (c3) and thus obtain a lower bound on *S_price*.

More precisely, since we have different vendors for the two components (*Pr.p_vendor = flamingo*, *Mb.m_vendor = oktal*), any potential discounts will be applied separately to each component. But *flamingo* doesn't offer discounts and the discount threshold for *oktal* is too high (*200*) to be applicable. Therefore, the system price will be: $S\_price = Pr.p\_price + Mb.m\_price \geq 220$ (due to (c3) and (c2)), which is inconsistent with the (c1) constraint $S\_price \leq 210$, so the combination of an *oktal* motherboard and a *flamingo* processor will be rejected.

Alternatively, we could acquire the processor from *oktal*, i.e. reduce *GPr:processor* (g1) with (r4-B), (r4-F) and (gh) to:

$$HPr:okt\_processor[p\_price->PP, ..] \tag{h5}$$

As before, (h5) will trigger (ic6) and propagate the price constraint $Pr.p\_price \geq 150.$ (c4)

But now the unfolding of *compute_discounted_price*(S, S_price) (g2) will be different, as both components are acquired from the same vendor (*Pr.p_vendor = oktal*, *Mb.m_vendor=oktal*), so that the discount is applicable to both components. In fact, since the undiscounted price $S\_price1 = Pr.p\_price + Mb.m\_price$ is above the discount threshold for *oktal* $S\_price1 \geq 220$ (due to (c4) and (c2), *oktal.discount_threshold = 200*), the system price will be: $S\_price = S\_price1 \cdot (1 - oktal.discount) - 0.9 \cdot S\_price$. Thus, the lower bound on *S_price* will be *198*, which is consistent with the (c1) constraint. Query planning has therefore retained only the following combination of sources: *okt_processor* and *okt_motherboard*, while discarding the other three possible combinations at planning time, so that only *okt_processor* and *okt_motherboard* are actually queried.

5 Source Capabilities

Information sources are viewed as *collections of source predicates* that can be accessed via a specialized query interface. The query planner reduces a query formulated in terms of model predicates to a query in terms of source predicates and constraints. However, since such a "global" query can involve source predicates from *several* information sources, it will have to be to *split* into sub-queries that can be treated by the separate information sources. Since each information source may have its own Web interface, we need to explicitly represent the *capabilities* of these interfaces. As opposed to traditional database query languages, such Web sources provide only limited query capabilities. For example, a specific Web interface may allow only certain types of selections and may also require certain parameters to be inputs (i.e. known at query time).

More precisely, the capabilities of a given information source are described using the following items:

- the *name* of the source
- the *source predicates* that can be accessed from this source, with (optional) input argument annotations (these can be Web pages, Web interfaces to databases, or even Web services)
- the *constraints* that can be treated (internally) in selections (as filters).

Parameters annotated with '+' denote inputs, assuming that

- input parameters have to be instantiated at query time
- the other parameters are completely uninstantiated at query time

The input-output specifications determine the dataflow in the query. Such specifications are especially important in the case of Web interfaces to databases, as well as for describing Web services. The plans produced by the query planner have to be refined in order to conform to these source capabilities.

We define a *precedence* relation over the variable occurrences in source predicates.

A variable occurrence X *directly precedes* another variable occurrence Y iff X occurs in a predicate that provides an input to a + variable of another predicate containing Y (e.g. $p(X,W)$, $q(+W,Y)$). The '*precedes*' relation is the transitive closure of the '*directly precedes*' relation.

We also say that a variable X *precedes* a predicate (literal) p iff X precedes some variable occurrence Y in p. We have similar notions of predicates preceding variables or other predicates.

Let $p(\overline{X})$ be a literal in a query plan. Since the + variables of p have to be instantiated before calling p, we have to make sure that all predicates preceding p have been called already.

A query plan is *consistent* w.r.t. the source capabilities iff the precedence relation on its literals is acyclic.

Since on the Web it will be virtually impossible to retrieve all records of source predicates with a very large number of such records, we additionally categorize sources as being either "*large*" or "*normal*".

Starting from a "logical" plan, we first try to assign to all "large" predicates binding patterns[7] with as many input(+) arguments as possible, while keeping the query

---

[7] A given source predicate can have several input-output *binding patterns*. For example *pubmed(+PMID, Title, Author)*, *pubmed(PMID, +Title, Author)*, *pubmed(PMID, +Title, +Author)*, etc.

plan consistent (i.e. acyclic). Once having assigned binding patterns to all predicates of the plan, we execute it (without considering later on alternative binding pattern assignments, since the different binding patterns only control the format of the query and not its answer set).

To further reduce the number of tuples retrieved from the sources (this being the most important efficiency bottleneck), we may take advantage of the sources that allow adding filters to the query (e.g. ask about motherboards *with prices bellow 200*). These *filters* can be constructed by propagating the user constraints from the query with other constraints from the source descriptions and the domain ontology. Of course, we can use as filters propagated constraints that refer exclusively to variables from the given predicate $p(\overline{X})$ and that match the source's capabilities.

However, there is an additional subtlety related to the necessity of making as few source calls as possible.

For example, in the case of the following query:

$?\text{-} p(X, Y), s(Z), q(+Y, V), Y+Z+V < 200, Y > 0, Z > 0, V > 0.$

We have to execute p before q in order to instantiate Y for q, but s can be called at any time. If s is called earlier than q (which is a natural thing to do if parallel plan execution is possible), then Z will be instantiated at the time of q's call.

Naively, one would be tempted to use all the current variable instantiations (say $Y=60, Z=100$) to obtain a reduced constraint $V<40$ to be used as a filter in the call $q(Y=60, V), V < 40$. However, every instantiation of Z will produce a different call to q and thus we would have to call q a large number of times. Even worse, the sets of tuples returned, e.g. by $q(Y=60, V), V < 40$; $q(Y=60), V<100$; etc. will (partially) overlap.

A better solution would be to propagate only the instantiations of the variables that (necessarily) precede q, i.e. $Y=60$, but not Z. In this case, the propagated constraint $V<140$ may be weaker, but it will be *the same for all bindings of* Z. Thus, a single query to q: $q(+Y=60, V), V<140$ will be enough, since we can reuse the tuples returned by it for all bindings of Z.

More precisely, let C be the set of constraints propagated from the user constraints in the query. When executing the source predicate call $p(\overline{X})$, we attach to it as filter the set of constraints $C(\overline{X}, \overline{X'}=\overline{x'})|_{SC}$ obtained by propagating from C the instantiations $\overline{X'}=\overline{x'}$ of the variables $\overline{X'}$ that precede p and retaining only those constraints that satisfy the source capabilities SC.

6 Conclusions and Future Work

An exhaustive comparison with other information integration systems is impossible, due to the very large number of such systems as well as to the lack of space. Briefly, while database oriented approaches to integration (such as *multi-databases* and *federated databases*) use *fixed* global schemas and are appropriate only if the information sources and users do not change frequently, we deal with *dynamically evolving* schemas (especially if the LAV modeling approach is employed). On the other hand, more *procedural* intelligent information integration approaches, like TSIMMIS [11] and even some declarative systems like MedLan [1] or HERMES [21], use explicit query reformulation rules[8], but *without the equivalent of our forward propagation rules* (which allow an early discovery and pruning of inconsistent plans before query execution). Our approach is closer to the more declarative systems like SIMS [2], Information Manifold [17] and Infomaster [6].

COIN [5] also uses a CLP framework (Eclipse) for abductive reasoning and CHRs for implementing integrity constraints. However, integrity constraints can be imposed in COIN *only on source predicates.* Thus, COIN domain knowledge reduces to Prolog reduction rules, which are used *only backwards* (during goal regression). The lack of forward propagation rules involving base predicates (and not just sources) makes the discovery of potential interactions between base predicates (and thus the full use of domain knowledge) impossible. Other related mediator-based Web integration systems are EMERAC [13] and Ariadne [15].

This paper extends our research related to the SILK intelligent information environment [3] to deal with the specificities of the Semantic Web. (The semi-structured nature of the data on the Web lead us to the use of an F-logic based internal reasoning level, while the limited source capabilities of Web resources and the high access costs required a different query planning strategy). A prototype implementation using plain Prolog (rather than F-logic) and CHR already exists. However, as shown in this paper, F-logic is a much more appropriate internal language for dealing with semi-structured data. We are currently working towards extending our system to use F-logic as internal reasoning language. This is non-trivial as there are no Prolog environments allowing a combination F-logic and CHR[9]. In this sense, our work is related to Xcerpt [4], an elegant declarative, rule-based query and transformation language for XML, for which a query planner is also currently under development.

Acknowledgements

We are grateful to François Bry and Sebastian Schaffert for insightful discussions. The present work has been partially supported by the REWERSE Network of Excellence of the European Community (http://www.rewerse.net).

References

1. Aquilino D., Asirelli P., Renso C., Turini F. MedLan: a Logic-based Mediator Language, IEI Technical Report B4-16, November 1997.
2. Arens Y., Knoblock C.A., Chun-Nan Hsu. Query Processing in the SIMS Information Mediator, Advanced Planning Technology, A. Tate (ed), AAAI Press, 1996.

---

[8] Such query templates correspond to our goal regression rules.
[9] The upcoming XSB Prolog release should contain both Flora2 and CHR, but their combination may not be straightforward (if at all possible).

3. Badea L., Tilivea D. Intelligent Information Integration as a Constraint Handling Problem, Proc. of the Fifth International Conference on Flexible Query Answering Systems (FQAS-2002), October 27 – 29, 2002, Copenhagen, Springer Verlag, pp. 12–27.
4. Berger S., Bry F., Schaffert S., Wieser C. Xcerpt and visXcerpt: From Pattern-Based to Visual Querying of XML and Semistructured Data. Proceedings VLDB03, Berlin, September 2003, http://www.xcerpt.org/.
5. Bressan S., Goh C.H. Answering queries in context. In Proceedings of the International Conference on Flexible Query Answering Systems, FQAS-98, Roskilde, 1998.
6. Duschka O.M., Genesereth M.R.. Infomaster - An Information Integration Tool. Tool. Proc. International Workshop "Intelligent Information Integration", KI-97, Freiburg, 1997.
7. Decker S., Sintek M. 'Triple - an RDF query, inference, and transformation language', in Proc. of the 2002 International Semantic Web Conference (ISWC-2002).
8. Decker S., Brickley D., Saarela J., Angele J. A Query and Inference Service for RDF. QL'98 – The Query Languages Workshop, World Wide Web Consortium, 1998.
9. Fensel D., Angele J., Decker S., Erdmann M., Schnurr H.P., Staab S., Studer R., Witt A., On2broker: Semantic-based Access to Information Sources at the WWW, Proceedings of WebNet, 1999, pp. 366–371.
10. Fruewirth T. Theory and Practice of Constraint Handling Rules, JLP 37:95–138, 1998.
11. Garcia-Molina H., Papakonstantinou Y., Quass D., Rajaraman A., Sagiv Y., Ullman J., Vassalos V., Widom J. The TSIMMIS approach to mediation: Data models and Languages. In Journal of Intelligent Information Systems, 1997.
12. Kifer M., Lausen G., Wu J. Logical foundations of object-oriented and frame-based languages, Journal of the ACM, Volume 42 , Issue 4 (July 1995), pp. 741–843.
13. Kambhampati S., Lambrecht E., Nambiar U., Nie Z., Senthil G. Optimizing Recursive Information Gathering Plans in EMERAC. Journal of Intelligent Information Systems. Vol. 22, No. 2., March 2004, p. 119–153.
14. Kakas A., Kowalski R., Toni F. The role of abduction in logic programming, Handbook of logic in AI and LP 5, OUP 1998, 235–324.
15. Knoblock, C. et al. The ARIADNE Approach to Web-Based Information Integration, in: International Journal of Cooperative Information Systems 10(1-2): pp. 145–169, 2001.
16. Levy A.Y. Logic-Based Techniques, in Data Integration Logic Based Artificial Intelligence, Jack Minker (ed). Kluwer, 2000.
17. Levy A.Y., Rajaraman A., Ordille J.J. Querying Heterogeneous Information Sources Using Source. Proc. 22nd VLDB Conference, Bombay, India. 1996.
18. Levy A.Y., Rousset M.C. Combining Horn Rules and Description Logics in CARIN. Artificial Intelligence Journal 104, September 1998.
19. Ludascher B., Himmeroder R., Lausen G., May W., Schlepphorst C. Managing Semistructured Data with FLORID: A Deductive Object-oriented Perspective. Information Systems, 23(8):589–613, 1998.
20. Marchiori M., Saarela J. Query+Metadata+Logic=Metalog, http://www.w3.org/TandS/QL/QL98/pp/metalog
21. Subrahmanian V.S. et al. HERMES: A heterogeneous reasoning and mediator system. http://www.cs.umd.edu/projects/hermes/overview/paper
22. Wiederhold G. Mediators in the architecture of future information systems, IEEE Comp. 25(3) 1992, 38–49.

Static Type-Checking of Datalog with Ontologies

Jakob Henriksson and Jan Małuszyński

Dept. of Computer and Information Science,
Linköping University, S 581 83 Linköping, Sweden
{x04jakhe, janma}@ida.liu.se

Abstract. We show how coupling of the emerging rule level of the Semantic Web to the existing ontology level can be achieved by static typing of web rules of a given application with classes of the ontology describing the application domain. This paper describes the principles and the implementation of a system that checks correctness of a given set of Datalog rules encoded in XML (according to the RuleML standard) wrt a type specification, where the Datalog predicates are typed with classes described by an OWL ontology. The type checker is based on a well-known verification technique for logic programs and employs the RACER reasoner for checking the verification conditions.

Keywords: Semantic Web, ontologies, rules, logic programs

1   Introduction

A question gaining recently wide interest is how to integrate rules with ontologies in the Semantic Web framework of the World Wide Web Consortium (W3C[1]). The ontology layer of the Semantic Web is already well defined and the commonly accepted ideas are reflected by the Web Ontology Language OWL[2]. The ontologies used in the context of the Semantic Web are expected to have a well-defined formal semantics. It is often argued that Description Logics (DLs) (see e.g. [BCM$^+$02]) are most suitable for that purpose, and indeed OWL DL, the core variant of OWL, is based on an expressive DL. On the other hand, there is so far no accepted standard for rules on the Semantic Web. Semantic web applications will certainly use different kinds of rules. This is reflected by the work done within RuleML[3] initiative which aims at defining mark-up for a family of rules. The basic language in this family is that of function-free Horn clauses (known as Datalog), which will most likely be used in many applications. Integration of such rules with ontologies is thus an important problem. A recent proposal in that direction [GHRS03] identifies a Description Logic, called Description Horn Logic (DHL), whose formulae can be transformed into equivalent Datalog rules, and the corresponding subset of Datalog, called Description

---

[1] http://www.w3.org/2001/sw
[2] http://www.w3.org/TR/owl-ref
[3] http://www.ruleml.org

H.J. Ohlbach and S. Schaffert (Eds.): PPSWR 2004, LNCS 3208, pp. 76–89, 2004.

Logic Programs. The Description Horn Logic is shown to be more expressive than the RDF-S fragment of the Description Logic (see [GHRS03] for the details). Thus, on the one hand it is practically relevant, and on the other hand it has complete tractable inference procedure. This is because any DHL ontology can be transformed into the equivalent Datalog program. This makes it possible to use complete and tractable inference procedures of Horn clauses for efficient answering of standard queries about classes and properties defined by a DHL ontology. The limitation of this elegant approach is that it does not apply to OWL but only to its restricted subset. The Description Logic Programs constitute also a restricted subset of Datalog. Thus, in this approach one achieves a complete fusion of ontology layer with rule layer by restricting the underlying logical formalisms: the Horn logic and the Description Logic. Another proposal for combining OWL and rules is the Semantic Web Rule Language (SWRL[4]) which extends OWL DL with Datalog rules built with unary and binary predicates. As pointed out in the proposal, this extension is undecidable. To our knowledge the issue of building practically relevant reasoners for SWRL has not been addressed yet.

In [Mal03] we suggested another approach to integration of Horn rules and ontologies, where classes of a given ontology are used as types for the arguments of the predicates in the rules. The rationale is that an ontology expressed in some Description Logic, (e.g. in OWL DL, which is based on an expressive description logic) provides a formal description of the domain, common for many applications, while rules describe application-specific relations on the domain. The link between the rules and the ontology is provided by defining (or inferring) types of the predicates. A type specification of a predicate associates classes of the ontology with argument positions of the predicate. As explained below, this makes it possible to formulate the notion of correctness of a program wrt a given type specification and to employ a well-known verification technique of logic programs for static type checking of Datalog programs. The check is done separately for every clause of a given Datalog program. It consists in generating some DL formulae which are to be proved wrt the given ontology. If all proofs succeed the clause is said to be *well-typed*. If all clauses of the program are well-typed then the program is correct wrt the type specification. A proof failure indicates potential typing errors, which may cause problems in use of the program. In the proposed approach the ontology reasoning is restricted to type checking[5] and is separated from runtime reasoning in Horn logic, necessary for querying the rule predicates. Thus the approach is generic, in the sense that it is not restricted to a particular DL, since any DL equipped with a specific reasoner can be used for type checking, and there is a possibility of extension of the type checker for dealing with extensions of Horn rules, e.g. for rules with negation. This paper presents this type checking method in more detail, describes briefly an experi-

---

[4] http://www.daml.org/rules/proposal/rules-all.html Draft version of 30 April 2004.
[5] The usual queries about the ontologies at hand can also be asked but this is not related to the issue of combining rules and ontologies.

mental system for type checking Datalog programs wrt to OWL ontologies, and illustrates its use on an example.

2   Typing Datalog Rules

In this Section we briefly outline our approach to type checking of rules as a special case of a more general technique for proving declarative properties of logic programs and we show how this technique can be applied for rules typed by classes of an ontology specified in a Description Logic.

2.1   Preliminaries

A Datalog rule is an implicitly universally quantified formula of the form

$$h \leftarrow b_1 \wedge \ldots \wedge b_n$$

where $n > 0$ and $h, b_1, \ldots, b_n$ are atomic formulae built over given alphabets of predicate symbols, constants and variables, and $\leftarrow$ is the implication connective. h is called the *head* of the rule, while the conjunction on the right hand side is called *the body*. A Datalog program P is a set of rules and ground atomic formulae (called *facts*). The least Herbrand model semantics (see e.g. [NM95])associates with each program P a set $\mathcal{M}_P$ of ground atomic formulae, which is also the set of all ground atomic logical consequences of the program.

Example 1. Consider the program consisting of the rule

$$uncle(U, X) \leftarrow father(Y, X), sibling(U, Y)$$

and facts $father(tom, john), sibling(bill, tom), sibling(john, mary)$ and $father(tom, mary)$.

   The least Herbrand model consists of all facts of this program and of the facts $uncle(bill, john)$ and $uncle(bill, mary)$.

   The least Herbrand model of a program is defined jointly by the rules and by the facts of the program. We expect that Datalog rules on the web will be used with different sets of facts distributed on the web. Thus for a given set of rules different sets of attached facts will result in different least Herbrand models. For example, adding the fact $sibling(bob, tom)$ to the example program above will extend its least Herbrand model with two additional facts $uncle(bob, john)$ and $uncle(bob, mary)$.

   Generally the constants of a program P represent elements of some application domain $\mathcal{D}$. Thus there exists a mapping $\mathcal{I}$ of the constants of P into objects in $\mathcal{D}$. We extend the mapping $\mathcal{I}$ to a logical interpretation over $\mathcal{D}$ where each n-ary predicate p is interpreted as the relation $p_\mathcal{I}$ consisting of those tuples $\langle \mathcal{I}(c_1), \ldots, \mathcal{I}(c_n) \rangle$ that $p(c_1, \ldots, c_n) \in \mathcal{M}_P$. This interpretation is also a model of P; we will call it the $\mathcal{I}$-induced model of P.

For example, if $\mathcal{I}$ maps the constants of our example to some persons Bill, John, Tom and Mary in the induced model Bill is the uncle of John and Mary.

The arguments of the relations of the $\mathcal{I}$-induced models will usually range over specific subsets of the domain, rather than over the whole domain. For example we would expect that an uncle of a person is a man and not a woman. In web applications the whole database of facts may not be accessible, or may dynamically change over time. Therefore it might be desirable to characterize a priori (a superset of) the range of each argument of the relation associated with a given predicate in the $\mathcal{I}$-induced model. We call this set the *type* of the argument. The *type of a predicate* is then the Cartesian product of the types of the respective arguments. More precisely for given program P and mapping $\mathcal{I}$ over $\mathcal{D}$ a type specification $\mathcal{T}$ associates with the i-th argument of an n-ary predicate p a subset $\mathcal{T}(p_i)$ of $\mathcal{D}$. Then by $\mathcal{T}(p)$ we denote the set $\mathcal{T}(p_1) \times ... \times \mathcal{T}(p_n)$.

Let $\mathcal{I}$ be a mapping of constants into a domain $\mathcal{D}$ and let $\mathcal{T}$ be a type specification of a program P. We say that P is correct wrt a type specification $\mathcal{T}$ iff for every predicate p in P the relation $p_{\mathcal{I}}$ in the $\mathcal{I}$-induced model is a subset of $\mathcal{T}(p)$.

Example 2. Consider a domain of people including, among others, the persons Bill, John, Tom and Mary. Naturally, the universe divides into two classes: *female* and *male* which are disjoint subsets of the set *person* including all elements of the domain.

For the program of Example 1 we consider the natural mapping $\mathcal{I}$ of constants into the considered domain, assigning the constant *mary* to person Mary, etc. We can check then that the program is correctly typed wrt the following type specification:

$$\mathcal{T}(father) = male \times person$$
$$\mathcal{T}(sibling) = person \times person$$
$$\mathcal{T}(uncle) \ = male \times person$$

This is because in any tuple of the relation *uncle* of the induced model the first argument is a male.

2.2   A Technique for Proving Type Correctness of Rules

Clearly the program, may or may not be correct wrt a given type specification. Verification of type correctness of a logic program is a special case of a more general problem of verification of a definite program wrt a specification, discussed by many authors (see e.g. Chapter 7 in [DM93] and references therein). In particular we adopt for our purposes the inductive proof method discussed in Section 7.2 of [DM93] and originating from Clark. Specialization of this method to our problem can be summarized by the following proposition.

Proposition 1. *Let P be a Datalog program, $\mathcal{T}$ a type specification for P over $\mathcal{D}$, and $\mathcal{I}$ be a mapping of the constants into the domain $\mathcal{D}$.*

If

- *for every ground fact $p(c_1, ..., c_n)$ in P we have $\mathcal{I}(c_i) \in \mathcal{T}(p_i)$ for $i = 1, ..., n$, and*
- *for every ground instance of a rule*

$$p0(\overline{c_0}) \leftarrow p1(\overline{c_1}) \wedge ... \wedge pk(\overline{c_k})$$

whenever $\mathcal{I}(\overline{c_i}) \in \mathcal{T}(pi)$ for $i = 1, ..., k$ then $\mathcal{I}(\overline{c_0}) \in \mathcal{T}(p0)$ where $\overline{c_i}$ denotes the respective vector of constants,

then P is correct wrt $\mathcal{T}$.

This proposition holds by soundness of the inductive proof method. It can be easily proved by a structural induction on the proof trees of the program. Intuitively, we want to check that the elements of the tuples in the $\mathcal{I}$-induced model are in the sets specified by a given type specification. The model is obtained by interpretation of constants in the least Herbrand model. Thus, the induced model consists of the tuples which are either directly indicated by facts (first condition of the proposition) or are obtained by the ground instances of the rules, using the T_P operator (see e.g. [NM95]). The type correctness of the latter is guaranteed by the second condition.

Notice that Proposition 1 only provides a sufficient condition. The method is not complete: a program may be correct wrt to a given type specification which does not satisfy the condition.

Example 3. Consider the program of Example 1 with type specification of Example 2.

In the following ground instance of the program rule:

$$uncle(mary, tom) \leftarrow father(john, tom), sibling(mary, john)$$

all body atoms are correctly typed but the head atom is not. Thus the program does not satisfy the conditions of Proposition 1, but, as discussed in Example 2 it is correct wrt the type specification.

In the considered example application of the rule to the facts of the program did not make it possible to obtain incorrectly typed conclusions. However, by adding to the program the correctly typed fact $sibling(ann, tom)$ would make it possible to obtain incorrectly typed conclusion that Ann is the uncle of John. This shows that in web applications the incompleteness of the considered proof method is not a problem, since we want the rules to work properly not only with the given fixed set of facts, but with all correctly typed facts. For this satisfaction of the verification conditions for the rule is not only sufficient but also necessary.

2.3   Specializing the Method to Types Defined in DL

We now discuss how conditions of Proposition 1 can be checked in practice, without generating ground instances of clauses and looking at interpretation of constants. A ground instance of a clause is obtained by binding each variable in a clause to a constant. Consider all occurrences of a variable X in a clause c. Generally it may have m occurrences in the body and p occurrences in the head. For each of them the type specification of the program predicates determines a type $T_i, i = 1, ..., m$ and $R_j, j = 1, ..., p$. To satisfy the second condition of the proposition it is necessary that

$$T_1 \cap ... \cap T_m \subseteq R_1 \cap ... \cap R_p$$

Such a condition should be generated and checked for each variable occurring in the clause. In addition one has to check that every constant occurring in the head is of the type required for its position. Formally, it is not necessary to check the types of the constants in the body, since a constant of wrong type will result in trivial satisfaction of the second condition of the proposition. This means that such a clause would never be applicable to correctly typed atoms. In practice it is desirable to perform this check in order to identify these useless clauses, which most likely were not intended by the programmer.

In order to be able to perform type checking described above we need a language for describing sets to be used as types. Following the Semantic Web approach we propose to adopt for that purpose the language of a Description Logic. A typing of a program P is thus specified as follows:

- We provide DL definitions T of concepts and roles (Tbox).
- We provide DL axioms A about individuals (Abox), so that for every constant a of P and for any given class expression C the formula $C(a)$ can be proved (or disproved) in the Description Logic from T and A.
- We assign to each n-ary predicate of P an n-tuple of class expressions built with the constructors of the DL over the primitive concepts of the ontology. Each model of T provides thus a typing of the program in the sense of Section 2.1.

Example 4. In most of the Description Logics the type specifications of Example 2 could be formulated as follows:
- Tbox:
$$person = male \sqcup female \quad male \sqcap female = \bot$$
- Abox:
$$male(john), male(tom), male(bill), female(mary)$$
- predicate assignment:
$$father : \quad (male, person)$$
$$sibling : \quad (person, person)$$
$$uncle : \quad (male, person)$$

We can now perform automatic type checking wrt to every model of this specification. For this

- using the Tbox, the Abox and the assignment of types to predicates we generate the formulae of the Description Logic, corresponding to the verification conditions described above,
- we prove the verification conditions using a complete DL reasoner.

If the proof succeeds, the program is correct wrt to the typing provided by any model of the ontology.

Example 5. The verification conditions for the rule of Example 1 and the type specification of Example 2 give rise to the following DL formulae:

$$person \sqsubseteq male, \quad person \sqsubseteq person$$

The first of them is not a logical consequence of the ontology, the other trivially holds.

As the research in DL resulted in several complete and efficient DL reasoners, we can choose any of them to implement a type checker for Datalog, as described above. In the rest of the paper we outline a prototype implementation of a type checker for Datalog types described in OWL and using a reasoner available on the web to perform type checking.

3   Implemented System Overview

We have implemented a prototype system which performs type checking of Datalog rules typed according to an ontology expressed in OWL DL. Being able to handle ontologies expressed in OWL is of importance since it supports commonly accepted ideas for a web ontology language. OWL is also a W3C Recommendation as of 10th February 2004.

RuleML defines mark-up for a family of rule languages of which Datalog is a member. Using a mark-up language such as RuleML allow for interoperability of the rules between different systems. An important notion of RuleML[6] for this work is the ability to associate a type with a variable or an individual (constant). This is accomplished by giving a value to the attribute *type* available for the *var* and *ind* tags. For example, `<var type=''type_name''>X</var>` associates the type *type_name* with the variable X in RuleML.

The input to the type checker is actually threefold: an ontology (in OWL), a rule-base (in RuleML) and a type specification. The type specification defines a mapping between predicates appearing in the Datalog rules and tuples of types as described in section 2. In the present version of the system a type specification is not given separately, but is assumed to be implicitly provided within the RuleML encoding of the Datalog rules in question. This should be done by providing class expressions as the values of the *type* attributes in RuleML for variables and constants in the rule-base marked up in RuleML. Since a variable in a rule appears at some argument position of a predicate p the specified type is assumed to be the type of this argument. Therefore, it is sufficient to specify the type only at one occurrence of p in all rules. Multiple definitions are allowed but should specify the same type for a given argument position of the predicate. The

---

[6] as of version 0.85.

type associated by the type attribute with a given occurrence of a constant is considered to be the type of this constant. For any occurrence of the constant in a rule its type should be subsumed by the type of the argument of the respective predicate.

The interface to the system is web-based and the type checker is implemented as a Java servlet which makes it easily available for testing purposes. Figure 1 shows the user interface where the input to the system is specified. The user must provide a rule-base marked up in RuleML and an ontology expressed in OWL DL according to which the rules are typed. The user has the option of providing a URI for each or load either of them from a local hard-drive.

Type checking of Datalog rules is carried out with the help of a DL reasoner (see section 3.1). The DL reasoner used in this system runs as a server process and the user has the option of using his/her own server instead of the default. This is convenient if the default server is not on-line for some reason or another. If the user chooses to use his/her own DL reasoner server a host address and a port number, to which the DL reasoner process listens, must be specified.

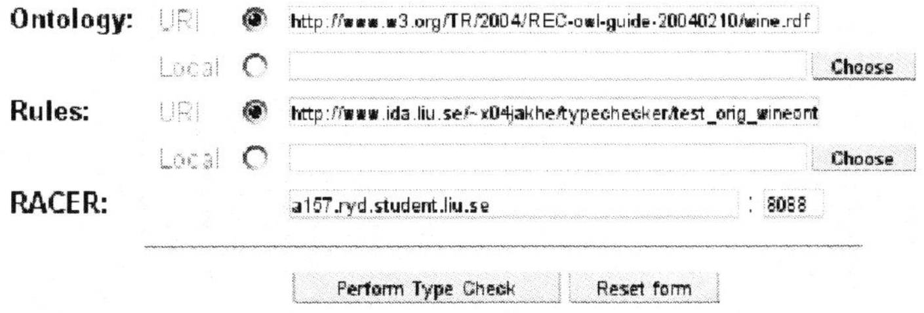

Fig. 1. User interface on the web

3.1 Choosing DL Reasoner

Type checking of Datalog rules consists of checking whether the DL formulae which are the verification conditions for the rules (as described in Section 2) are logical consequences of a given ontology. Since the ontologies we are concerned with are formalized in a DL, we are in need of a DL reasoner to be a subcomponent of the implemented type checker. Research in Description Logic has resulted in several efficient DL reasoners for highly expressive DLs. One such reasoner is the RACER system[7]. One of the main reasons for choosing the RACER reasoner for use in the type checking system is because of its support for OWL documents. It is possible to tell RACER the location (via an URI) of an OWL document (i.e. an ontology) whereupon it is loaded into the reasoner. Once the ontology is loaded into RACER it is possible to send queries to the reasoner, e.g. to check whether some DL formula is a logical consequence of the loaded ontology.

---

[7] http://www.sts.tu-harburg.de/ r.f.moeller/racer/

Interaction with RACER is made possible through socket communication using the JRacer API (in Java) available on the RACER home-page. Strings of commands are simply sent to RACER for execution whereupon an answer is given, also in the form a string, which is interpreted in an appropriate manner.

3.2   System Details

Figure 2 shows an overview of the internals of the type checker. The input to the system, i.e. the ontology and the rules, are provided through a HTML form as seen in figure 1. This information is posted to the Java servlet which then performs the necessary steps to type check the rules. First, the ontology is loaded into RACER which is conveniently done due to RACERs support of OWL documents. A URI reference to the ontology can be handled by RACER. Next, the rule-base (in RuleML) is parsed and the type specification is derived from the types explicitly given to each variable and individual. Once the rule-base is parsed the necessary verification conditions for type correctness are constructed. As described earlier these verification conditions are DL formulae being membership checks $(C(x))$ and inclusions (subsumption) checks $(B_1 \sqcap \ldots \sqcap B_n \sqsubseteq H_1 \sqcap \ldots \sqcap H_m)$. The verification conditions are sent to the RACER reasoner to verify whether the formulae are logical consequences of the ontology. When some condition is found not to be a logical consequence of the given ontology the user is informed of which condition failed and the reason for it.

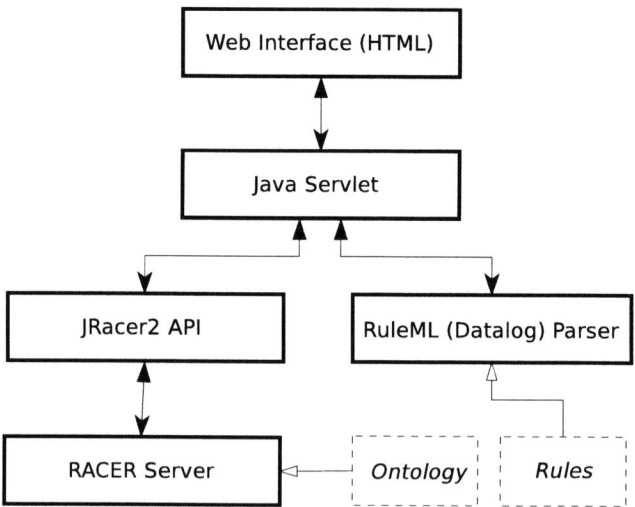

Fig. 2. System overview

When a verification condition fails the user is presented with the failing rule in a Prolog-syntax (as complement to the rather verbose RuleML) together with (this is optional) the corresponding RuleML mark-up actually sent as input to the type checker.

3.3   Error Handling

An important aspect of the prototype type checking system is to give adequate feedback to users regarding errors that occur. Apart from the obvious error of type incorrect rules there are also other issues which the user must be informed of. Important checks performed by the system and upon failure reported to the user include the following:

- Type expressions are not class expressions of the underlying ontology,
- Rules are not safe, i.e. there are variables which only occur in the head of a rule and not in the body,
- The rule-base document is not well-formed, i.e. an invalid rule-base document,
- The rule-base document does not validate in accordance with the accompanying RuleML (Datalog) DTD, i.e. illegal or invalid constructs are used in the mark-up of the rules.

4   An Example

We adopt an example from [DLNS98] where a hybrid language $\mathcal{AL}$-log is defined. The language consists of a structural component (a DL) and a relational component (Datalog). The example we adopt includes an ontology, formalized by the DL formulae shown in figure 3. The ontology describes the terminology used in an academic setting which includes concepts such as *FullProfessor*, *FacultyMember*, *Course* and *Topic* among others and properties such as *teaching*.

$FullProfessor \sqsubseteq FacultyMember$
$NonTeachingFullProfessor = FullProfessor \sqcap \neg \exists Teaching.Course$
$AdvancedCourse \sqcup BasicCourse = Course$
$AdvancedCourse \sqcap BasicCourse \sqsubseteq \bot$

Fig. 3. Axioms of Academic ontology in abstract syntax

In our example we encode the same axioms in OWL. The indented meaning of the rule in figure 4 is to state whether or not a student may do his/her thesis with a certain faculty member. The typing of the program is given in figure 5.

Thus, for this rule the following validity conditions must hold.

1. $Student \sqsubseteq Student$
2. $FullProfessor \sqcap \exists teaching.AdvancedCourse \sqsubseteq FacultyMember$

```
mayDoThesis(X, Y) :-
        curriculum(X, Z),
        expert(Y, Z).
```

Fig. 4. Example rule for Academic domain

mayDoThesis $\to< Student, FacultyMember >$
curriculum $\to< Student, Topic >$
expert $\to< FullProfessor \sqcap \exists teaching.AdvancedCourse, Topic >$

Fig. 5. Typing of the Academic example

The first condition holds trivially while the second one is more complex and more difficult to prove. The type checking system with the ontology loaded can easily and quickly decide whether the condition holds or not. In this case the condition will be proved, thus the rule is shown to be type correct w.r.t. the type specification.

Now suppose we use the same rule as in figure 4 but this time type check w.r.t the type specification in figure 6.

mayDoThesis $\to< Student, FullProfessor \sqcap \exists teaching.AdvancedCourse >$
curriculum $\to< Student, Topic >$
expert $\to< FullProfessor, Topic >$

Fig. 6. Another typing of the Academic example

Again we get two validity conditions that must hold.

1. $Student \sqsubseteq Student$
2. $FullProfessor \sqsubseteq FullProfessor \sqcap \exists teaching.AdvancedCourse$

Again the first condition holds. The second one, on the other hand, does not hold and the error is reported by the system, i.e. there is a type failure. The output from the system can be seen in figure 7. To the left the rule is presented in Prolog syntax with the addition of having the types of the variables come after the variable separated with a comma. To the right of the rule the user has the option of showing the verbose RuleML code which corresponds to the rule on the left. Below these two parts the reason for the type failure is given in a less formalized English sentence.

5   Discussion and Further Work

We elaborated on our previous suggestion [Mal03] on static typing of Datalog rules by classes of an ontology formalized in a DL. The proposed typing

Ontology http://www.ida.liu.se/~x04jakhe/thesis.owl already loaded, not reloaded.
Rule Database. http://www.ida.liu.se/~x04jakhe/thesis.ruleml

Rule: unnamed	
mayDoThesis(X:Student , Y:(and FullProfessor (some teaching AdvancedCourse))) :- curriculum(X:Student , Z:Topic), expert(Y:FullProfessor , Z:Topic).	[View RuleML code]

Reason for type error:

The concept (and http://www.ida.liu.se/~x04jakhe/thesis.owl#FullProfessor (some http://www.ida.liu.se/~x04jakhe/thesis.owl#teaching http://www.ida.liu.se/~x04jakhe/thesis.owl#AdvancedCourse)) does not subsume the concept http://www.ida.liu.se/~x04jakhe/thesis.owl#FullProfessor

1 of 1 rules were not type correct
Done.

Fig. 7. Report of a type error

method is a specialization of a general method for proving declarative properties of logic programs, where the properties are specified and proved in a Description Logic. The approach has thus a solid formal foundation. It is generic in the sense that it is not a priori restricted to any particular Description Logic. For any chosen DL a type checker based on (possibly remote) access to a specific DL reasoner can be easily implemented along the lines discussed in this paper. We implemented an experimental version of a type checker for types being classes specified in OWL, where the verification conditions are checked in RACER.

The presented approach shows a rigorous way of coupling the emerging rule level of the Semantic Web with the ontology level. In contrast to the approaches of [GHRS03] and of SWRL it is a kind of loose coupling, rather than a full integration. In contrast to the SWRL we can use any complete reasoner for the chosen DL. The advantage of our approach is that it is generic and allows for using of the unchanged ontology reasoners for type checking of rules. On the other hand, it strictly separates static type checking from reasoning on the rule level, where the ontology reasoning is not involved.

At present our type checker can only work with total type specifications, providing types of all predicates in the rules. As an aid to the rule designer one could allow a *partial typing*, predicates mapped by the typing to tuples where all types are not explicitly stated. For this a kind of *type inference* for the missing types is needed. By introducing new class names for unspecified types one can still generate the verification conditions for the rules. They can be seen as *type constraints*. Type checking of a rule-base would render a number of such constraints. The constraints could be introduced into the ontology in the DL reasoner whereupon the consistency of the ontology would be checked. If the ontology is found to be inconsistent it would mean that the type constraints introduced are inconsistent and are therefore unsolvable. On the other hand, if the ontology is still consistent then a solution to the type constraints exists and the rule-base is considered type correct.

For interoperability reasons we have chosen to represent rules in RuleML. However, RuleML like any XML syntax is very verbose. For better communication with the rule designer a more human-friendly representation would be desirable, with both way transformation into RuleML. Also the present way of specifying types as attributes within RuleML rules does not seem to be a good solution in long range. Especially, for large rule bases the scattered type specification in the present form would be very inconvenient. It is not clear how a separate type specification would be encoded but perhaps the DIG[8] language would be a starting point.

We believe that our approach can be extended to other kinds of rules relevant for the Semantic Web; for that we should first find and investigate Semantic Web applications employing both rules and ontologies.

Acknowledgment

This research has been funded by the European Commission and by the Swiss Federal Office for Education and Science within the 6th Framework Programme project REWERSE number 506779 (cf. `http://rewerse.net`).

The authors acknowledge the valuable comments obtained from the anonymous reviewers which helped very much in preparation of the final version of the paper.

References

[BCM+02]   F. Baader, D. Calvanese, D. McGuiness, and D. Nardi, and P. Patel-Schneider(eds.). *The Description Logic Handbook*. Cambridge University Press, 2002.

[DLNS98]   F. M. Donini, M. Lenzerini, and D. Nardi, and A. Schaerf. AL-log: Integrating Datalog and Description Logics. *Intelligent Information Systems*, 10(3):227–252, 1998.

[DM93]   P. Deransart and J. Małuszynski. *A Grammatical View of Logic Programming*. MIT Press, 1993.

[GHRS03]   B. N. Grosof, I. Horrocks, R. Volz, and S. Decker. Description Logic Programs: Combining Logic Programs with Description Logic. In *Proc. 12th International World Wide Web Conference*, pages 48–57, ACM Press, 2003. http://www2003.org/cdrom/papers/refereed/p117/p117-grosof.html.

---

[8] http://dl-web.man.ac.uk/dig/index.shtml

[Mal03]   Jan Maluszynski. On integrating rules into the semantic web. In *Electronic Notes in Theoretical Computer Science*, volume 86, Elsevier, 2003.

[NM95]   U. Nilsson, and J. Małuszyński. *Logic, Programming and Prolog*. John Wiley, 2 edition, 1995. Second Edition.

Reasoning About Temporal Context Using Ontology and Abductive Constraint Logic Programming

Hongwei Zhu, Stuart E. Madnick, and Michael D. Siegel

MIT Sloan School of Management
30 Wadsworth Street, MA, 02142, USA
{mrzhu, smadnick, msiegel}@mit.edu
http://interchange.mit.edu/coin

Abstract. The underlying assumptions for interpreting the meaning of data often change over time, which further complicates the problem of semantic heterogeneities among autonomous data sources. As an extension to the Context Interchange (COIN) framework, this paper introduces the notion of temporal context as a formalization of the problem. We represent temporal context as a multi-valued method in F-Logic; however, only one value is valid at any point in time, the determination of which is constrained by temporal relations. This representation is then mapped to an abductive constraint logic programming framework with temporal relations being treated as constraints. A mediation engine that implements the framework automatically detects and reconciles semantic differences at different times. We articulate that this extended COIN framework is suitable for reasoning on the Semantic Web.

1 Introduction

The Web, and many other data sources, accumulate a large amount of data over time. In certain cases, it is even required by law for organizations to store historical data and make sure it is accurate and easy to retrieve[1]. It is critical that the retrieved data can be correctly interpreted, especially in the context of the Semantic Web where users or agents make decisions based on information coming from multiple autonomous sources. This well known semantic heterogeneity problem is further complicated when the semantics of data not only differs across sources, but also changes over time.

As an example, suppose an arbitrage specialist in New York City wants to study longitudinal stock price differences among exchanges. Within several keystrokes and mouse clicks at Yahoo Finance site, he retrieves the historical prices for Daimler-Chrysler at New York and Frankfurt exchanges, see Figure 1. He is astonished by what he sees: 1) the prices at the exchanges are extraordinarily different (*what an arbitraging opportunity*); and 2) the price at Frankfurt plunged by almost a half at the

---

[1] See Robert Sheier on "Regulated storage" in ComputerWorld, 37(46), November 17, 2003. Health Insurance Portability Act requires healthcare providers keep records till two years after death of patients; Sarbanes-Oxley Act requires auditing firms retain records of financial statements.

H.J. Ohlbach and S. Schaffert (Eds.): PPSWR 2004, LNCS 3208, pp. 90–101, 2004.
© Springer-Verlag Berlin Heidelberg 2004

turn from 1998 to 1999 (*too bad if someone bought the stock right before the price decline*)! Possible conclusions from the observations are in parentheses.

Date	Open	High	Low	Close	Volume	Adj Close*
6-Jan-99	105.25	105.74	103.92	105.13	2,061,200	90.49
5-Jan-99	99.05	103.43	98.93	103.31	2,634,600	88.92
4-Jan-99	99.66	100.69	98.08	98.99	3,441,400	85.20
31-Dec-98	94.49	94.55	93.21	93.51	506,900	80.49
30-Dec-98	94.97	95.34	94.18	94.18	391,300	81.06
29-Dec-98	96.13	96.25	95.64	95.95	1,195,700	82.58
28-Dec-98	95.64	96.43	95.16	95.64	1,707,800	82.32
6-Jan-99	90.10	92.40	89.30	92.30	13,950,500	86.67
5-Jan-99	86.80	88.60	86.10	86.80	12,329,300	81.51
4-Jan-99	83.50	88.50	82.50	87.50	13,660,200	82.16
30-Dec-98	166.30	167.90	164.50	164.50	4,934,820	154.47
29-Dec-98	166.00	166.50	164.50	165.00	5,039,660	154.94
28-Dec-98	159.50	167.80	159.30	166.50	9,748,480	156.34

* Close price adjusted for dividends and splits.

Fig. 1. Stock prices for Daimler-Chrysler from Yahoo. Top: New York; Bottom: Frankfurt

These are wrong conclusions based on false observations, all resulted from unresolved heterogeneous and changing semantics. Here, not only are the currencies for stock prices different at the two exchanges, but the currency at Frankfurt exchange also changed from German Marks to Euros at the beginning of 1999. Once the data is transformed into the analyst context, i.e., all prices in US dollars, it can be seen that there is neither significant arbitraging opportunity nor abrupt price plunge for this stock. Unfortunately, the technologies used by the analyst do not sufficiently represent and make use of the semantics of the data being exchanged.

The example illustrates the kinds of problems that the Semantic Web aims to solve. Context Interchange (COIN) framework [7, 10], originated from the semantic data integration research tradition, shares the common goal and provides an extensible solution to semantic heterogeneity problems. COIN is a web-based mediation approach with several distinguishing characteristics:

- Detection and reconciliation of semantic differences are a system service and are transparent to users;
- Mediation does not require that any semantic differences between each source-receiver pair to be specified a priori, rather, it only needs a declarative description of data semantics and the methods of reconciling possible differences. Semantic differences are detected and reconciled at the time of query; and
- Mediation is implemented in abductive constraint logic programming. As a result, it allows for knowledge level query and can generate *intensional* answers as well as *extensional* answers. Efficient reasoning is achieved by combining abduction with concurrent constraint solving.

With the temporal extension presented in this paper, COIN is capable of processing static semantic heterogeneities as well as those that change over time. As elaborated later, these features make COIN suitable for the Semantic Web. In this paper, we describe the COIN framework with a focus on the representation and reasoning of changing semantics. The use of SQL is for convenience purpose and should not be construed as a constraint of the framework, which will become clear as we describe the logic formalism of COIN.

2 Context Interchange by Example

Before a formal definition is given, we call implicit metadata knowledge such as the currency for price *context* and the history of time varying metadata *temporal context*. The temporal context in the previous example is quite simple. To illustrate the COIN approach, let's consider a slightly more complicated example in Figure 2, where various aspects of data semantics in a company financials data source change at different times.

Context *c_src*	Context *c_target*
1. All *monetary values* are in French Francs until 2000 and in Euros afterwards;	1. All *monetary values* are always in USD;
2. All *monetary values* have a scale factor of 1M until 1999, 1K until 2001, and 1M from 2002	2. All *monetary values* always have a scale factor of 1K
3. *Profit* is tax excluded until 2000, tax included afterwards	3. *Profit* is always tax included
4. All *other numbers* have a scale factor of 1 until 2001 and 1K afterwards	4. All *other numbers* always have a scale factor of 1K

Financials

Year	Num_Employee	Profit	Tax
...			
1999	5100	4.2	1.1
2000	12000	13000	2500
2001	25.3	20000	4800
2002	30.6	35.3	7.97
...			

Query Q1:

```
Select Year,Num_Employee,Profit
From Financials
Where 2000=<Year;
```

Fig. 2. Temporal context example. Various aspects of data semantics change at different times

This example involves one data source with asynchronously changing semantics shown on the left side, and one data receiver, whose context is stated on the right side in Figure 2. The situation becomes much more difficult for humans to handle when there are multiple sources being used to serve multiple receivers – each with a potentially different context. Although our design is intended for the more complex case, we will use the simple situation of Figure 2 for presentation purposes. We distinguish two kinds of temporal contexts: 1) *representational* – different representations for the same concept, e.g., different currencies and scale factors for monetary values; and 2) *ontological* – similar concept with slight differentiation, e.g., profit with taxes included or excluded. In resolving ontological differences, representational differences of related concepts should be resolved as well.

In this example, the user knows what can be queried from the source but is unaware of the context differences. This is similar to how the Web is typically used. Clearly, a direct execution of the sample query Q1 in Figure 2 over the source will return data that is not correct in the user context. With COIN, however, the user can issue the query and expect that the results can be correctly interpreted in his context. To relieve the users of the burden of keeping track of and reconciling context differences, data semantics of sources and receivers need to be explicitly recorded as a set of context axioms and elevation axioms with reference to an ontology. As shown in Figure 3, the Context Mediator detects context differences at run time and rewrites user queries into mediated queries (*MQ*) that reconcile these differences. The MQ can be returned to the user as an *intensional* answer to the original query, or it can be sent to the query optimizer to generate an optimized query plan for the executioner to retrieve data, perform necessary conversions, and assemble the data records as an *extensional* answer. So when query Q1 is issued, the mediator can generate the following MQ1:

```
MQ1: Select Year, Num_Employee*0.001, Profit*O.Rate+Tax*O.Rate
     From Financials, (Select Rate from Olsen, Financials
           where Expressed='FRF' and Exchanged='USD' and Date=Year) O
     Where Year=2000
     Union
     Select Year, Num_Employee*0.001, Profit*O.Rate
     From Financials, (Select Rate from Olsen, Financials
           where Expressed='EUR' and Exchanged='USD' and Date=Year) O
     Where Year=2001
     Union
     Select Year, Num_Employee, Profit*O.Rate*1000
     From Financials, (Select Rate from Olsen, Financials
           where Expressed='EUR' and Exchanged='USD' and Date=Year) O
     Where 2002=<Year;
```

MQ1 considers all the semantic changes since year 2000 and reconciles the semantic differences between the source and the receiver through three sub-queries. Note an auxiliary data source *Olsen* for currency conversion is introduced in MQ1. The execution of an optimized MQ1 will return the dataset whose values have been transformed to conform to the user context.

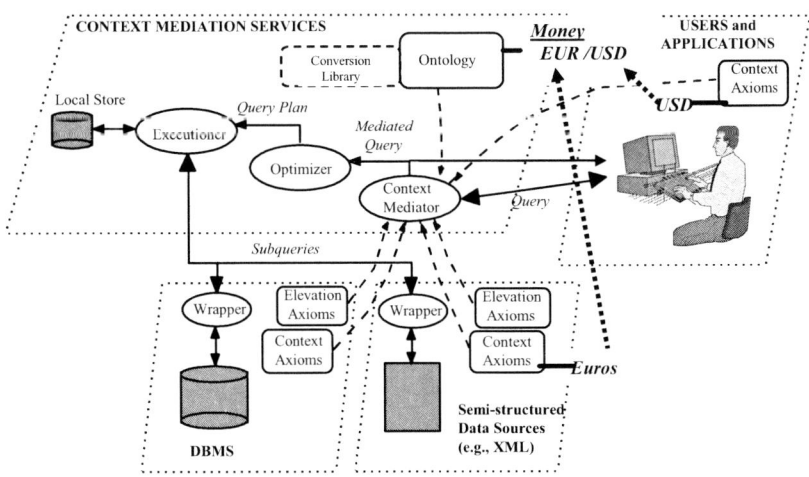

Fig. 3. Architecture of the COIN system

3 Temporal Context in COIN Framework

The example in Figure 2 can be understood with the notion of *context* as in [17]. Each tuple in the *Financials* table represents a statement about the company, which is true only within the given context *c_src*. Each statement is not true when it is directly restated in the *c_target* context. The COIN framework provides a logic formalism for describing context and a mediation service for restating statements from source contexts in the receiver context. For example, it is true that the number of employees in 1999 is 5100 in the *c_src* context, which can be expressed as

$$\bar{c}: \quad ist(c\_src, num\_employee(1999, 5100)).$$

a correct restatement of which in the *c_target* should be

$$\bar{c}: \quad ist(c\_target, num\_employee(1999, 5.1)).$$

because the scale factors in the two contexts are different.

The COIN system automates the process that restates the facts from the source context in the target context. This is achieved by formally capturing context knowledge and automatically detecting and reconciling context differences.

The original COIN framework was based on a snapshot data model that lacks the capability of describing and reasoning about changes of semantics. We will describe the ongoing research that non-trivially extends COIN to represent and process temporal context, the understanding of which can be benefited by a brief introduction to the existing COIN framework; further details can be found in [7, 10].

3.1 Overview of the COIN Framework

The COIN framework consists of a formalism for context knowledge representation and a service of query mediation and execution. Knowledge representation in COIN is based on an object oriented deductive data model that consists of three components:

- Ontology – to define the semantic domain using a collection of semantic types and their relationships. A type can be related to another in three ways: 1) as a subtype or super-type (e.g., *profit* is a subtype of *monetary value*; 2) as a named attribute (e.g., *temporal entity* such as year is a temporal attribute of *profit*); and 3) as a modifier or contextual attribute, whose value is specified in context axioms and can functionally determine the interpretation of instances of the type that has this modifier (e.g., *monetary value* type has a scale factor modifier). There is a distinguished type *basic* in the ontology that serves as the super type of all the other types and represents all primitive data types. Objects are instances of the defined types;
- Elevation axioms – to establish correspondences between data elements in sources and the types in the ontology, e.g., tax in the example in Figure 2 corresponds to *monetary value* in the ontology; and
- Context axioms – to specify the values of modifiers for each source or receiver and the conversions for transforming an object in one context to another. The context of each source or receiver is uniquely identified with a context label, e.g.,

c_src and *c_target* in the example. The value specification for modifiers can be a simple value assignment or a set of rules that specify how to obtain the value. Thus, conceptually a context can be thought to be a set of <*modifier, object*> pairs, where *object* is a singleton in most non-temporal cases.

These components can be naturally represented using F-Logic [15], which has rich constructs for describing types and their relationships and has formal semantics for inheritance and overriding. Attributes and modifiers are represented as functions or methods of the defined types; since modifier values vary by context, methods for modifiers are parameterized with a context label. Comparison between objects is only meaningful when performed in the same context, i.e., suppose *x* and *y* are objects,

$$x \overset{c}{\Diamond} y \Leftrightarrow x[value(c) \rightarrow u] \wedge y[value(c) \rightarrow v] \wedge u \Diamond v.$$

where $\Diamond$ is one of the comparison operators for primitives in $\{=, \neq, <, \leq, >, \geq, \dots\}$, and the *value* method is a parameterized function that returns the primitive value of an object in the specified context *c*.

The detection and reconciliation of context differences are through a mediation engine implemented in abductive constraint logic programming, details of which are provided later.

3.2 Representation of Temporal Context

For temporal context representation, the ontology is augmented with explicit time concepts such as the ones defined in DAML Time Ontology [12]. Temporal entity is the most general concept and can be further specialized into time *instant* and time *interval*. Any other concepts or types whose value or semantics change over time are related to temporal concepts via named attributes or modifiers in the COIN ontology, e.g., *monetary value* has a temporal attribute of type *temporal entity*, which can be described in F-Logic as:

$$monetaryValue[tempAttr \Rightarrow temporalEntity].$$

A graphical representation of the ontology for the example is given in Figure 4.

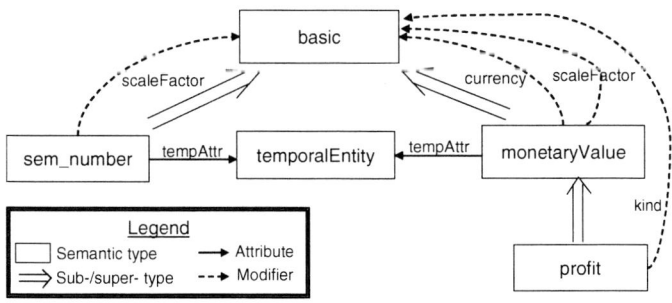

Fig. 4. A graphical representation of the example ontology

The changing semantics of data is captured by specifying the history of the modifiers. Thus modifiers are multi-valued over the entire history; but at any point in time, there is only a single valid value for each modifier. For example, to describe the temporal context regarding the currency in the example, we first declare in the ontology that *currency* is a multi-valued *modifier* for *monetary value*:

$$monetaryValue[currency(ctxt) \Rrightarrow basic].$$

Next, we specify the values and their corresponding time intervals using the following context axiom (which corresponds to two clauses in clausal form):

$$\forall X : monetaryValue \; \exists Y : basic \vdash$$
$$X[currency(c\_src) \rightarrow Y] \wedge$$

$$(Y[value(c\_src) \rightarrow 'FRF'] \leftarrow X[tempAttr \rightarrow T] \wedge T \in_t \overset{c\_src}{I_{\leq 2000}}) \wedge \tag{1}$$

$$(Y[value(c\_src) \rightarrow 'EUR'] \leftarrow X[tempAttr \rightarrow T] \wedge T \in_t \overset{c\_src}{I_{2001\leq}}).$$

where $\vdash$ is used for pre-declaration for object types, $I_{\leq 2000}$ represents the time interval up to year 2000 and $\in_t$ is a temporal inclusion relation, which can be translated into a set of comparisons between time points by introducing functions that return the beginning and ending points of an interval:

$$\forall T : temporalEntity, I : temporalEntity \vdash$$
$$T \overset{c}{\in_t} I \Leftrightarrow (begin(I) \overset{c}{\leq} begin(T)) \wedge (end(T) \overset{c}{\leq} end(I)).$$

Conceptually, we can think of temporal context as a set of *<modifier, history>* pairs with *history* being a set of *<object, time_interval>* pairs or a set of time-stamped objects.

Another way of thinking about history specification is to regard it as a set of rules with applicability of each being constrained by an appropriate temporal relation. With this view, temporal context representation is analogous to *data level context* in snapshot based COIN, by *data level context* we mean that within a named context a modifier can have different values depending on other characteristics of the object. [11] gives an example of this kind where the scale factor for *monetary value* is 1 if it is not in Japanese Yen and is 1000 if otherwise:

$$\forall X : monetaryValue \; \exists Y : basic \vdash$$
$$X[scaleFactor(c) \rightarrow Y] \wedge$$

$$(Y[value(c) \rightarrow 1] \leftarrow X[currency(c) \rightarrow Z] \wedge Z \overset{c}{\neq} 'JPY') \wedge$$

$$(Y[value(c) \rightarrow 1000] \leftarrow X[currency(c) \rightarrow Z] \wedge Z \overset{c}{=} 'JPY').$$

This data level context specification is similar to temporal context especially after the temporal relation is transformed into a set of comparisons between time points. Thus temporal context is analogous to data level context even though they are conceptually quite different. This analogy suggests that the mediation engine for snapshot COIN can be extended with additional rules for temporal relations to process temporal context.

Because modifiers are single valued at any given point in time, the conversion functions for temporal context handling are the same as those in snapshot COIN. Earlier we described conversions as part of context specification. Through parameterization, a conversion function can be defined more generally to be used in multiple contexts. For example, the following currency conversion function can be used to convert monetary values from any arbitrary context $c1$ to any other arbitrary context $c2$:

$$x : monetaryValue \vdash$$
$$x[cvt(currency, c2) @ c1, u \rightarrow v] \leftarrow$$
$$x[currency(c1) \rightarrow C_f] \wedge x[currency(c2) \rightarrow C_t] \wedge x[tempAttr \rightarrow T] \wedge$$
$$olsen\_(A, B, R, D) \wedge C_f \overset{c2}{=} A \wedge C_t \overset{c2}{=} B \wedge T \overset{c2}{=} D \wedge$$
$$R[value(c2) \rightarrow r] \wedge v = u * r. \tag{2}$$

where *olsen_* corresponds to an external relation that gives exchange rate between two currencies on any specified date.

A recent effort [8] introduced automatic conversion composition based on equational relationships between contexts, e.g., given conversions between 1) base price and tax-included price; and 2) tax-included price and final price, the conversion between base price and final price can be composed using symbolic equation solvers.

3.3 Mediation with Abductive Constraint Logic Programming

The task of mediation is to translate a user query that assumes everything is in user context to a mediated query (*MQ*) that reconciles context differences detected during the mediation process; when the MQ is subsequently executed, facts stated in source contexts are correctly restated in the user context. This task corresponds to the abductive logic programming (ALP) framework [13] very well, *i.e.*, the user query corresponds to the observation in ALP and the MQ, which is derived from knowledge representation axioms to incorporate all necessary conversions, serves as the abductive explanation to the user query. As we see earlier, temporal relations in temporal context representation can be considered as temporal constraints over the time domain, which suggests constraint solving is necessary. It follows that mediation can be implemented with the abductive constraint logic programming (ACLP) [14] where abduction, consistency checking, and constraint propagation are interleaved.

As an extension to ALP, ACLP is a triple $<\mathcal{P}, \mathcal{A}, IC>$, where $\mathcal{P}$ is a constraint logic program, $\mathcal{A}$ is a set of abducible predicates different from the constraint predicates, and IC is a set of integrity constraints over the domains of $\mathcal{P}$. Query answering in ACLP is that given a query $q(X)$, generate a set of abductive hypothesis Δ and a substitution θ so that $\mathcal{P} \cup \Delta$ entails $q(\vec{X})\theta$ and is consistent; Δ consists of abducible predicates and simplified constraints.

The COIN framework can be straightforwardly mapped to ACLP. Knowledge representation in COIN can be translated into an equivalent normal Horn program [1]; or alternatively, the knowledge representation can be directly expressed in first order Horn clauses. This corresponds to $\mathcal{P}$. Predicates and arithmetic operators allowed by the query languages of the sources and other callable external functions constitute $\mathcal{A}$. We also allow constraints to be abducibles. IC consists of integrity constraints in data sources and any constraints introduced in the user query.

Abductive inference in COIN is a modified SLD-resolution [6] in that literals corresponding to predicates in data sources are abducted without evaluation; constraints over non-temporal types are also directly abducted. Constraints introduced in user query, by the conversion functions, and related to *temporal entity* types are evaluated after they are abducted. The prototype is implemented using constraint logic programming environment ECLiPSe (http://www.icparc.ic.ac.uk/eclipse/) with the extension of Constraint Handling Rules (CHR) [9]. Naturally, we use the constraint store to collect the abucibles; when a constraint is abducted, applicable CHR rules will be triggered to simplify/propagate the constraint or signify a failure to cause backtracking of abduction. At the end of a successful resolution, predicates in the constraint store constitute the abductive answer.

The current implementation is an enhancement to the procedure described in [4] with significant extensions to handle conversion composition [8] and temporal context. We will focus on temporal context handling, thus we only briefly describe the procedure here and refer readers to [4] for other details.

The mediator accepts queries in clausal form. Auxiliary components in our prototype translate a SQL query into its equivalent logic form for mediation and translate the MQ back into SQL for query planning and execution. The example query can be translated to the following clausal form:

$$\leftarrow answer(y, n, p).$$
$$answer(y, n, p) \leftarrow financials(y, n, p, t) \wedge 2000 \leq y.$$

where we use predicate *answer* to simulate *projection*. This query is naïve in the sense that it directly references the primitive objects in data sources without the concern about potential context differences. The query is further translated into a well formed context-aware query by 1) replacing each primitive object with its Skolemized semantic counterpart as specified in elevation axioms. We call a so transformed relation a *semantic relation*; 2) replacing comparison operators for non-temporal objects with $\lozenge^{c\_target}$; 3) replacing comparison for temporal objects with temporal relations (e.g., replacing $\leq$ with *tle_*, which stands for inclusive *before*); and 4) introduce the parameterized *value* function for each projected object; as defined earlier, $\lozenge^{c\_target}$ also introduces *value* function calls. After this transformation, the naïve query becomes:

$$answer(y, n, p) \leftarrow financials\_(sk_y, sk_n, sk_p, sk_t) \wedge tle\_(sk_{2000}, sk_y) \wedge$$
$$sk_y[value(c\_target) \rightarrow y] \wedge sk_n[value(c\_target) \rightarrow n] \wedge$$
$$sk_p[value(c\_target) \rightarrow p].$$

This is the query that is fed to the mediator. Literals corresponding to semantic relations are unified with elevation axioms and the corresponding source predicates are abducted. Constraints are abducted and immediately processed if corresponding CHR rules exist; abduction backtracks after a failure in constraint process. Value functions are processed with the following algorithm:

```
For each value function
  Find direct and inherited modifiers of the object
  For each modifier
    Compare modifier values in source and target contexts
```

```
     If they differ
       Find conversion function for the object
       If not found, find conversion function of parents
       If not found, invoke function composition
       Invoke found/composed conversion and return a primitive
 If no modifier, return the primitive value of the object ■
```

This algorithm implements the semantics and simulates non-monotonic inheritance afforded in the knowledge representation language. It is recursive in that modifiers are objects, comparison of which introduces *value* function calls; declaratively defined conversions usually introduce *value* function calls as well.

Given the well formed query, the resolution of the first literal generates the abducible *financials*(y_0, n_0, p_0, t_0). Similarly $tle(2000, y_0)$ is abducted into the constraint store when $tle\_(sk_{2000}, sk_y)$ is resolved. The object corresponding to Year attribute has no modifier, thus this sub-goal succeeds without generating any abducible. The other two *value* function calls will non-trivially involve the above algorithm. For elucidation purpose, let's focus on the resolution for value function call on *profit* object. Modifier *kind* for describing whether taxes are included is directly found; other modifiers including *currency* and *scale factor* are found through inheritance from *monetary value* type. Let's focus on the conversion for currency differences. In the conversion function for currency, a *value* function call (3rd line in formula 2) is made to find the currency in the source, which will find the first rule for history specification that essentially says before year 2000 the currency is 'FRF' (3rd line in formula 1). Further resolution will post $tle(y_0, 2000)$ into the constraint sotre. This constraint, along with the constraint $tle(2000, y_0)$ that was posted earlier, will trigger the following CHR rule:

```
antisymmetry @ X tle Y, Y tle X <=> X=Y.
```

which is a simplification rule that replace the two *tle* temporal constraints with a single equality constraint. There are other CHR rules for handling cases such as transitivity, overlapping, and inconsistency. When this resolution finishes successfully, the constraint store contains all the abudcibles that can be translated into the first sub-query in MQ1. With backtracking, all the other answers are found.

Although finding the values of all modifiers with non-conflicting temporal constraints is a combinatorial search, many of the search branches are very shallow, e.g., given the constraint introduced in user query, the search branch that tries scale factor before 1999 fails immediately after this temporal constraint is posted into the store.

4   Discussion

With the extension of temporal context handling, the COIN framework is now capable of solving a much wider range of semantic heterogeneity problems. Any changes in representational and ontological semantics can be represented and reasoned about within the extended COIN framework. For example, [5] describes a spatio-temporal scenario where historic statistics of the economy (e.g., GDP) and the environment (e.g., CO_2 emissions) of each sovereign country is stored in several sources. Let us consider a user who performs longitudinal studies in the Balkans and is used to using 'YUG' to refer to the geographic area bounded by the former Yugoslavia. Because the area has gone through a series of balkanizations, notably in 1991 the region broke up into five sovereign states, the user's query that worked before the broken-up would stop working correctly afterwards. With COIN, however, the query continues to work correctly once the temporal context is appropriately encoded. We have successfully tested this scenario with our prototype. The MQ, which will not be shown here, is about a page long because it needs to combine data from appropriate individual countries, convert currency differences for each, and reconcile other context differences (e.g., scale factors, etc.).

This Balkans example is interesting because it demonstrates that the extended COIN framework can process different aggregation rules that are applicable at different time periods. There are many accounting rules of this nature. Just like in our solution approach we draw analogy between temporal context and non-temporal data level context, there are also analogous non-temporal aggregation rules. For example, instead of depending on time periods, it depends on purposes (SEC filing, risk assessment, taxation, etc) that the rules differ for whether the total revenue of a corporation should include those of foreign branches, subsidiaries, subsidiaries of branches and subsidiaries, and other companies majority-owned by the corporation. As is demonstrated in the Corporate Householding research [16], COIN framework can be applied to this scenario as well to represent and reasoning about those complex rules.

The analogy between temporal context and data level context is important. It allows us to use computationally more mature technologies such as constraint solving to reconcile temporal context differences. This was not obvious when we first approached the problem of changing semantics because the nature of the problem naturally suggests the use of temporal logics.

The COIN framework is applicable to the Semantic Web for several reasons. Although we used relational sources in the example, COIN is not restricted to the relational data model because the framework is in fact based on an object oriented logic model, which is expressive enough to encompass non-relational data sources. The ACLP based implementation of the mediator generates the MQ from a set of abducibles, which include predicates admissible by most query languages, be it relational, keyword based, or ontology based. More importantly, the COIN framework relies on the description of data semantics, not on the description of the semantic differences; the latter are automatically detected and reconciled when a query is issued. This is very well in line with the Semantic Web, where each source furnishes a description of its semantics for agents from other contexts to process. And lastly, a recent extension to the basic COIN system added an ontology merging capability to allow large applications to be built by merging separate ontologies [7]. This is very similar to how agents work with distributed ontologies on the Semantic Web.

In this paper we assumed that time is uniformly represented in all sources and receivers. In reality, temporal entities can be heterogeneous across systems. For future research, we would like to extend the notion of temporal context to deal with semantic heterogeneities among temporal entities. This may be achieved by introducing the full Time ontology into knowledge representation. The conversions for reconciling these sorts of heterogeneity can be implemented as external function calls to web services that specifically handle time zones, calendars, and granularities [2, 3].

Acknowledgements

The work reported herein was supported, in part, by the Singapore-MIT Alliance (SMA) and the Malaysia University of Science and Technology (MUST)-MIT collaboration.

References

1. S. Abiteboul, G. Lausen, H. Uphoff, E. Waller, "Methods and Rules", SIGMOD Rec., 22(2), pp. 32-41, 1993.
2. C. Bettini, "Web services for time granularity reasoning," TIME-ICTL'03, 2003.
3. C. Bettini, S. Jajodia, and X. S. Wang, Time Granularities in Databases, Data Mining, and Temporal Reasoning: Springer, 2000.
4. S. Bressan, C.H. Goh, T. Lee, S. Madnick, M. Siegel, "A Procedure for Mediation of Queries to Sources in Disparate Context", ILPS'97, 1997.
5. N. Choucri, S. Madnick, A., Moulton, M. Siegel, H. Zhu, "Information Integration for Counter Terrorism Activities: The Requirement for Context Mediation1", IEEE Aerospace Conference, 2004.
6. K. Eshgi, Kowalski, R. "Abduction Compared with Negation as Failure", Proceedings of 6th Intl Conf. on Logic Programming, 1989.
7. Firat, "Information Integration using Contextual Knowledge and Ontology Merging," PhD Thesis, MIT, 2003.
8. A. Firat and S. Madnick and B. Grosof, "Financial information integration in the presence of equational ontological conflicts", WITS, 2002.
9. T. Frühwirth, "Theory and Practice of Constraint Handling Rules," Journal of Logic Programming, 37, pp. 95-138, 1998.
10. C.Goh, "Representing and Reasoning about Semantic Conflicts in Heterogeneous Information Systems", PhD Thesis, MIT, 1997
11. C. Goh, S. Bressan, S. Madnick, and M. Siegel, "Context Interchange: New Features and Formalisms for the Intelligent Integration of Information," ACM TOIS, vol. 17, pp. 270-293, 1999.
12. J. R. Hobbs, "A DAML Ontology of Time," LREC, 2002.
13. A.C. Kakas, R.A. Kowalski, F. Toni, "Abductive Logic Programming", Journal of Logic Programming, 2(6), pp. 719-770, 1993.
14. A.C. Kakas, A. Michael, and C. Mourlas, "ACLP: Integrating Abduction and Constraint Solving," Journal of Logic Programming, 44, pp. 129-177, 2000.
15. M. Kiffer, G. Laussen, J. Wu, "Logic Foundations of Object-Oriented and Frame-based Languages", J. ACM, 42(4), pp. 741-843, 1995.
16. S. Madnick, R. Wang, X. Xian, "The Design and Implementation of a Corporate Householding Knowledge Processor to Improve Data Quality", JMIS, 20(3), pp. 41-69, 2004.
17. J. McCarthy, "Generality in Artificial Intelligence", CACM, 30(12), pp. 1030-1035, 1987.

Towards a Multi-calendar Temporal Type System for (Semantic) Web Query Languages

François Bry and Stephanie Spranger

University of Munich, Munich 80538, Germany
{bry,spranger}@pms.ifi.lmu.de
http://www.pms.ifi.lmu.de

Abstract. Time is omnipresent on the (Semantic) Web. However, formalism like XML, XML Schema, RDF, OWL and (Semantic) Web query languages have, if any, only very limited notions of temporal data types and temporal theories built-in. Recently, the development of Web Services for temporal operations has begun. In this article, we describe a connection, possibly the first one, between such Web Services and Web formalisms: A proposal of a *type system* for temporal and calendric data, called *multi-calendar temporal type system* seamlessly integrated into a host (query) language. The type system's associated type checking methods are beyond the scope of this article. For proof-of-concept purposes, the Web and Semantic Web query language Xcerpt has been chosen.

1   Introduction

Time is omnipresent on the Web or Semantic Web (for short (Semantic) Web). Many Web sites and pages implicitly or explicitly refer to temporal and calendric data. Many advanced (Semantic) Web applications like web-based information and appointment scheduling systems and so-called adaptive Web systems refer to temporal and calendric data, as well. Most existing or foreseen mobile computing applications refer not only to locations but also to time. For example, a mobile application listing pharmacies in the surrounding of a user will preferably only mention those that are currently open, i.e. it refers to rather sophisticated temporal and calendric data. The temporal and calendric data involved are most often rather complex, sometimes involving different calendars (e.g. cultural calendars like the Gregorian and the Islamic and business calendars) with various regulations and lots of irregularities (e.g. leap years), and "trimmed to fit" individual use. For example, one might think of the Web sites of a university announcing lectures, courses, examinations, consultation hours of professors, etc. within a teaching term, or a personal appointment book containing entries like business conferences or personal work out times during the summer period. How to represent, query, and process such kind of time and cal-

---

Acknowledgement: This research has been funded by the European Commission and by the Swiss Federal Office for Education and Science within the 6th Framework Program project REWERSE number 506779 (cf. http://rewerse.net).

H.J. Ohlbach and S. Schaffert (Eds.): PPSWR 2004, LNCS 3208, pp. 102–117, 2004.

endar data on the (Semantic) Web, i.e. using Web formalisms like XML, XML Schema, RDF, OWL, and (Semantic) Web query languages?

On the one hand, those formalisms developed for the (Semantic) Web have, if any, only very limited notions of temporal datatypes and temporal theories built-in. The W3C standard XML Schema, for example, supports some temporal data types which are restricted to the Gregorian calendar without multi-calendar reasoning, e.g. no "calendar cast primitives". Furthermore, only some operations over temporal data types for temporal computation and/or reasoning in XQuery implementing XMLSchema are supported. On the other hand, several time and calendar theories have been investigated and developed for a long time from different perspectives: (1) In Artificial Intelligence, temporal logics and calculi and temporal constraint reasoning independent of calendars have been investigated, e.g. [1, 2, 3, 4, 5]. (2) In temporal databases, algebraic representations for time and calendars have been theoretically investigated, e.g. [6, 7, 8]. It is however not clear, neither how these general methods can be applied to both real time dealing with irregularities (e.g. leap seconds[1] and castings between different calendars) and temporal types, nor how static type checking and type inferencing as needed when types are integrated in programming or query languages can be performed. (3) Several algorithms for calendrical calculations [9] are developed and implemented allowing for various calendar-based calculations. Recently, the development of some Web Services for temporal operations have begun [10, 11].

In this article, we describe a (possibly first) connection between such Web Services and Web formalisms: A proposal of a *type system* for temporal and calendric data, called *multi-calendar temporal type system*, seamlessly integrated into the Web and Semantic Web query language Xcerpt [12]. This article is devoted to the language of the type system. Its associated type checking methods are beyond the scope of this article. Static type checking is as useful and desirable with temporal and calendric data types as it is with whatever other data type. It makes error detection at compile time possible, and it improves code generation, as well. Specific aspects of calendar systems make static type checking for such data an interesting challenge. The temporal type system is *open* inasmuch that the type system is neither restricted to a particular calendar nor to specific temporal or calendric data. Instead, a programmer can specify any professional, cultural, religious, etc. time concept his/her application might need. The type system provides a small, but powerful, declarative set of *type constructors, selectors,* and, as they are sometimes called, *mutators*. Note that, for example the temporal data types defined in XML Schema are specified without such type operators.

This article is organized as follows. Section 1 is this introduction. Section 2 sketches the major concepts of the time model used for the multi-calendar temporal type system. Section 3 introduces the multi-calendar temporal type system: the type constructors and selectors and its module structure, and this section exemplifies the type system's expressiveness. Section 4 gives perspectives for proof-of-concept of the multi-calendar temporal type system. Finally, Section 5 concludes this article.

---

[1] International System of Units(SI), http://www.bipm.org/en/si/

2   Time Model

The time model used for the multi-calendar temporal type system combines interval-based temporal logics, in particular Allen's interval calculus [2] with the concept of 'hierarchical time lines' to represent time and so-called calendar units like 'hour' or 'day' (often realized as time granularities, e.g. in [6,7,8]). In the present time model, however, hierarchical time lines are realized as *time partitions* of a *time domain* and *selections* of time partitions. Additional concepts are *durations* and *time intervals* over those time partitions (resp. selections), improving and simplifying the layered time model presented in [13].

The time domain is the set of time points used to interpret time and calendar concepts. A time point is a non-divisible moment of time which is much smaller than the smallest extend of time which can be modeled in the type system.

Definition 1 (Time Domain). *The* time domain *is a pair $(\mathcal{T},<_{\mathcal{T}})$ where $\mathcal{T}$ is an infinite set and $<_{\mathcal{T}}$ is a total order on $\mathcal{T}$ such that $\mathcal{T}$ is not bounded for $<_{\mathcal{T}}$. If $(\mathcal{T},<_{\mathcal{T}})$ is a time domain, then an element $t \in \mathcal{T}$ is called* time point.

To introduce hierarchical time lines, the time domain can be partitioned into countable finite many, finite or infinite parts in the time domain $(\mathcal{T},<_{\mathcal{T}})$.

Definition 2 (Time Partition of $(\mathcal{T},<_{\mathcal{T}})$ and Parts). *Let $(\mathcal{T},<_{\mathcal{T}})$ be a time domain. Then $\mathcal{P} \subset \mathcal{P}(\mathcal{T})$ (i.e. a subset of the powerset of $\mathcal{T}$) is a* time partition *of $(\mathcal{T},<_{\mathcal{T}})$, if*

1. *all sets of $\mathcal{P}$ are non-empty,*
2. *if for all $t_i \in p$ and for all $t_j \in q$ with $t_i, t_j \in \mathcal{T}$, p and q sets in $\mathcal{P}$ $t_i <_{\mathcal{T}} t_j$, then $p < q$,*
3. *any two distinct sets of $\mathcal{P}$ are disjoint, and*
4. *every time point of $\mathcal{T}$ belongs exactly to one of the sets of $\mathcal{P}$, i.e. $\mathcal{T}$ is the union of the sets of $\mathcal{P}$.*

A set p of a time partition $\mathcal{P}$ is called part.

With Definition 2, the calendar units `hour`, `day`, `week`, and `month` of the Gregorian calendar are time partitions, and `2004-05-05` (using the notation of the ISO 8601 standard for dates and time[2]) is a part of `day`. Note that in a concrete implementation, a part of a time partition may be represented by an interval in the time domain.

Infinite sets of gapped subsets of a time partition are called *selections*. The set of all Saturdays is a selection of the time partition `day`, for example.

Time Partitions are related in the sense that the parts of one time partition may be further aggregated by a specific set of parts of another time partition to form one part in an *including* time partition.

---

[2] http://www.iso.ch/iso/en/prods-services/popstds/datesandtime.html

Definition 3 (Include Relation). *Let $\mathcal{P}$ and $\mathcal{Q}$ be two time partitions. $\mathcal{P}$ includes $\mathcal{Q}$ ($\mathcal{P} \trianglerighteq \mathcal{Q}$) if for each part $p \in \mathcal{P}$ there exists a set S of parts in $\mathcal{Q}$ such that $p = S$. Then $\mathcal{Q}$ is* included in $\mathcal{P}$ *($\mathcal{Q} \trianglelefteq \mathcal{P}$).*

With Definition 3, day $\trianglelefteq$ day, day $\trianglelefteq$ week, day $\trianglelefteq$ month, but not week $\trianglelefteq$ month (if the Gregorian calendar is used). The *include* relation introduces a partial order over time partitions.

The *include* relation permits to specify and relate time partitions in terms of included time partitions as further "aggregations" of the time domain to larger parts. The larger parts are specified by durations of parts of the included time partition which need to be anchored in the included time partition.

In the multi-calendar temporal type system, the include relation is realized as a typing relation, called *include typing relation* between types.

To measure the amount of time in a time partition (resp. a selection), for example 4 weeks (in the time partition week), durations are defined.

Definition 4 (Duration). *Let $\mathcal{P}$ be a time partition or a selection of a time partition. Then a* duration d *in $\mathcal{P}$ is a signed integral number of parts of $\mathcal{P}$, i.e. an amount of time with known length but no specific starting or ending point.*

A time interval is a not necessarily connected, possibly infinite, anchored number of parts of a time partition (resp. selection) with the constraints that the parts in a time interval are totally ordered and disjoint.

Definition 5 (Time Interval). *Let $\mathcal{P}$ be a time partition or a selection of a time partition. Then a* time interval I *is a finite or infinite collection of pairwise disjoint, totally ordered intervals $[p, q]$, $p, q \in \mathcal{P}$ where $p \leq q$.*

With Definition 5, [2003-03,2003-08] (using the notation of the ISO 8601 standard for dates and time[3]) is a time interval of time partition month.

3   The Multi-calendar Temporal Type System

This section introduces and exemplifies the syntactic forms of the type system, i.e. its type constructors and selectors which are similar to base types and structured types in programming languages like integers, strings, and lists with appropriate operations over these types and the type system's module structure.

3.1   Base Types

In general, a base type is a set of simple, unstructured values such as numbers or booleans with appropriate primitive operations for manipulating these values, pre-defined in the type system. Base types are also called atomic types, because they have no internal structure as far as the type system is concerned. A *base type* in the temporal type system is a base type in this sense, and in the sense, that

---

[3] http://www.iso.ch/iso/en/prods-services/popstds/datesandtime.html

it is the reference type for any further type declared (w.r.t. include Definition 3), using type constructors of the type system.

The type system supports a single base type called *reference time partition type*. A reference time partition type is a set of *parts* of some chosen reference time partition whose parts are indexed by integers – plus appropriate primitive operations to manipulate these values. A *reference time partition* is a time partition of the time domain according to Definition 2 with a *fixed part* in the time domain indexed by 1. A reference time partition with a fixed part is required for a computer implementation of the multi-calendar temporal type system to reckon time: Fix an arbitrary starting point as 1 in the time domain, and specify any other part of this time partition by giving a number relative to that fixed point. The duration of any part of the reference time partition is 1.

The reference time partition type with a fixed part in the time domain provides a semantics for any further type declared (see below Section 3.2 for details). In particular, conversions to and from this reference type to other types become possible which can be expressed by mappings to and from some chosen reference time partition, of course with a fixed part anchored in the time domain. This enables processing of dates and times from arbitrary types and/or calendars and type casting. Note that the reference time partition must be chosen such that any further time partition may be declared directly or indirectly in terms of the reference time partition.

In the type system, the reference time partition type `Ref` has the constant 1 (intended to represent the fixed part of the reference time partition) and the operations `next` (successor part) and `previous` (predecessor part) to enumerate the parts of the reference time partition, and the duration of any part of type `Ref` is 1 `Ref`.

For example, we may chose the time partition `second` as the reference time partition type `Ref` with midnight at the onset of Thursday, January 1 of year 1970 (Gregorian) as fixed point second 1 (according to Unix time). It is thus the first second of the first minute and the first hour; this assumption is correct[4] and valid for any civil calendar in use today. The duration of a second in type `second` is 1 `second`.

In the concrete syntax of the type system, i.e. the syntax used by some programmer, the reference time partition type is referenced by its name, e.g. `second`. A part (i.e. a *value* of the reference time partition type) is specified by its integer index (e.g. `second(2)`). In addition to the (integer) index (relative to the fixed point) for each part of this reference time partition, textual values to represent dates and times for input and output of the type's values are supported, as well. We suggest to choose the ISO Standard 8601 for Dates and Time[5] as textual representation format in the type system; then `second(1)` might equally be used with '1970-01-01T00:00:00', for example.

---

[4] International System of Units (SI), http://www.bipm.org/en/si/
[5] http://www.iso.ch/iso/en/prods-services/popstds/datesandtime.html

3.2   Structured Types

This section introduces the different ways of building structured types in the multi-calendar temporal type system, using type constructors and selectors.

Time Partitions. Many programs need to deal with time partitions whose parts are aggregations of sets of parts of the reference time partition. These time partitions can be (directly or indirectly) constructed from the reference time partition. The type mechanism that supports this kind of programming with arbitrary time partitions is *time partition type*. The elements of a time partition type are called *parts*.

A time partition is a data structure that specifies a partition of the time domain into finite or infinite parts (cf. Definition 2), possibly of different durations, by an aggregation of sets of parts of the reference time partition or another, already declared, time partition as follows: A time partition type specifies the first part, the durations, and an ordered finite periodic pattern of parts of different durations, possibly with finite many exceptions such that all parts of a time partition are clearly located by possibly infinite (convex) intervals in the time domain. The type constructor for time partition types is `timepartition`. For every time partition T, the type

```
timepartition d₁[named n₁]>> ... >> dₘ[named nₘ] where anchor=a
```

describes a time partition T whose parts are constructed from an already declared time partition S such that time partition T *includes* time partition S, and S is *included in* T (cf. Definition 3). With the type constructor `timepartition`, $d_i, i \in \{1, ..., m\}$ are durations in an already declared time partition S, and a, the anchor, is the first part of a set of parts of S determining the first part of the time partition T. The order of the durations of the parts of time partition T is syntactically committed by $>>$, connecting the anchored durations in the given periodic order, called *periodic pattern* which may be nested. Exceptions in the durations of the parts of some time partition (e.g. leap seconds in the specification of the time partition `minute`) are captured by a common `case` expression (which may be nested). Subsets of a time partition T may be named by [named n_i], $i \in \{1...m\}$. Each named subset of T builds a subtype of T usable as any other type declared. An additional syntactic form of the type constructor `timepartition` is provided, where the parts in the periodic pattern of the time partition declared can be numbered:

```
timepartition 1:d₁[named n₁] ... m:dₘ[named nₘ] where anchor=a
```

The fundamental property of time partitions is that T(i), the ith part of time partition T can be computed according to the specifications in the type declaration for T quickly for any value $i \in \mathbb{Z}$ at run time. i is called the *(integer) index* of the ith part of the time partition T relative to its first part (i.e. its anchor) located in the time domain. Of course, as it is the case for the reference time partition type, each part of a time partition type has an additional textual value representation of dates and times for input and output of type values.

Let's consider a small example. We declare the time partition `teaching_term` (according to teaching terms at Bavarian universities where winter terms always begin in October) by an aggregation of the time partition `month` (of the Gregorian calendar), assuming that `month` is already declared, as follows:

```
type teaching_term = timepartition
                     1: 6 month named winterterm
                     2: 6 month named summerterm
              anchored_at month(10);
```

With this type declaration, a part of type `teaching_term` has a duration of 1 `teaching_term`, and the teaching_term indexed by 1 is defined by including 6 months starting with the month indexed by 10. The ith part of the time partition `teaching_term` is `teaching_term(i)`. `winterterm` is a subtype of `teaching_term` that can be used in the same way as the type `teaching_term`.

Selectors. So far, we have studied the type constructor for time partitions totally covering the time domain $(\mathcal{T},<_{\mathcal{T}})$ in terms of Definition 2. But people frequently use particular selected, gapped subsets of a partition like `Saturday` of the partition `day` or `the 8'o clock news` of the partition `hour`: `Saturday` is the infinite set of every 6th part out of a period of 7 parts of `day` and `the 8'o clock news` is an infinite set of every 8th part out of any period of 24 parts of `hour`.

Selectors construct subtypes of a type by selecting specific sets of its supertype. We accomplish this by formalizing the intuition that any type S constructed by a selector is more informative than the type T, S is constructed from. We say S is a *subtype* of T, written S $<:$ T[6], to mean that any part of S can safely be used in a context where a part of T is expected. For types T_1, T_2, ..., and $i \in \mathbb{Z}$, the following selectors are supported. The selectors are subsequently explained by examples (using time and calendar concepts of the Gregorian calendar).

Selector	Syntactic From	Conditions
select	`select` T_1`(i) where` $<$ condition $>$	
select_during	`select_during(i,`T_1`,`T_2`)`	$T_1 \trianglelefteq T_2$
select_overlaps	`select_overlaps(i,`T_1`,`T_2`)`	neither $T_1 \trianglelefteq T_2$ nor $T_1 \trianglerighteq T_2$
includes	T_1 `includes` T_2	$T_1 \trianglerighteq T_2$
included_in	T_1 `included_in` T_2	$T_1 \trianglelefteq T_2$
union	T_1 `union` T_2	$T_1,T_2 <: T_3$
intersects	T_1 `intersects` T_2	$T_1,T_2 <: T_3$
minus	T_1 `minus` T_2	$T_1,T_2 <: T_3$
join	T_1 `join` T_2	$T_1,T_2 <: T_3$
shift	`shift(`T_1`,d)`	d :: duration of T_1

With the selector `select`, specific sets of a type can be selected using constraints over the type's parts expressed by *conditions* the parts must satisfy, usable after the keyword `where`. For example, the subtype `winterterm` of the type `teaching_term`, i.e. always the first out of two teaching terms, can be declared as follows:

---

[6] Denoting *predicate subtyping* constraining the parts of T satisfying a *selector*.

```
(1) type winterterm = select teaching_term(i) where i mod 2==1;
```

This selector comes with an additional syntactic form which provides a rather textual representation to formulate simple conditions, e.g.

```
(2) type winterterm = select teaching_term
        anchored_at teaching_term(1) in_period 2 teaching_term;
```

Note that the syntactic form (2) is merely syntactic sugar for the form (1).

The selectors select_during and select_overlaps enable to select subsets of parts of a time partition T_1 by locating specific parts in another time partition T_2 where the parts of the time partition T_1 are either *during, start,* or *finish* [2] those of T_2 (i.e. T_1 is included in T_2) or might *overlap* [2] those of T_2 (i.e. T_1 is not included in T_2). For example,

```
type  christmas_day  =  select_during(25,day,december);
type  1stweek_winterterm  =  select_overlaps(1,week,winterterm);
```

With these type declarations christmas_day is a subtype of day, locating always the 25th part of type day in each part of type december, and 1stweek_winterterm is a subtype of week, locating always the first part of week that possibly overlaps with the respective part of type winterterm. The select_overlaps selector is used, because the type week is not included in the type winterterm.

The selectors includes and included_in select included (resp. including) parts of type T_1 in type T_2. For example,

```
type  christmas_week  =  week  includes  christmas_day;
```

specifies the set of all those weeks which include a Christmas Day.

The shift selector shifts each part of type T by a duration of type Duration of T. For example, the *4th* Advent can be specified as the Sunday in the week before the week including Christmas Day.

```
type Advent4=shift(sunday included_in christmas_week),-7 day);
```

The three selectors union, minus, and intersects are the usual set-theoretic operations over types. They can be, for example, used to declare the following calendar types:

```
type  weekend_days  :=  sunday  union  saturday;
type  weekday  =  day  minus  weekend;
type  sunday&lastday_month  =  sunday  intersects  lastday_month;
```

The set of all weekend days is the union of all Saturdays and Sundays, any weekday is the difference of days and weekend days, and those Sundays which are also the last day of some month are straightforwardly declared by union, minus, and intersects, respectively.

To declare a type weekend instead of weekend_days, for example, whose parts have the length of two consecutive days, the selector join over types T_1 and T_2 both having the same supertype can be used, concatenating the parts of both types.

Durations. Many programs dealing with time make use of means to measure time or specifying extends of temporal events in terms of *durations*. A duration is a signed integral number of parts in any type with known length but no specific starting or ending parts.

The type constructor `duration of T` describes for any type T a duration drawn from the type T. A duration value of type `duration of T` formed by a signed number and a type T is written q T where $q \in \mathbb{Q}$. For example `YearsOfStudy` has a duration of 9 teaching_terms (at a Bavarian university).

```
YearsOfStudy::duration of teaching_term = 9 teaching_term;
```

Note that type annotation is not required for duration types in the type system, because type inferencing is supported. For example, the duration of the variable `YearsOfStudy` may be declared without previous type annotation.

Time Intervals. For many programs dealing with time it is useful to have a mechanism to specify somehow related parts in some time partition building particular *time intervals*. The type mechanism that supports this kind of programming with time intervals is *time interval type*. A time interval is a finite or infinite sequence of possibly non-connected parts of some time partition where the parts are ordered and pairwise disjoint. For example, my holidays in 2003 between 8 to 14 April and 29 July to 6 August is a time interval in time partition `day`.

The type constructor for time intervals is `timeinterval`. For every type T, the type `timeinterval of T` describes finite or infinite ordered sequences of possibly non-connected parts whose elements are drawn from T.

Time intervals can be constructed by the following syntactic forms, i.e. by the following value constructors.

– The *empty* time interval (with elements of type T) is written `[]::T`.
– A time interval constructed by its *ending points* t_1 and t_2 (both of type T), including all parts between t_1 and t_2 of T, is written `[`t_1`..`t_2`]::T`.
– A time interval constructed by a *duration* q T (of type `duration of T`) and an *anchor* t (of type T) is written `q T from t::T`, meaning that q consecutive parts of T are included in the time interval where t is the first of those parts.
– A possibly infinite time interval constructed by a *selector* s (cf. Section 3.2) (of type T), possibly an *anchor* t_1 and possibly an *endpoint* t_2 (both of type T) is written `s [from `t_1`] [to `t_2`]::T`, meaning that those parts of T satisfying s between a possible anchor t_1 and a possible endpoint t_2 are included in the constructed time interval.

Time intervals constructed in one of the previously introduced forms can be related by a *comma* operator, interpreted as a concatenation of time intervals.

Let's turn attention to the following example. We assume that the types `day`, `month`, and `sunday` (all of the Gregorian calendar) are already declared.

```
Holidays03 = [2003-04-08..2003-04-14],[2003-07-29..2003-08-06];
KickoffMeeting = 4 day from 2004-03-01;
ClubMeeting = select_during(2,sunday,month) from 2004-02-15;
```

The variable `MyHolidays03` is of type time interval of days as previously illustrated. `KickoffMeeting` is a time interval of four consecutive days starting with day 2004-03-01 (and ending with day 2004-03-04). And `ClubMeeting` is a time interval including always the second Sunday of each month starting with day 2004-02-15. As illustrated, type annotation is also not required for variables and constants of type `timeinterval`, because type inferencing is supported.

3.3   Modules

Types in the multi-calendar temporal type system are declared within a *module*. A module defines a scope for a finite set of type declarations belonging together. A module has the following syntactic form:

```
CALENDAR [qualified] MY_CALENDAR
  (* finite set of type declarations *)
END
```

The attribute `qualified` is optional. If used, the declarations made in this module are restricted to the scope of this module. If the module is imported, i.e.

```
CALENDAR ANOTHER_CALENDAR
  import MY_CALENDAR;
  (* finite set of type declarations *)
END
```

then declaration `d` made within the module `MY_CALENDAR` and used in the module `ANOTHER_CALENDAR` is accessed by `MY_CALENDAR.d`. Thus, the name `d` might also be used for a declaration within the module `ANOTHER_CALENDAR`. For example, if the Gregorian calendar is declared in a qualified module `GREGORIAN` containing a type `christmas_day` and the Julian calendar is declared in another qualified module `JULIAN` containing also the type `christmas_day`, then Julian and Gregorian Christmas can be used together within some program using the dot notation: `GREGORIAN.christmas_day`[7] and `JULIAN.christmas_day`[8], respectively. That means, qualified calendar modules provide a means for dealing with context-dependent temporal and calendric data.

3.4   Examples

Let us consider a detailed example on programming with the multi-calendar temporal type system. Example 1 is an exemplary declaration of the Gregorian calendar, and Example 2 is an exemplary declaration of the arithmetic Islamic calendar in which months follow a pattern set. In this example, the declarations

---

[7] 25 December.
[8] 7 January.

of the Islamic calendar are based on those of the Gregorian calendar (i.e. the calendar declarations are directly related), to enable straightforward comparison and casting of Islamic and Gregorian calendar concepts in some program. This can be realized by declaring one time partition of the Islamic calendar in terms of a time partition of the Gregorian calendar, and subsequently relating any further type declaration to this time partition and the system's fixed part in time. Note that the type system also supports the possibility to declare the Islamic calendar independent of the Gregorian calendar, both only with relation to the reference time partition type, for example.

For the following examples, we assume that the time partition second is the pre-defined *reference time partition type* with midnight at the onset of Thursday, January 1 of year 1970 (Gregorian), according to Unix time, as fixed part second 1. Furthermore, we assume that the following relations and a function are pre-defined such that they are usable in the subsequent examples: (1) leapYear is a pre-defined relation that returns true if a given Gregorian month falls into a Gregorian leap year, otherwise it returns false; (2) islamicLeapYear is a pre-defined relation that returns true if a given Islamic month falls into an Islamic leap year, otherwise it returns false; and (3) sunset(Locale) is a pre-defined function that returns the time in local mean time for a given Locale.

Example 1. (**Gregorian Calendar**)

```
CALENDAR GREGORIAN
  type minute = timepartition 60 second anchored_at second(1);
  type hour = timepartition 60 minute anchored_at minute(1);
  type day = timepartition 24 hour anchored_at hour(1);
  type week = timepartition 7 day anchored_at day(-2); (* begin on Mondays *)
  type month = timepartition
                    1:  31 day named january
                    2:  case
                              leapYear  = 29 day named february
                            | otherwise = 28 day named february
                        end
                    3:  31 day named march
                    4:  30 day named april
                    5:  31 day named may
                    6:  30 day named june
                    7:  31 day named july
                    8:  31 day named august
                    9:  30 day named september
                   10:  31 day named october
                   11:  30 day named november
                   12:  31 day named december
                anchored_at day(1);
  type year = timepartition 12 month anchored_at month(1);
  with select day(i) where i mod 7 == j
    type monday    = j == 5
    type tuesday   = j == 6
    type wednesday = j == 0
    type thursday  = j == 1
    type friday    = j == 2
    type saturday  = j == 3
    type sunday    = j == 4
  end
END
```

The Gregorian calendar is declared straightforward using some of the previously introduced type constructors defining specific sets with the intended meaning. Exceptions are captured using case expressions which are usable within any type declaration, e.g. the declaration of type month to capture the irregularity of Gregorian months due to Gregorian leap year rules. In Example 1 it is demonstrated how type declarations can be group using the with ...end construct, declaring weekdays, for example.

In real life minutes contain leap seconds from time to time. This phenomenon can also be expressed in the type system:

```
type minute = timepartition case
                            minute(1051200)      = 70 second
                          | containsLeapSeconds = 61 second
                          | otherwise           = 60 second
                          end
                anchored_at second(1);
```

assuming that containsLeapSeconds is a pre-defined relation that returns true if a given minute contains leap seconds, otherwise it returns false.

Note that type declarations for the most important Christian and Orthodox holidays are straightforward when using the temporal type system, extending the program given in Example 1 only by a few lines.

Now let us consider declarations for the Islamic calendar.

Example 2. **(Islamic Calendar)**

```
CALENDAR ISLAMIC
import GREGORIAN;
 type i_day =shift(day,distance(sunset(Locale),midnight));
 type i_week =timepartition 7 i_day anchored_at i_day(-1); (*begin on Sundays*)
 type i_month =timepartition
                1:  30 i_day named muharram
                2:  29 i_day named safar
                3:  30 i_day named rabiI
                4:  29 i_day named rabiII
                5:  30 i_day named jumadaI
                6:  29 i_day named jumadaII
                7:  30 i_day named rajab
                8:  29 i_day named sha'ban
                9:  30 i_day named ramadan
                10: 29 i_day named shawwal
                11: 30 i_day named dhu al-qa'da
                12: case
                        islamicLeapYear = 30 i_day named dhu_al_hijja
                      | otherwise       = 29 i_day named dhu_al_hijja
                    end
                anchored_at i_day(-286);
 type i_year = timepartition 12 month anchored_at i_month(1);
 with select day(i) where i mod 7 == j
   type yaum_al-ahad     = j == 4      (* Sunday    *)
   type yaum_al-ithnayna = j == 5      (* Monday    *)
   type yaum_al-thalatha = j == 6      (* Tuesday   *)
   type yaum_al-arba'a   = j == 0      (* Wednesday *)
   type yaum_al-hamis    = j == 1      (* Thursday  *)
   type yaum_al-jum'a    = j == 2      (* Friday    *)
   type yaum_al-as-sabt  = j == 3      (* Saturday  *)
 end
END
```

In Example 2 we define an explicit relation between the Gregorian and the Islamic calendar. In the Islamic calendar, the chosen fixed part, i.e. midnight at the onset of Thursday, January 1 of year 1970 (Gregorian) corresponds to 22 October 1398 (Islamic). Note that an Islamic day begins at sunset of the previous Gregorian day and ends at sunset of the next Gregorian day. The sunset depends on a specific location. However, Islamic days are also defined by a period of 24 hours. The aspect of sunset is only of interest if we talk of evening or for determining the beginning of Islamic holidays. An Islamic type i_day may thus simply be declared by a shift according to sunset of the Gregorian calendar type day as illustrated in Example 2. The other time partition of this calendar are then straightforward declared in the expected manner.

Note that type declarations also for the most important Islamic holidays are straightforward when using the temporal type system, extending the program given in Example 2 only by a few lines.

4   Perspective: Integration into the Web Query Language Xcerpt

With the multi-calendar temporal type system, we develop a type language for time and calendar concepts with which the programmer can declare concepts of his/her needs within a (intern or extern) *module,* seamlessly integrated into a host (query) language. For proof-of-concept purposes, we have chosen the (Semantic) Web query language Xcerpt [12] as host language for the type system. The multi-calendar temporal type system integrated into the (Semantic) Web query language Xcerpt is intended to support temporal *adaptive Web systems*[9], formulating queries independent of a particular web-based application and/or a particular temporal or calendric context.

For explicitly ascribing a particular type to an Xcerpt term, we write "t::T" for "the term t which we ascribe the type T". A value or object v of some type defined in a module can be used as an Xcerpt term appearing in an Xcerpt program simply by using its name v.

Let us consider an oversimpled database (Example 3) of a travel agency containing air journey offers during the summer period as it is defined for the traveling industry (a type declaration for type summer is illustrated in the calendar JOURNEY used by some travel agency). The offers come with destination, price-per-week, and bookable elements. A person inquiries the travel agency for a one week journey during his summer vacations, which he/she has defined in the module JOURNEY, as well in the time interval MyVacation04 (of type timeinterval of day). The module in Example 3 imports the Gregorian calendar module declared in Example 1 such that its declarations can be used in the module JOURNEY.

---

[9] Adaptation basically means delivering and/or rendering data in a context-aware manner, i.e. combining parts of Web data depending on context specified, e.g. by some user model, parameters of the rendering, or time and location of some user.

Example 3. (**Data Term and Query**)

```
CALENDAR JOURNEYS
    import_calendar GREGORIAN;
    type summer = june join july join august join september;
    Summer2004 = 2004 includes summer;
    MyVacation04 = [2004-07-19..2004-08-22];
END


air_journeys {                            }
  season { Summer2004 }
  journey {                                  CONSTRUCT
    destination { "Santorini" },               destinations { all var Dest }
    price-per-week { "329  " },              FROM
    bookable { [2004-06-01..2004-06-20] or     air_journeys {{
              [2004-07-17..2004-08-04] or        journey {{
              [2004-09-15..2004-09-22] }           var Dest ⤳ destination,
  },                                               bookable { var Booking }
  journey {                                    }}
    destination { "Sicily" },              }} where {
    price-per-week { "461  " },               zip_some_contains(var Booking,
    bookable { [2004-06-24..2004-07-23] or  (MyVacation04 includes week))
              [2004-08-02..2004-08-19] }        }
  }, ...                                    END
```

With Example 3, the tourist looks for a week which is included in his/her summer vacations in year 2004. This is expressed by the function `includes` casting the time interval `MyVacation04` to a time interval of weeks of the same time period. At least one of these weeks must be contained in one of the bookable time intervals. This is expressed with the relation `zip_some_contains`, generalizing Allen's interval relation *contains* [2] such that each of the bookable time intervals are related to each of the weeks according to the contains relation, returning true if at least one week is contained in one of the bookable time intervals.

Note that several functions and relations over values of any type are supported, e.g. Allen's interval relations [2], casting functions, and functions to relate parts and/or time intervals and durations. Relations over types can be used in an Xcerpt condition box (i.e. the `where`-part of an Xcerpt query), and functions over temporal and calendric types supported with the temporal type system can be used within relations and in an Xcerpt CONSTRUCT-part.

5   Conclusion

This article has introduced the type constructors and selectors of a multi-calendar temporal type system seamlessly integrated into a host (query) language. Its associated type checking methods have not been considered in this article.

The type constructors and selectors of the type system, presented in this article, form a small and simple, but powerful set: As illustrated in this article, different calendars like the Gregorian and the Islamic calendar can be defined; the Hebrew calendar, which is slightly more complicated than the addressed ones, may also be defined in the temporal type system. Furthermore, several time and calendar notions used in a university context and in a business context have been defined in the type system. For proof-of-concept purposes, we currently implement the introduced type constructors and selectors and several functions and operations over temporal types in the (Semantic) Web query language Xcerpt.

The type constructors and selector of the temporal type system, presented in this article, are designed to provide a means for modeling typed time and calendar data in (Semantic) Web queries in a declarative way integrated into its host language, to allow for context-aware queries, and to enable static type checking. A type amenable to static type checking, i.e. at compile time before the actual value in some program is computed, must be "value independent". For this reason, a type like `working_week` which depends on concrete values like the US holiday Independence Day being in each year at *4th* July must be derived from a more general time partition type. Note that other time models for calendars are value dependent (e.g. [6,7]). Type checking and type inferencing types in the multi-calendar temporal type system is an interesting challenge due to specific aspects of time concepts and calendar systems. For example, type equivalence since a type like `4thAdvent` might be declared in different ways, however defining the same time, or type casting, because casting type `week` to type `month` information is lost that cannot be recovered. In addition, two interesting typing relations *includes* and *subtype of* between temporal and calendric types exist. Beyond this, several relations and functions supported over temporal and calendric types are *polymorph*.

References

1. McDermott, D. V.: A temporal Logic for Reasoning about Processes and Plans. Cognitive Science **6** (1982) 101–155
2. Allen, J. F.: Maintaining Knowledge about temporal Intervals. Communications of the ACM **26** (1983) 832–843
3. van Benthem, J.: The Logic of Time. Studies in Epistemology, Logic, Methodology, and Philosophy of Science. D. Reidel Publishing Company (1983)
4. Gabbay, D.M., Hodkinson, I., Reynolds, M.: Temporal Logic. Mathematical Foundations and Computational Aspects, Vol. 1. Oxford University Press Inc. New York (1994)
5. Vila, L.: A Survey on temporal Reasoning in Artificial Intelligence. Artificial Intelligence **7** (1994) 4–28
6. Chandra, R., Segev, A., Stonebraker, M.: Implementing Calendars and temporal Rules in next Generation Databases. In: Proc. Int. Conf. on Data Engineering. (1994) 264–273
7. Bettini, C., Jajodia, S., Wang, X. S.: Time Granularities in Databases, Data Mining, and temporal Reasoning. Springer Verlag, Berlin (2000)
8. Ning, P., Wang, X. S., Jajodia, S.: An Algebraic Representation of Calendars. In: the Annuals of Mathematics and Artificial Intelligence (Kluwer), to appear. (2001)
9. Dershowitz, N. Reingold, E. M.: Calendrical Calculations: The Millennium Edition. Cambridge University Press (2001)
10. Ohlbach, H. J.: WebCal, an advanced Calendar Server. In: Technical Report. University of Munich. (2003)

11. Bry, F., Lorenz, B., Ohlbach, H. J., Spranger, S.: On Reasoning on Time and Location on the Web. In: Proc. Workshop on Principles and Practice of Semantic Web Reasoning, LNCS 2901, Springer-Verlag. (2003)
12. Schaffert, S. Bry, F.: Querying the Web Reconsidered: A Practical Introduction to Xcerpt. In: Technical Report, PMS-FB-2004-7. University of Munich. (2004)
13. Bry, F., Spranger, S.: Temporal Constructs for a Web Language. In Proc. 4th Workshop on Interval Temporal Logics and Duration Calculi (ESSLLI). (2003)

Calendrical Calculations with Time Partitionings and Fuzzy Time Intervals[*]

Hans Jürgen Ohlbach

Institut für Informatik, Universität München
Oettingenstr. 67
D-80538 München, Germany

Abstract. This paper presents a piece in a big mosaic which consists of formalisms and software packages for representing and reasoning with everyday temporal notions. The kernel of the mosaic consists of several layers. At the bottom layer there are a number of basic datatypes for elementary temporal notions. These are time points, crisp and fuzzy time intervals and partitionings for representing periodical temporal notions like years, months, semesters etc. Partitionings can be arranged to form 'durations' (e.g. '2 semester and 1 month'). Each formalism in the bottom layer comes with its own functions and relations.

The second layer is presented in this paper. It contains a number of basic functions which use time points, intervals, partitionings and durations simultaneously. The functions are introduced and motivated with temporal expressions in natural language.

The third layer, which is not presented in this paper, uses the functions and relations of the lower layers as building blocks in a specification language for specifying complex temporal notions.

The whole mosaic contains a number of other formalisms, in particular a representation of calendar systems, and various databases with information about temporal notions.

1   Motivation and Introduction

The phenomenon of *time* has many different facets which are investigated by different communities. Physicists investigate the flow of time and its relation to physical objects and events. Temporal logicians develop abstract models of time where only the aspects of time are formalized which are sufficient to model the behaviour of computer programs and similar processes. Linguists develop models of time which can be used as semantics of temporal expressions in natural language. More and more information about facts and events in the real world is stored in computers, and many of them are annotated with temporal information. Therefore it became necessary to develop computer models of the

---

[*] This research has been funded by the European Commission and by the Swiss Federal Office for Education and Science within the 6th Framework Programme project REWERSE number 506779 (cf. http://rewerse.net).

H.J. Ohlbach and S. Schaffert (Eds.): PPSWR 2004, LNCS 3208, pp. 118–133, 2004.
© Springer-Verlag Berlin Heidelberg 2004

use of time on our planet, which are sophisticated enough to allow the kind of computation and reasoning that humans can do. Examples are 'calendrical calculations' [4], i.e. formal encodings of calendar systems for mapping dates between different calendar systems. Other models of time have been developed in the temporal database community [2], mainly for dealing with temporal information in databases. This work is becoming more important now with the emergence of the Semantic Web [1]. Informal, semi-formal and formal temporal notions occur frequently in XML documents, and need be 'understood' by XML query and transformation mechanisms.

The formalisms developed so far approximate the real use of time on our planet to a certain degree, but still ignore important aspects. In the WebCal project [3] we aim at a very detailed modelling of the temporal notions which can occur in semi-structured data. The WebCal system consists of a kernel and several modules around the kernel. The kernel itself consists of several layers. At the bottom layer there are a number of basic datatypes for elementary temporal notions. These are time points, crisp and fuzzy time intervals [8, 9], and partitionings for representing periodical temporal notions like years, months, semesters etc. [10, 11]. The partitionings can be specified algorithmically or algebraically. The algorithmic specifications allows one to encode phenomena like leap seconds, daylight savings time regulations, the Easter date, which depends on the moon cycle etc. Partitionings can be arranged to form 'durations' (e.g. '2 semester and 1 month'). Each formalism in the bottom layer comes with its own functions and relations.

The second layer, the *mixed function layer*, is presented in this paper. It contains a number of basic functions which use time points, intervals, partitionings and durations simultaneously. The functions are introduced and motivated with temporal expressions in natural language.

The third layer, which is not yet worked out in detail, uses the functions and relations of the lower layers as building blocks in a specification language for specifying complex temporal notions. A first version of this language has been presented in [6, 7].

Since the mixed function layer uses the formalisms from the first layer, we briefly introduce this layer and then define the mixed functions.

2   Time Points and Time Intervals

The flow of time underlying most calendar systems corresponds to a time axis which is isomorphic to the real numbers $\mathbb{R}$. Therefore we take as time points just real numbers. Since the most precise clocks developed so far, atomic clocks, measure the time in discrete units, it would be sufficient to resrict the representation of time points to integers, but this is not important for the purposes of this paper. It becomes an issue for concrete implementations.

The next important datatype is that of time intervals. Time intervals can be crisp or fuzzy. With fuzzy intervals one can encode notions lake 'around noon' or 'late night' etc. This is more general and more flexible than crisp intervals. Therefore the WebCal system uses fuzzy intervals as basic interval datatype.

Fuzzy Intervals are usually defined through their membership functions [12, 5]. A membership function maps a base set to a real number between 0 and 1. The base set for fuzzy time intervals is a linear time axis, isomorphic to the real numbers.

Definition 1 (Fuzzy Time Intervals). *A fuzzy membership function is a total function* $f : \mathbb{R} \mapsto [0,1]$ *which does not need to be continuous, but it must be integratable. The fuzzy interval* i_f *that corresponds to a fuzzy membership function* f *is* $i_f \overset{\text{def}}{=} \{(x,y) \subseteq \mathbb{R} \times [0,1] \mid y \leq f(x)\}$. *Given a fuzzy interval* i *we usually write* $i(x)$ *to indicate the corresponding membership function.*

A fuzzy time interval may consist of several subintervals or components. *Let* $Comp(i)$ *the the components of* i. ∎

This definition comprises single or multiple crisp or fuzzy intervals like these:

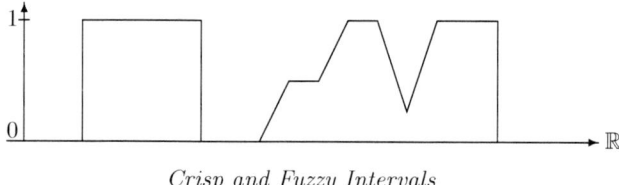

Crisp and Fuzzy Intervals

The fuzzy intervals can also be infinite. For example, the term 'after tonight' may be represented by a fuzzy value which rises from fuzzy value 0 at 6 pm until fuzzy value 1 at 8 pm and then remains 1 ad infinitum.

Fuzzy time intervals may be quite complex structures with many different characteristic features. The simplest ones are *core* and *support*. The core $C(i)$ is the part of the interval i where the fuzzy value is 1, and the support $S(i)$ is the subset of $\mathbb{R}$ where the fuzzy value of i is non-zero. In addition one can define the *kernel* $K(i)$ as the part of the interval i where the fuzzy value is *not* constant ad infinitum, i.e. the kernel is the smallest convex interval in $\mathbb{R}$ such that $i(x)$ is constant for x outside $K(i)$. Fuzzy time intervals with finite kernel are of particular interest because although they may be infinite, they can easily be implemented with finite data structures.

Fuzzy time intervals can be measured in various ways. Besides the size $|i| \overset{\text{def}}{=} \int i(x) \, dx$, one can locate the position of the core, support and kernel. i^{fO} and i^{lO} are the first and last time coordinates of O, where O is either C (core) or S (support) or K (kernel). One can also measure the maximal fuzzy value $\hat{i}$. This should, but need not be 1. Let i^{fm} be the time coordinate of the first point with $i(i^{fm}) = \hat{i}$ and let i^{lm} be the last such point.

Fuzzy intervals are represented by their *envelope polygons*. These polygons represent the membership functions.

Definition 2 (Envelope Polygon). *The envelope polygon* I *of a fuzzy time interval is a finite sequence of points* $p_0, \ldots, p_n$. *Each point* p *is a tuple* $(p.x, p.y)$ *consisting of the time coordinate* $p.x$ *and the fuzzy value coordinate* $p.y$.

$p_i.x \leq p_{i+1}.x$ *must hold for all* i.
We usually identify the envelope polygon with the fuzzy set itself.   ■

The details of the fuzzy intervals and the operations used in the WebCal system are presented in [8, 9]. The only aspect of fuzzy time intervals which is of some importance for this paper are the set operations ∪ (union), ∩ (intersection) and \ (set difference) for fuzzy intervals. There is no unique definition of these operations for fuzzy intervals. Therefore one has to state, which definition is being used. A definition of intersection which takes the minimum of the membership functions, and a corresponding definition of union which takes the maximum of the membership functions is very natural, but not the only choice. In this paper we can leave it open, which version is to be used. In the implementation one can choose a particular one, or one can leave it as an extra parameter, and the application system has to make the choice.

3   Partitionings

The WebCal system uses the concept of *partitionings* of the real numbers to model periodical temporal notions. In particular, the basic time units years, months etc. are realized as partitionings. Other periodical temporal notions, for example semesters, school holidays, sunsets and sunrises etc. can also be modelled as partitionings.

A partitioning of the real numbers $\mathbb{R}$ may be, for example, $(..., [-100, 0[, [0, 100[, [100, 101[, [101, 500[, ...)$. The intervals in the partitionings need not be of the same length (because time units like years are not of the same length either). The intervals can, however, be enumerated by natural numbers (their *coordinates*). For example, we could have the following enumeration

$$... \; [-100 \; 0[\; [0 \; 100[\; [100 \; 101[\; [101 \; 500[\; ...$$
$$... \quad\quad -1 \quad\quad 0 \quad\quad 1 \quad\quad 2 \quad\quad ...$$

We use *labelled partitionings*. The labels are names for the partitions. For example, the labels for the 'day' partitioning can be 'Monday', 'Tuesday' etc.

The formal definition for labelled partitionings of $\mathbb{R}$ which is used in this paper is:

Definition 3 (Labelled Partitionings). *A partitioning P of the real numbers $\mathbb{R}$ is a sequence* $... [t_{-1}, t_0[, [t_0, t_1[, [t_1, t_2[, ...$ *of half open intervals in $\mathbb{R}$ with integer boundaries, such that either the sequence is infinite at one or both ends, or it is preceded by an infinite interval* $]-\infty, t[$ *(the* start partition*) or/and it is ended by an infinite interval* $[t, +\infty[$ *(the* end partition*).*

For a time point t and a partitioning P let t^P be the P-partition containing t.

A coordinate mapping *of a partitioning P is a bijective mapping between the intervals in P and a subset of the integers. Since we always use one single coordinate mapping for a partitioning P, we can just use P itself to indicate the mapping. Therefore let p^P be the* coordinate *of the partition p in P.*

For a coordinate i let i^P be the partition which corresponds to i.
For a time t let $t^{PP} \stackrel{\text{def}}{=} (t^P)^P$ be the coordinate of the P-partition containing t.
A Labelling L is a finite sequence of strings $l_0, \ldots, l_{n-1}$.
A labelling $L = l_0, \ldots, l_{n-1}$ is turned into a labelling *function $L_P(p)$ for a partitioning P as follows:*

$$L_P(p) \stackrel{\text{def}}{=} \begin{cases} l_{p^P \bmod n} & \text{if } p \text{ is finite} \\ \text{'startPartition'} & \text{if } p = [-\infty, t[\\ \text{'endPartition'} & \text{if } p = [t, +\infty[\end{cases}$$

where p is a partition in P.   ∎

An important operation which involves partitionings is the '*shift*' function. $shift(t, 1, month)$, for example, shifts the time point t by one month. Since the length of the partitions may be different, such a shift function is usually *not continuous*. For example, if the time point t is in January, a shift of 1 month may mean a shift of 31 days, whereas if t is in February, a shift of 1 month may mean a shift of 28 days. The details of the *shift* functions for time points are not important for this paper. We must, however, keep in mind that the *shift* function is in general not continuous.

The *shift* function can have an extra Boolean parameter SG (for Skip Gaps). If it is true then all partitions labelled 'gap' are skipped when the actual shift is computed. All functions defined below can have this extra parameter when they use the *shift* function. The formalism of labelled partitionings, together with various algorithmic and symbolic specification mechanisms for labelled partitionings, is presented in [10].

4   Durations

The partitionings are the mathematical model of periodic time units, such as years, months etc. This offers the possibility to define *durations*. A duration may, for example, be '3 months and 2 weeks'. Months and weeks are represented as partitionings, and 3 and 2 denote the number of partitions in these partitionings. The numbers need not be integers, but can be arbitrary real numbers.

A duration can be interpreted as the length of an interval. In this case the numbers should not be negative. A duration, however, can also be interpreted as a time shift. In this interpretation negative numbers make perfectly sense. $d = (-2\ week), (3\ month)$, for example, denotes a backward shift of 2 weeks followed by a forward shift of 3 months.

Definition 4 (Duration). *A duration $d = (d_0\ P_0), \ldots, (d_k\ P_k)$ is a list of pairs where the d_i are real numbers and the P_i are partitionings.*

If a duration is interpreted as a shift of a time point, it may be necessary to turn the shift around, in the backwards direction. Therefore the inverse of a duration is defined:

$$-d \stackrel{\text{def}}{=} (-d_k\ P_k), \ldots, (-d_0\ P_0)$$ ∎

For example, if $d = (3\ month), (2\ week)$ then $-d = (-2\ week), (-3\ month)$.

Definition 5 (shift for Durations). *Given a function $shift(t, m, P)$, which shifts a time point t by m partitions of the partitioning P, we define a corresponding* shift *function for durations:*

$$shift(t, d) \stackrel{\text{def}}{=} shift(\dots shift(shift(t, d_0, p_0), d_1, p_1) \dots, d_k, p_k)$$

where t is a time point and $d = (d_0, p_0), \dots, (d_k, p_k)$ is a duration. ∎

5   Operations on Points, Intervals and Partitionings

In this section we introduce a number of operations which involve points, intervals, partitionings and durations simultaneously. Together with the operations for the individual datatypes they form the basic building blocks for a specification language for temporal notions.

Since the intervals are represented by their envelope polygons, there is the choice to define the operations directly on the envelope polygons, or on the abstract notion of interval. In the implementation they must operate on the envelope polygons, but it makes sometimes things clearer if they are defined on the abstract level.

It turned out that even quite simple operations become very complex and need many parameters if all the details of fuzzy intervals and partitionings are taken into account. Therefore it is necessary to introduce the operations informally first, and to motivate and discuss the details before the formal definition is presented.

5.1   Shift and Extend

The first operation is the 'shift' operation for intervals. Suppose we have an interval of two hours, and want to shift it by one week. The two hours may be the time for a meeting, and the meeting is shifted to next week. This sounds simple, but the details can be really tricky. The problem is that durations (1 month, 1 week etc.) can denote intervals of different length. In January, for example, a duration of 1 month means 31 days. In February it means only 28 days. This causes that the shift function for time points is not continuous. The distance $(shift(t, 1\ month) - t)$ depends on the position of t, and this holds for all meaningful definitions of '$shift$'. As an extreme case, take the interval [January 31, February 1[. If we shift the two time points separately, we can get [February 31, March 1[, which is equivalent to [March 3, March 1[. That is definitely not what one wants. In order to avoid that the intervals get distorted, one must choose a time point as the anchor point for the shift, and compute the size of the shift for this anchor point. If we choose January 31 in the above example as anchor point, we get a shift of 31 days, and the result is [March 3, March 5[. If we choose February 1, the result is [March 1, March 3[.

In principle one can choose any time point as anchor point, but this causes another problem. If the interval consists of several subintervals, it might not be desirable to choose one anchor point for all subintervals. Therefore the shift function defined below uses a symbolic representation for the anchor point. This way the shift function allows one to shift the subintervals separately. For example, if the interval consists of one subinterval in January and one in February, and we shift it by 1 month, then the interval in January is shifted by 31 days, and the interval in February is shifted by 28 days.

Definition 6 (Shift). *Let* $I = (p_0, \ldots, p_n)$ *be an envelope polygon. Let* D *be a duration. 'componentwise' is a Boolean flg. ' anchorpoint' is one of the keywords 'fm' (first maximum), 'fS' (first Support), 'fC' (first Core), 'fK' (first Kernel), 'lm' (last maximum), 'lS' (last Support), 'lC' (last Core), 'lK' (last Kernel).*

We define the function $shift(I, D, componentwise, anchorpoint)$ *first for the case componentwise = false:*

$$shift(I, D, false, anchorpoint) \stackrel{\text{def}}{=} ((p_0.x + d, p_0.y), \ldots, (p_n.x + d, p_n.y))$$

where $d \stackrel{\text{def}}{=} shift(I^{anchorpoint}, D) - I^{anchorpoint}$.

In the case componentwise = true, the components of the interval are shifted separately.

$$shift(I, D, true, anchorpoint) \stackrel{\text{def}}{=} \bigcup_{J \in Comp(I)} shift(J, D, false, anchorpoint)$$

The result is undefined if the anchor point is the infinity. ∎

This definition of 'shift' guarantees that finite intervals are not distorted. The gaps between components, however, can be distorted if $componentwise = true$ is chosen. It can even happen that the shifted components overlap or they change their ordering.

Extend: The 'extend' function defined below extends an interval by a given duration. It corresponds to phrases like 'for two more hours'. It can also shrink intervals when the duration is negative. 'extend' is quite similar to the 'shift' function. The difference is that 'extend' shifts only a part of the interval to make it wider or shorter. The choices we have for the 'extend' function are: one can extend the interval at the left or at the right side; one can extend only the outermost subinterval, or all subintervals separately, and one can choose the anchor point for computing the shift.

An extended fuzzy interval has still the same shape as the original one. It has only become longer. It is also possible to shrink a fuzzy interval while preserving its shape more or less. To do this one has to cut it into two pieces, shift one piece and compute the intersection of the first piece with the shifted second piece.

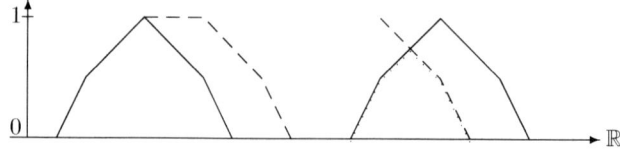

Extending and Shrinking a Fuzzy Interval

Definition 7 (Extend). *Let $I = (p_0, \ldots, p_n)$ be an envelope polygon. Let D be a duration. 'front' and 'componentwise' are Boolean flags. anchorpoint is one of the keywords 'fm' (first maximum), 'fS' (first Support), 'fC' (first Core), 'fK' (first Kernel), 'lm' (last maximum), 'lS' (last Support), 'lC' (last Core), 'lK' (last Kernel).*

We define $extend(I, D, front, componentwise, anchorpoint)$ first for the case componentwise = false:

Let $d \stackrel{\text{def}}{=} shift(I^{anchorpoint}, D) - I^{anchorpoint}$, and let $p_l \stackrel{\text{def}}{=} I^{fm}$ and $p_k \stackrel{\text{def}}{=} I^{lm}$.

$extend(I, D, true, false, anchorpoint)$
$$\stackrel{\text{def}}{=} \begin{cases} ((p_0.x - d, p_0.y), \ldots, (p_l.x - d, p_l.y), p_l \ldots, p_n) & \text{if } d > 0 \\ ((p_0.x - d, p_0.y), \ldots, (p_l.x - d, p_l.y)) \cap (p_l \ldots, p_n) & \text{otherwise.} \end{cases}$$

$extend(I, D, false, false, anchorpoint)$
$$\stackrel{\text{def}}{=} \begin{cases} (p_0, \ldots, p_k, (p_k.x + d, p_0.y), \ldots, (p_n.x + d, p_l.y)) & \text{if } d > 0 \\ (p_0, \ldots, p_k) \cap ((p_k.x + d, p_0.y), \ldots, (p_n.x + d, p_l.y)) & \text{otherwise.} \end{cases}$$

In the case componentwise = true, the components of the interval are extended separately.

$extend(I, D, front, true, anchorpoint)$
$$\stackrel{\text{def}}{=} \bigcup_{J \in Comp(I)} extend(J, D, front, false, anchorpoint).$$

The result is undefined if the anchor point is the infinity. ∎

5.2   Which

The next function can be used to answer queries like 'which day in the week is now' or 'in which week in the year is the time point t'. The parameters are $which(t, P, Q, inclusion, SG)$. t is the time point for which we want to get the information. P and Q are partitionings. For example, P could be the 'week' partitioning and Q could be the 'year' partitioning. *inclusion* is a control parameter for determining what counts as the first P partition in the Q partitioning. The problem can be best illustrated with weeks and years. Since weeks and years are not synchronized, the beginning of a year need not be the beginning of a week. It is therefore a matter of convention what counts as the first week in a year. It could be the first week which is completely contained in the year, it could be the first week which overlaps with the year, or it could be the first week whose lager part is in the year. The latter one is the condition which is commonly being used. Therefore *inclusion* is one of the keywords 'subset', 'overlap' and 'bigger_part_inside'.

The last parameter, SG (for Skip Gaps) controls whether partitions labelled 'gap' are counted or not. If $SG = true$ then they are skipped, otherwise they are counted.

The 'which' function is a partial function. There are various conditions which can cause $which(t, P, Q, inclusion, IG)$ to be undefined. For example, if $SG = true$ and the label of t^Q is 'gap' then the function call is undefined. Another example is when the role of P and Q is reversed and we ask, for example, 'which year in the week is now', with the condition $inclusion = subset$. No meaningful answer is possible in this case.

'which' first locates the Q-partition containing t. Then it determines the first P-partition in this Q-partition. Finally it counts the number of P-partitions which must be traversed until t is reached.

Definition 8 (Which). *Let t be a time point, let P and Q be partitionings. SG is a Boolean flag, and ' inclusion' is one of the keywords 'subset', 'overlap' and 'bigger_part_inside'. P and Q can be labelled.*

$which(t, P, Q, inclusion, IG)$

$$\stackrel{\text{def}}{=} \begin{cases} undefined & if\ SG = true\ and\ L_Q(t^Q) = \text{'gap'} \\ undefined & if\ n\ is\ undefined \\ \min_k(t \in (n+k)^P) & if\ SG = false \\ \min_k(t \in (n+k)^P) - gaps(n,k) & if\ SG = true\ and\ L((n+k)^P) \neq \text{'gap'} \\ undefined & otherwise \end{cases}$$

where n is the coordinate of the first P-partition within the Q-partition that contains t:

$$n \stackrel{\text{def}}{=} \begin{cases} n' & if\ n'\ is\ defined\ and\ (SG = false\ or\ L_P(n'^P) \neq \text{'gap'}) \\ undefined\ otherwise \end{cases}$$

The computation of n' depends on the 'inclusion' parameter.

Case *inclusion = subset:*

$$n' \stackrel{\text{def}}{=} \begin{cases} (t^Q_{[)})^{PP} & if\ (t^Q_{[)})^P \subseteq t^Q \\ (t^Q_{[)})^{PP} + 1 & if\ ((t^Q_{[)})^{PP} + 1)^P \subseteq t^Q \\ undefined & otherwise \end{cases}$$

Case *inclusion = bigger_part_inside:*

$$n' \stackrel{\text{def}}{=} \begin{cases} (t^Q_{[)})^{PP} & if\ |(t^Q_{[)})^P \cap t^Q| \geq |(t^Q_{[)})^P \setminus t^Q| \\ (t^Q_{[)})^{PP} + 1 & |((t^Q_{[)})^{PP} + 1)^P \cap t^Q| \geq |((t^Q_{[)})^{PP} + 1)^P \setminus t^Q| \\ undefined & otherwise \end{cases}$$

Case *inclusion = overlap:*

$$n' \stackrel{\text{def}}{=} (t^Q_{[)})^{PP}.$$

The auxiliary function 'gaps' counts the number of partitions between n and k which are labelled 'gap'

$$gaps(n,k) \stackrel{\text{def}}{=} \Sigma_{i=n}^k \begin{cases} 1\ if\ L_P(i^P) = \text{'gap'} \\ 0\ otherwise \end{cases}$$

∎

5.3   Extract

We define two 'extract' functions. Both extract certain parts of given intervals. The first one, 'extractL' extract partitions from given intervals which are labelled with a given label. For example, if the days in the day-partitioning are labelled 'Monday', 'Tuesday' etc., one can use extractL to extract all Tuesdays from a given interval. The parameters are $extractL(I, label, P, inclusion, intersection)$. I is the interval, *label* is the label and P is the labelled partitioning. '*inclusion*' is one of the keywords 'subset', 'bigger_part_inside' or 'overlaps'. It controls the relationship between the interval I and the partition p with the right label. If, for example, $inclusion = subset$ then p must be a subset of the support of I. '*intersection*' is a Boolean flag. It controls whether the result consists of just the partitions, or the partitions intersected with I.

Definition 9 (ExtractL). *Let I be an interval, 'label' a label, P a labelled partitioning with labelling L_P, 'inclusion' one of the key words 'subset', 'bigger_part_inside' or 'overlaps' and 'intersection' a Boolean flag. We define the function extractL:*

$$extractL(I, label, P, inclusion, intersection)$$

$$\stackrel{\text{def}}{=} \bigcup_{p \in P, L(p)=label, C(p)} \begin{cases} p \cap I & \text{if } intersection = true \\ p & \text{otherwise} \end{cases}$$

where

$$C(p) \stackrel{\text{def}}{=} \begin{cases} p \subseteq S(I) & \text{if } inclusion = \text{ 'subset'} \\ |p \cap S(I)| \geq |p \setminus S(I)| & \text{if } inclusion = \text{ 'bigger\_part\_inside'} \\ p \cap I \neq \emptyset & \text{otherwise} \end{cases}$$ ∎

The next function, '$extractD$' can extract a subinterval of a certain *duration* from an interval. It can, for example, be used to extract the second fortnight in a year. The parameters are

$$extractD(I, O, D, componentwise, boundaries, forward, inclusion, intersection)$$

I is the interval from which subintervals are to be extracted. O (for offset) is a duration. It determines the offset for the interval to be extracted. For example, if the second fortnight is to be extracted, we need an offset of one fortnight. $O = ((2, week))$ could be used in this case. D is the duration of the interval to be extracted. Both, the offset, and the duration must be positive. Otherwise the extractD function is undefined. *componentwise* is a flag. If it is false then only one single subinterval is extracted. If it is true then a subinterval of each component of I is extracted. '*boundaries*' is one of the keywords 'support', 'core' or 'kernel'. It determines the part of the interval I which is to be used for the extraction. *forward* is a Boolean flag. If it is true then the offset is computed from the start of the interval I. Otherwise it is computed from the end of the interval. '*inclusion*' is one of the keywords 'align', 'subset', 'bigger_part_inside' or 'overlaps'. It is used in the functions *startpoint* and *endpoint* and determines exactly from where the offset is computed. In the above example, one would choose $inclusion = bigger\_part\_inside$. This causes that the usual convention that the first week in a year (or any other interval) is the week whose bigger part is in the interval. '*intersection*' is again a Boolean flag. If it is true then the time interval which is determined by the offset and the duration is intersected with I. Otherwise this time interval is returned, even if its intersection with I is empty. This feature can, for example, be used to compute the second fortnight from now. It is sufficient to have an interval I which is just one second long. With the flags $inclusion = align$ and $intersection = false$ one would get the 2 weeks interval.

The $extractD$ function needs two auxiliary functions $startpoint$ and $endpoint$. They compute the exact start and endpoint for the offset.

Definition 10 (Startpoint, Endpoint). *Let t be a time point, P a partitioning and 'inclusion' one of the keywords 'align', 'subset', 'bigger_part_inside' or 'overlap'. We define the two functions*

$startpoint(t, P, inclusion)$ *and* $endpoint(t, P, inclusion)$:

$$startpoint(t, P, \text{`align'}) \stackrel{\text{def}}{=} t$$

$$startpoint(t, P, \text{`subset'}) \stackrel{\text{def}}{=} \begin{cases} t^P_[& \text{if } t = t^P_[\\ t^P_] & \text{otherwise} \end{cases}$$

$$startpoint(t, P, \text{`bigger\_part\_inside'}) \stackrel{\text{def}}{=} \begin{cases} t^P_[& \text{if } t - t^P_[\le t^P_] - t \\ t^P_] & \text{otherwise} \end{cases}$$

$$startpoint(t, P, \text{`overlap'}) \stackrel{\text{def}}{=} t^P_[$$

$$endpoint(t, P, \text{`align'}) \stackrel{\text{def}}{=} t$$

$$endpoint(t, P, \text{`subset'}) \stackrel{\text{def}}{=} \begin{cases} t^P_[& \text{if } t = t^P_[\\ (t^{P^P} - 1)^P_[& \text{otherwise} \end{cases}$$

$$endpoint(t, P, \text{`bigger\_part\_inside'}) \stackrel{\text{def}}{=} \begin{cases} t^P_] & \text{if } t - t^P_[\ge t^P_] - t \\ t^P_[& \text{otherwise} \end{cases}$$

$$endpoint(t, P, \text{`overlap'}) \stackrel{\text{def}}{=} \begin{cases} t^P_[& \text{if } t = t^P_[\\ (t^P_] & \text{otherwise} \end{cases}$$

The next auxiliary function $intersect(i, I, inclusion, intersection)$ checks whether the interval i is an admissible part of the result of $extractD$. This depends on the control parameter '*inclusion*' which determines the relationship between i and the original interval I. The second parameter '*intersection*' controls whether i itself should be the result, or the intersection of i with $S(I)$.

Definition 11 (Intersect). *Let $i = [t_1, t_2[$ be a crisp interval, and let I be a fuzzy interval. Let 'inclusion' be one of the keywords 'subset', 'bigger_part_inside' or 'overlap'. Let 'intersect' be a Boolean flag.*
    We define

$intersect(i, I, inclusion, intersection)$

$$\stackrel{\text{def}}{=} \begin{cases} i \cap S(I) & \text{if } keep = true \text{ and } intersect = true \\ i & \text{if } keep = true \text{ and } intersect = false \\ \emptyset & \text{otherwise} \end{cases}$$

where

$keep = true \; iff \; inclusion = \text{'subset'} \; and \; i \subseteq S(I) \; or$
$\qquad\qquad inclusion = \text{'bigger\_part\_inside'} \; and \; |i \cap S(I)| \geq |i \setminus S(I)| \; or$
$\qquad\qquad inclusion = \text{'overlap'} \; and \; i \cap S(I) \neq \emptyset$

Definition 12 (ExtractD). *Let I be an interval, let $O = ((n_0, P_0), \ldots)$ (for offset) and D (for duration) be two durations. 'componentwise', 'forward' and 'intersection' are three Boolean flags. 'boundaries' is one of the keywords 'support', 'core' or 'kernel' and 'inclusion' is one of the keywords 'align', 'subset', 'bigger_part_inside' or 'overlaps'.*

We define the function
$extractD(I, O, D, componentwise, boundaries, forward, inclusion, intersection)$
as follows:

$$Let \; [a, b[\stackrel{\text{def}}{=} \begin{cases} [I^{fS}, I^{lS}[& if \; boundaries = \text{'support'} \\ [I^{fC}, I^{lC}[& if \; boundaries = \text{'core'} \\ [I^{fK}, I^{lK}[& otherwise \end{cases}$$

be the relevant boundaries for extracting the interval. The extractD function is undefined if one of the boundaries is infinite.

$$Let \; t_0 \stackrel{\text{def}}{=} \begin{cases} startpoint(a, P_0, inclusion) \; if \; forward = true \\ endpoint(b, P_0, inclusion) \quad otherwise \end{cases}$$

t_0 *is the start point for computing the offset.*

$$Let \; [t_1, t_2[\stackrel{\text{def}}{=} \begin{cases} [shift(t, O), shift(t_1, D)[& if \; forward = true \\ [shift(t_2, -D), shift(t, -O)[& otherwise \end{cases}$$

be the interval to be extracted.

$extractD(I, O, D, false, boundaries, forward, inclusion, intersection)$
$\qquad \stackrel{\text{def}}{=} intersect([t_1, t_2[, I, inclusion, intersection).$
extracts one subinterval from I.
$extractD(I, O, D, true, parameters)$

$$\stackrel{\text{def}}{=} \begin{cases} \bigcup_{J \in Cmp(I)} extractD(J, O, D, false, parameters) \\ \quad if \; componentwise = true \\ extractD(I, O, D, false, parameters) \quad otherwise \end{cases}$$

extracts a subinterval from each component.
'parameters' stands for 'boundaries, forward, inclusion, intersection'.　■

A simplified version of '$extractD$' needs no duration D, but only an offset O, and extracts instead of an interval, just the start point of the interval.

6　Split

The function 'split' splits an interval into several intervals of a given duration. As an example for its use, suppose we want to define a function 'Weekend(I)', which extracts from the interval I all weekends. One way to do this would be to partition the interval I into intervals of one week length, and then to use the function $extractD$ to extract from each week the sixth and the seventh day. The function

$$split(I, D, componentwise, boundaries, forward, inclusion, sequencing,$$
$$intersect)$$

is controlled by a whole bunch of parameters. The flag '$componentwise$' indicates whether the interval I is split as a whole, or whether its components are split separately. The keyword '$boundaries$' determines whether the support of I, the core of I or the kernel of I is to be split. The flag '$forward$' indicates whether the interval is to be split from left to right or from right to left. $inclusion$ is a further keyword. It controls where to start with the splitting and determines the relationship between the split parts and the interval I. For example, if $inclusion = subset$ then all split parts must be a subset of the support if I. The keyword '$sequencing$' becomes relevant when the duration D is not a single partition, but something mixed. If, for example, $D = (1week, 3day)$ we want to split I into intervals of length 1 week plus 3 days. There are three different options. The first possibility is to partition I sequentially without gaps. The second possibility is to synchronize the split parts with the 'week' partitioning. That means each split part starts with the start of a week. Since the length of the split parts is not a multiple of a week length, we must either leave gaps (second possibility) or compute overlapping split parts (third possibility).

Finally the '$intersect$' flag controls whether the sequence of partitions is the result of split, or whether the partitions are intersected with I.

The 'split' function needs two auxiliary functions, '$advance$' and '$retract$'. Depending on the value of the keyword 'sequencing' they compute the start point of the next split part. '$advance$' is used for forward splitting and '$retract$' is used for backward splitting.

Definition 13 (Advance and Retract). *Let t be a time point, P a partitioning and sequencing one of the key words 'sequential', 'overlap' or 'with_gaps'. We define the function 'advance':*

$$advance(t, P, sequencing) \stackrel{\text{def}}{=} \begin{cases} t & \text{if } sequencing = \text{'sequential'} \\ t^P{}_[& \text{if } sequencing = \text{'overlap'} \text{ or } t = t^P{}_[\\ t^P{}_] & \text{otherwise} \end{cases}$$

We define the function 'retract:

$$retract(t, P, sequencing) \stackrel{\text{def}}{=} \begin{cases} t & \text{if } sequencing = \text{'sequential'} \\ t^P{}_] & \text{if } sequencing = \text{'overlap'} \text{ or } t = t^P{}_] \\ t^P{}_[& \text{otherwise.} \end{cases}$$
∎

Definition 14 (Split). *Let I be an interval and $D = ((n_0, P_0), \ldots)$ be a duration. Let 'boundaries' be one of the keywords 'support', 'core' or 'kernel'. Let 'componentwise', 'forward' and 'intersect' be Boolean flags. Let ' inclusion' be* *one of the keywords 'subset', 'bigger_part_inside' or 'overlap', and let 'sequencing' be one of the key words 'sequential', 'overlap' or 'with_gaps'.*

We define the function split:

$split(I, D, componentwise, boundaries, forward, inclusion, sequencing,$
$\quad intersect)$ *which computes a list* $(S_0, \ldots)$ *of intervals.*

Case componentwise = false:

Let $[a, b[\stackrel{\text{def}}{=} \begin{cases} [I^{fS}, I^{lS}[& \text{if boundaries} = \text{'support'} \\ [I^{fC}, I^{lC}[& \text{if boundaries} = \text{'core'} \\ [I^{fK}, I^{lK}[& \text{otherwise} \end{cases}$

be the relevant boundaries for splitting the interval. The split function is unde-fined if one of the boundaries is infinite.

Let $t_0 \stackrel{\text{def}}{=} \begin{cases} startpoint(a, P_0, inclusion) & \text{if } forward = true \\ endpoint(b, P_0, inclusion) & \text{otherwise} \end{cases}$

be the start point for computing the split.

We compute a first sequence S'_i *of intervals:*

if $forward = true$ *then*

$S'_0 \stackrel{\text{def}}{=} [t_0, shift(t_0, D)[$ *and* $S'_{i+1} \stackrel{\text{def}}{=} [s, t[$ *where* $s \stackrel{\text{def}}{=} advance(S'_{i]}, P_0, sequencing)$ *and* $t \stackrel{\text{def}}{=} shift(s, D)$.

The sequence S'_i *is computed until* $S'_{i]} \geq b$.

if $forward = false$ *then*

$S'_0 \stackrel{\text{def}}{=} [shift(t_0, -D), t_0[$ *and* $S'_{i+1} \stackrel{\text{def}}{=} [s, t[$ *where* $t \stackrel{\text{def}}{=} retract(S'_{i[}, P_0, sequencing)$ *and* $s \stackrel{\text{def}}{=} shift(t, -D)$.

The sequence S'_i *is computed until* $S'_{i[} \leq a$.

The final sequence $(S_0, \ldots)$ *is now obtained from the* S'_i *by computing*

$S_i \stackrel{\text{def}}{=} intersect(S'_i, I, inclusion, intersect)$

and removing the empty intervals from the sequence.

Case componentwise = true:

$split(I, D, true, parameters) \stackrel{\text{def}}{=} \bigcup_{J \in Comp(I)} split(J, D, false, parameters)$

where parameters stands for
'boundaries, forward, inclusion, sequencing, intersect'.

$\bigcup$ *does in this case not mean set union, but appending the lists of intervals, and removing duplicates.*   ∎

An appication for the '*split*' function is the representation of clock times. For example, the interpretation of '8:30 am' could be the set of all time points corresponding to 8:30 am. Alternatively it could mean a function mapping an interval I to the time points in I which corresponds to 8:30 am. This could be achieved as a composition of the '*split*' function and the '*extract*' function.

7   Summary

In this paper a number of basic operations have been defined which operate on time points, crisp and fuzzy time intervals, partitionings and durations. Together with the functions and relations defined for each of these datatypes separately, they form the building blocks for a powerful specification language for temporal notions. This language can then be used as a computational semantics for temporal expressions in structured and semistructured data, and for XML and database query languages.

The functions at the mixed function layer were chosen to be *minimal* and *powerful*. Minimal means that they cannot be decomposed into simpler functions. Powerful means that as many different operations on fuzzy time intervals as possible can be defined by combining the mixed functions and the functions at the lower layer. So far, this is not such a formal notion as the general notion of computable functions. Experience and practical applications will show whether other functions need to be added.

The functions will be available in the WebCal system. This system is developed for processing complex temporal notions as realistically as possible, i.e. without any approximations and abstractions. A prototype, which does not yet contain all the functions proposed in this paper is currently being tested.

References

1. T. Berners-Lee, M. Fischetti, and M. Dertouzos. *Weaving the Web: The Original Design and Ultimate Destiny of the World Wide Web.* Harper, San Francisco, September 1999. ISBN: 0062515861.
2. Claudio Bettini, Sushil Jajodia, and Sean X. Wang. *Time Granularities in Databases, Data Mining and Temporal Reasoning.* Springer Verlag, 2000.
3. François Bry, Bernhard Lorenz, Hans Jürgen Ohlbach, and Stephanie Spranger. On reasoning on time and location on the web. In N. Henze F. Bry and J. Malusyński, editors, *Principles and Practice of Semantic Web Reasoning*, volume 2901 of *LNCS*, pages 69–83. Springer Verlag, 2003.
4. Nachum Dershowitz and Edward M. Reingold. *Calendrical Calculations.* Cambridge University Press, 1997.
5. Didier Dubois and Henri Prade, editors. *Fundamentals of Fuzzy Sets.* Kluwer Academic Publisher, 2000.
6. Hans Jürgen Ohlbach. About real time, calendar systems and temporal notions. In H. Barringer and D. Gabbay, editors, *Advances in Temporal Logic*, pages 319–338. Kluwer Academic Publishers, 2000.
7. Hans Jürgen Ohlbach. Calendar logic. In I. Hodkinson D.M. Gabbay and M. Reynolds, editors, *Temporal Logic: Mathematical Foundations and Computational Aspec ts*, pages 489–586. Oxford University Press, 2000.
8. Hans Jürgen Ohlbach. Fuzzy time intervals and relations – the FuTIRe library. Technical report, Inst. f. Informatik, LMU München, 2004. See http://www.pms.informatik.uni-muenchen.de/mitarbeiter/ohlbach/systems/FuTIRe.
9. Hans Jürgen Ohlbach. Relations between fuzzy time intervals. In *Proceedings of Time04*, 2004. To appear.

10. Hans Jürgen Ohlbach. The role of labelled partitionings for modelling periodic temporal notions. http://www.informatik.uni-muenchen.de/mitarbeiter/ohlbach/homepage/publications/PRP/abstracts.shtml, 2004. To be published.
11. Hans Jürgen Ohlbach. The role of labelled partitionings for modelling periodic temporal notions. In *Procceedings of Time04*, 2004. To appear.
12. L. A. Zadeh. Fuzzy sets. *Information & Control*, 8:338–353, 1965.

DR-DEVICE: A Defeasible Logic System for the Semantic Web

Nick Bassiliades[1], Grigoris Antoniou[2], and Ioannis Vlahavas[1]

[1]Department of Informatics, Aristotle University of Thessaloniki
GR-54124 Thessaloniki, Greece
{nbassili, vlahavas}@csd.auth.gr
[2]Institute of Computer Science, FO.R.T.H.
P.O. Box 1385, GR-71110, Heraklion, Greece
antoniou@ics.forth.gr

Abstract. This paper presents DR-DEVICE, a system for defeasible reasoning on the Web. Defeasible reasoning is a rule-based approach for efficient reasoning with incomplete and inconsistent information. Such reasoning is, among others, useful for ontology integration, where conflicting information arises naturally; and for the modeling of business rules and policies, where rules with exceptions are often used. In this paper we describe these scenarios in more detail along with the implementation of the DR-DEVICE system, which is capable of reasoning about RDF data over multiple Web sources using defeasible logic rules. The system is implemented on top of CLIPS production rule system and builds upon R-DEVICE, an earlier deductive rule system over RDF data that also supports derived attribute and aggregate attribute rules. Rules can be expressed either in a native CLIPS-like language, or in an extension of the OO-RuleML syntax. The operational semantics of defeasible logic are implemented through compilation into the generic rule language of R-DEVICE. The paper includes a use case of a semantic web broker that reasons defeasibly about renting apartments based on buyer's requirements (expressed RuleML defeasible logic rules) and seller's advertisements (expressed in RDF).

1 Introduction

The development of the Semantic Web [14] proceeds in layers, each layer being on top of other layers. At present, the highest layer that has reached sufficient maturity is the ontology layer in the form of the description logic based languages of DAML+OIL [18] and OWL [20].

The next step in the development of the Semantic Web will be the logic and proof layers, and rule systems appear to lie in the mainstream of such activities. Moreover, rule systems can also be utilized in ontology languages. So, in general rule systems can play a twofold role in the Semantic Web initiative: (a) they can serve as extensions of, or alternatives to, description logic based ontology languages; and (b) they can be used to develop declarative systems on top of (using) ontologies. Reasons why rule systems are expected to play a key role in the further development of the Semantic Web include the following:

H.J. Ohlbach and S. Schaffert (Eds.): PPSWR 2004, LNCS 3208, pp. 134–148, 2004.
© Springer-Verlag Berlin Heidelberg 2004

1. Seen as subsets of predicate logic, monotonic rule systems (Horn logic) and description logics are orthogonal; thus they provide additional expressive power to ontology languages.
2. Efficient reasoning support exists to support rule languages.
3. Rules are well known in practice, and are reasonably well integrated in mainstream information technology.

Possible interactions between description logics and monotonic rule systems were studied in [26]. Based on that work and on previous work on hybrid reasoning [28] it appears that the best one can do at present is to take the intersection of the expressive power of Horn logic and description logics; one way to view this intersection is the Horn-definable subset of OWL.

This paper is devoted to a different problem, namely conflicts among rules. Here we just mention the main sources of such conflicts, which are further expanded in section 2. At the ontology layer: (a) default inheritance within ontologies, (b) ontology merging; and at the logic and reasoning layers: (a) rules with exceptions as a natural representation of business rules, (b) reasoning with incomplete information.

Defeasible reasoning is a simple rule-based approach to reasoning with incomplete and inconsistent information. It can represent facts, rules, and priorities among rules. This reasoning family comprises defeasible logics ([35], [6]) and Courteous Logic Programs [24]. The main advantage of this approach is the combination of two desirable features: enhanced representational capabilities allowing one to reason with incomplete and contradictory information, coupled with low computational complexity compared to mainstream nonmonotonic reasoning.

In this paper we report on the implementation of a defeasible reasoning system for reasoning on the Web, called DR-DEVICE. Its main characteristics are the following:

- Its user interface is compatible with RuleML [15], the main standardization effort for rules on the Semantic Web.
- It is based on a CLIPS-based implementation of deductive rules ([10], [11]). The core of the system consists of a translation of defeasible knowledge into a set of deductive rules, including derived and aggregate attributes. However, the implementation is declarative because it interprets the not operator using Well-Founded Semantics [21].

2 Conflicting Rules on the Semantic Web

In this section we describe in more detail certain scenarios that justify the need for defeasible reasoning on the Semantic Web.

Reasoning with Incomplete Information. In [4] a scenario is described where business rules have to deal with incomplete information: in the absence of certain information some assumptions have to be made which lead to conclusions not supported by classical predicate logic. In many applications on the Web such assumptions must be made because other players may not be able (e.g. due to communication problems) or willing (e.g. because of privacy or security concerns) to provide information. This is the classical case for the use of nonmonotonic knowledge representation and reasoning [33].

Rules with Exceptions. Rules with exceptions are a natural representation for policies and business rules [5]. And priority information is often implicitly or explicitly available to resolve conflicts among rules. Potential applications include security policies ([9], [29]), business rules [2], personalization, brokering, bargaining, and automated agent negotiations [22].

Default Inheritance in Ontologies. Default inheritance is a well-known feature of certain knowledge representation formalisms. Thus it may play a role in ontology languages, which currently do not support this feature. In [23] some ideas are presented for possible uses of default inheritance in ontologies. A natural way of representing default inheritance is rules with exceptions, plus priority information. Thus, nonmonotonic rule systems can be utilized in ontology languages.

Ontology Merging. When ontologies from different authors and/or sources are merged, contradictions arise naturally. Predicate logic based formalisms, including all current Semantic Web languages, cannot cope with inconsistencies. If rule-based ontology languages are used (e.g. DLP [26]) and if rules are interpreted as defeasible (that is, they may be prevented from being applied even if they can fire) then we arrive at nonmonotonic rule systems. A skeptical approach, as adopted by defeasible reasoning, is sensible because it does not allow for contradictory conclusions to be drawn. Moreover, priorities may be used to resolve some conflicts among rules, based on knowledge about the reliability of sources or on user input). Thus, nonmonotonic rule systems can support ontology integration.

3   An Introduction to Defeasible Logics

The basic characteristics of defeasible logics are:

- Defeasible logics are rule-based, without disjunction.
- Classical negation is used in the heads and bodies of rules, but negation-as-failure is not used in the object language (it can easily be simulated, if necessary [6], [8]).
- Rules may support conflicting conclusions.
- The logics are skeptical in the sense that conflicting rules do not fire. Thus consistency is preserved.
- Priorities on rules may be used to resolve some conflicts among rules.
- The logics take a pragmatic view and have low computational complexity.

A *defeasible theory* D is a couple $(R,>)$ where R a finite set of rules, and $>$ a superiority relation on R. In expressing the proof theory we consider only propositional rules. Rules containing free variables are interpreted as the set of their variable-free instances.

There are three kinds of rules: *Strict rules* are denoted by $A \rightarrow p$, and are interpreted in the classical sense: whenever the premises are indisputable then so is the conclusion. An example of a strict rule is "Professors are faculty members". Written formally: `professor(X)` $\rightarrow$ `faculty(X)`. Inference from strict rules only is called *definite inference*. Strict rules are intended to define relationships that are definitional in nature, for example ontological knowledge.

Defeasible rules are denoted by $A \Rightarrow p$, and can be defeated by contrary evidence. An example of such a rule is `professor(X)` $\Rightarrow$ `tenured(X)` which reads as follows: "Professors are typically tenured".

Defeaters are denoted as $A \sim> p$ and are used only to prevent some conclusions, not to actively support conclusions. An example of such a defeater is `assistant-Prof(X) ~> ¬tenured(X)` which reads as follows: "Assistant professors may be not tenured".

A *superiority relation* on R is an acyclic relation > on R (that is, the transitive closure of > is irreflexive). When $r_1 > r_2$, then r_1 is called *superior* to r_2, and r_2 *inferior* to r_1. This expresses that r_1 may override r_2. For example, given the defeasible rules

```
r₁: visiting-professor(X) => professor(X)
r₂: professor(X) => tenured(X)
r₃: visiting-professor(X) => ¬tenured(X)
```

no conclusive decision can be made about whether a visiting professor is tenured, because rules r_2 and r_3 contradict each other. But if we introduce a superiority relation > with $r_3 > r_2$, then we can indeed conclude that a visiting professor is not tenured.

A formal definition of the proof theory is found in [6]. A model theoretic semantics is found in [32].

4 The DR-DEVICE System

The DR-DEVICE system consists of two major components (Fig. 1): the RDF loader/translator and the rule loader/translator. The former accepts from the latter (or the user) requests for loading specific RDF documents. The RDF triple loader downloads the RDF document from the Internet and uses the ARP parser [34] to translate it to triples in the N-triple format. Both the RDF/XML and N-triple files are stored locally for future reference. Furthermore, the RDF document is recursively scanned for namespaces which are also parsed using the ARP parser. The rationale for translating namespaces is to obtain a complete RDF Schema in order to minimize the number of OO schema redefinitions. Fetching multiple RDF schema files will aggregate multiple RDF to OO schema translations into a single OO schema redefinition. Namespace resolution is not guaranteed to yield an RDF schema document; therefore, if the namespace URI is not an RDF document, then the ARP parser will not produce triples and DR-DEVICE will make assumptions, based on the RDF semantics [27], about non-resolved properties, resources, classes, etc.

All N-triples are loaded into memory, while the resources that have a `URI#anchorID` or `URI/anchorID` format are transformed into a `ns:anchorID` format if `URI` belongs to the initially collected namespaces, in order to save memory space. The transformed RDF triples are fed to the RDF triple translator which maps them into COOL objects, according to the mapping scheme in section 4.1. Notice that as RDF triples are mapped to objects they get deleted.

The rule loader accepts from the user a URI (or a local file name) that contains a defeasible logic rule program in RuleML notation [15]. The RuleML document may also contain the URI of the input RDF document on which the rule program will run, which is forwarded to the RDF loader. The RuleML program is translated into the native DR-DEVICE rule notation using the Xalan XSLT processor [37] and an XSLT stylesheet. The DR-DEVICE rule program is then forwarded to the rule translator.

The rule translator accepts from the rule loader (or directly from the user) a set of rules in DR-DEVICE notation and translates them into a set of CLIPS production rules. The translation of the defeasible logic rules is performed in two steps: first, the defeasible logic rules are translated into sets of deductive, derived attribute and aggregate attribute rules of the basic R-DEVICE rule language (section 5.1), and then, all these rules are translated into CLIPS production rules ([10], [11]). When the translation ends, CLIPS runs the production rules and generates the objects that constitute the result of the initial rule program or query. Finally, the result-objects are exported to the user as an RDF/XML document through the RDF extractor.

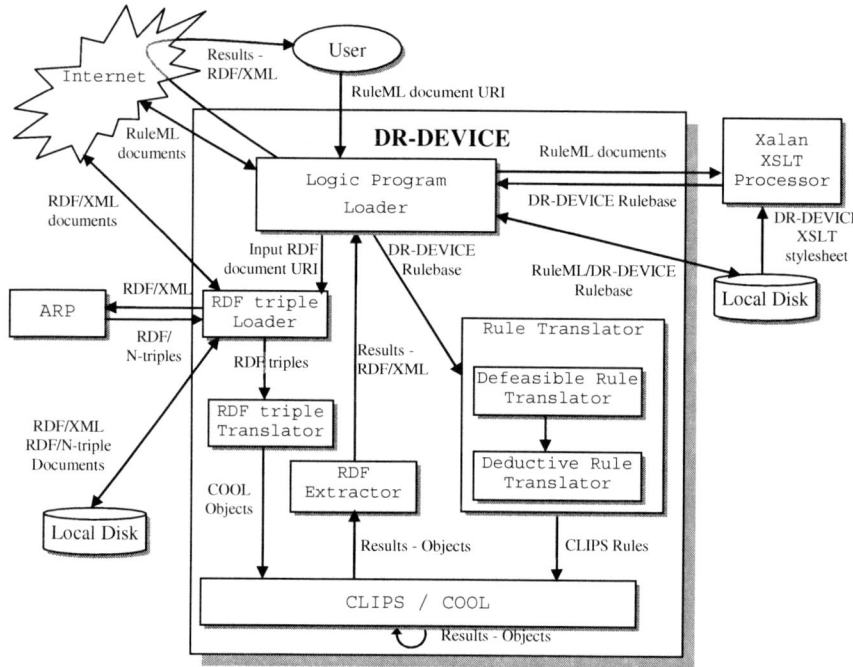

Fig. 1. Architecture of the DR-DEVICE system

4.1 The R-DEVICE System

In this subsection we give a brief overview of the R-DEVICE system which is the basis for building DR-DEVICE. R-DEVICE ([10], [11]) is a deductive object-oriented knowledge base system, which transforms RDF triples into objects and uses a deductive rule language for querying and reasoning about them.

Triple-to-Object Mapping Scheme

R-DEVICE imports RDF data into the CLIPS production rule system [17] as COOL objects. The main difference between the RDF data model and our object model is that we treat properties both as first-class objects and as attributes of resource objects. In this way properties of resources are not scattered across several triples as in most other RDF storage and querying systems, resulting in increased query performance due to less joins. The main features of this mapping scheme are the following:

- Resource *classes* are represented both as COOL classes and as direct or indirect instances of the `rdfs:Class` class. This binary representation is due to the fact that COOL does not support meta-classes. Class names follow the `ns:anchorID` format, while their corresponding instances have an object identifier with the same name, surrounded by square brackets.
- All *resources* are represented as COOL objects, direct or indirect instances of the `rdfs:Resource` class. The identifier of a resource object is the same as the URI address of the resource, except if their address can be abbreviated to a `ns:label`.
- Finally, *properties* are direct or indirect instances of the class `rdf:Property`. Furthermore, properties are defined as slots (attributes) of their domain class(es). The values of properties are stored inside resource objects as slot values. Actually, RDF properties are multislots, i.e. they store lists of values, because a resource can have multiple times the same property attached to it.

The descriptive semantics of RDF data may call for dynamic redefinitions of the OO schema, which are handled by R-DEVICE.

The Rule Language of R-DEVICE

R-DEVICE features a powerful deductive rule language which is able to express arbitrary queries both on the RDF schema and data, including recursion, stratified negation, ground and generalized path expressions over the objects, derived attributes and aggregate, grouping, and sorting functions, mainly due to the second-order syntax of the rule language which is efficiently translated into sets of first-order logic rules using metadata. R-DEVICE rules define views which are materialized and incrementally maintained. Finally, users can use and define functions using the CLIPS host language. R-DEVICE belongs to a family of previous such deductive object-oriented rule languages ([12], [13]). Deductive rules are implemented as CLIPS production rules and their syntax is a variation of the CLIPS syntax. Examples of rules can be found in the next section, as well as in [36].

5   The Defeasible Logic Language of DR-DEVICE

There are three types of rules in DR-DEVICE, closely reflecting defeasible logic: strict rules, defeasible rules, and defeaters. Rule type is declared with keywords `strictrule`, `defeasiblerule`, and `defeater`, respectively. For example, the following rule construct represents the defeasible rule r4: `bird(X) => flies(X)`.

```
(defeasiblerule r4
  (bird (name ?X))
 =>
  (flies (name ?X)))
```

Predicates have named arguments, called slots, since they represent CLIPS objects. DR-DEVICE has also a RuleML-like syntax [15]. The same rule is represented in RuleML notation (version 0.85) as follows:

```
<imp>
   <_rlab><ind type="defeasiblerule">r4</ind></_rlab>
   <_head>
     <atom>    <_opr><rel>bird</rel></_opr>
               <_slot name="name"><var>X</var></_slot>
     </atom>
   </_head>
   <_body>
     <atom>    <_opr><rel href="flies"/></_opr>
               <_slot name="name"><var>X</var></_slot>
     </atom>
   </_body>
</imp>
```

We have used the `type` attribute inside the `ind` element of the rule label (`_rlab`) to denote rule type. However, several features of defeasible logic and its DR-DEVICE implementation could not be captured by the latest RuleML DTDs, so we have developed a new DTD using the modularization scheme of RuleML, extending the Datalog with strong negation DTD.

Superiority relations are represented as attributes of the superior rule. For example, the following rule r5 is superior to rule r4 that has been presented above.

```
(defeasiblerule r5
   (declare (superior r4))
   (penguin (name ?X))
 =>
   (not (flies (name ?X))))
```

In RuleML notation, there is a `superiority` attribute in the rule label.

```
<imp>
   <_rlab superior="r4"><ind type="defeasiblerule">r5</ind></_rlab>
...
</imp>
```

Classes and objects (facts) can also be declared in DR-DEVICE; however, the focus in this paper is the use of RDF data as facts. The input RDF file(s) are declared in the `rdf_import` attribute of the `rulebase` (root) element of the RuleML document. There exist two more attributes in the `rulebase` element: the `rdf_export` attribute that declares the address of the RDF file with the results of the rule program to be exported, and the `rdf_export_classes` attribute that declares the derived classes whose instances will be exported in RDF/XML format. Further extensions to the RuleML syntax, include function calls that are used either as constraints in the rule body or as new value calculators at the rule head. Furthermore, multiple constraints in the rule body can be expressed through the logical operators: _not, _and, _or. Examples of all these can be found in the next section (Fig. 5, Fig. 6).

5.1 Translating Defeasible Rules

The translation of defeasible rules into R-DEVICE rules is based on the translation of defeasible theories into logic programs through a meta-program ([31]). We use the meta-program to guide defeasible rule compilation. Each *defeasible rule* in DR-DEVICE is translated into a set of 5 R-DEVICE rules:

- A *deductive* rule that generates the derived defeasible object when the condition of the defeasible rule is met.
- An aggregate attribute "*support*" rule that stores the rule ids of the rules that can potentially prove positively or negatively the object.
- A derived attribute "*overruled*" rule that stores the rule id of the rule that has overruled the positive or the negative proof of the defeasible object, if the rule condition has been at least defeasibly proven, and if the rule has not been defeated by a superior rule.
- A derived attribute "*defeasibly*" rule that defeasibly proves either positively or negatively an object, if the rule condition has been at least defeasibly proven, if the opposite conclusion has not been definitely proven and if the rule has not been overruled by another rule.
- A derived attribute "*defeated*" rule that stores the rule id of the rule that has defeated overriding rules when the former is superior to the latter, if the rule condition has been at least defeasibly proven. A "defeated" rule is generated only for rules that have a superiority relation, i.e. they are superior to others.

Strict rules are handled in the same way as defeasible rules, with an addition of a derived attribute rule (called *definitely* rule) that definitely proves either positively or negatively an object, if the condition of the strict rule has been definitely proven, and if the opposite conclusion has not been definitely proven.

Defeaters are much weaker rules that can only overrule a conclusion. Therefore, for a defeater only the "overruled" rule is created, along with a deductive rule to allow the creation of derived objects, even if their proof status cannot be supported by defeaters.

Execution Order. The order of execution of all the above rule types is as follows: "deductive", "support", "definitely", "defeated", "overruled", "defeasibly". Moreover, rule priority for stratified defeasible rule programs is determined by stratification. Finally, for non-stratified rule programs rule execution order is not determined. However, in order to ensure the correct result according to the defeasible logic theory for each derived attribute rule of the rule types "definitely", "defeated", "overruled" and "defeasibly" there is an opposite "truth maintenance" derived attribute rule that undoes (retracts) the conclusion when the condition is no longer met. In this way, even if rules are not executed in the correct order, the correct result will be eventually deduced because conclusions of rules that should have not been executed can be later undone.

DR-DEVICE has been extensively tested using a tool that generates scalable test defeasible logic theories that comes with Deimos, a query answering defeasible logic system [30].

6   Use Case of Defeasible Reasoning Over RDF Data

In this section we present a full example of using DR-DEVICE rules in a brokered trade application that takes place via an independent third party, the broker. The broker matches the buyer's requirements and the sellers' capabilities, and proposes a transaction when both parties can be satisfied by the trade. In our case, the concrete application (which has been adopted from [7]) is apartment renting and the landlord takes the role of the abstract seller.

---

1. *Apartment Requirements*
  - Carlos is looking for an apartment of at least 45m^2 with at least 2 bedrooms.
  - If it is on the 3rd floor or higher, the house must have an elevator.
  - Also, pet animals must be allowed.
2. *Price Requirements*
  - Carlos is willing to pay $300 for a centrally located 45m2 apartment, and $250 for a similar flat in the suburbs.
  - In addition, he is willing to pay an extra $5 per m2 for a larger apartment, and $2 per m2 for a garden.
  - He is unable to pay more than $400 in total.
3. *Preferences*
  - If given the choice, he would go for the cheapest option.
  - His 2nd priority is the presence of a garden.
  - Lowest priority is additional space.

Fig. 2. Verbal description of Carlo's (a potential renter) requirements

```
<!DOCTYPE rdf:RDF [
    ...
    <!ENTITY carlo "http://.../dr-device/carlo/carlo.rdf#">
]>
<rdf:RDF
    ...
    xmlns:carlo="&carlo;">

    <carlo:apartment rdf:about="&carlo;a1">
        <carlo:bedrooms rdf:datatype="&xsd;integer">1</carlo:bedrooms>
        <carlo:central>yes</carlo:central>
        <carlo:floor rdf:datatype="&xsd;integer">1</carlo:floor>
        <carlo:gardenSize rdf:datatype="&xsd;integer">0</carlo:gardenSize>
        <carlo:lift>no</carlo:lift>
        <carlo:name>a1</carlo:name>
        <carlo:pets>yes</carlo:pets>
        <carlo:price rdf:datatype="&xsd;integer">300</carlo:price>
        <carlo:size rdf:datatype="&xsd;integer">50</carlo:size>
    </carlo:apartment>
    ...
</rdf:RDF>
```

Fig. 3. RDF document for available apartments

Available apartments reside in an RDF document (Fig. 3). The requirements of a potential renter, called e.g. Carlo, are shown in Fig. 2. These requirements are expressed in DR-DEVICE's defeasible logic rule language as shown in Fig. 4 (in native CLIPS-like syntax). Rules r1 and r2 cover some of the first set of requirements in Fig. 2, rules r7 and r9 represent requirements from the second set and rules r10, r11 from the third. Finally, rules cheapest1 and cheapest2 calculate the cheapest of the acceptable apartments. The complexity of the rule `cheapest2` is due to the lack of conflicting literals support in DR-DEVICE.

```
(import-rdf "http://.../dr-device/carlo/carlo.rdf")
(export-rdf "http://.../dr-device/carlo/export-carlo.rdf" acceptable rent)
(defeasiblerule r1
   (carlo:apartment (carlo:name ?x))
 =>
   (acceptable (apartment ?x)))
(defeasiblerule r2
   (declare (superior r1))
   (carlo:apartment (carlo:name ?x) (carlo:bedrooms  ?y&:(< ?y 2)))
 =>
   (not (acceptable (apartment ?x))))
...
(defeasiblerule r7
   (carlo:apartment (carlo:name ?x) (carlo:size ?y&:(>= ?y 45))
                    (carlo:gardenSize ?z) (carlo:central "yes"))
 =>
   (calc (bind ?a (+ 300 (* 2 ?z) (* 5 (- ?y 45)))))
   (offer (apartment ?x) (amount ?a)))
...
(defeasiblerule r9
   (declare (superior r1))
   (offer (apartment ?x) (amount ?y))
   (carlo:apartment (carlo:name ?x) (carlo:price ?z&:(< ?y ?z)))
 =>
   (not (acceptable (apartment ?x))))
(defeasiblerule cheapest1
   (acceptable (apartment ?x))
 =>
   (cheapest (apartment ?x)))
(defeasiblerule cheapest2
   (declare (superior cheapest1))
   (acceptable (apartment ?x))
   (carlo:apartment (carlo:name ?x) (carlo:price ?z))
   (acceptable (apartment ?y&~?x))
   (carlo:apartment (carlo:name ?y) (carlo:price ?w&:(< ?w ?z)))
 =>
   (not (cheapest (apartment ?x))))
...
(defeasiblerule r10
   (cheapest (apartment ?x))
 =>
   (rent (apartment ?x)))
(defeasiblerule r11
   (declare (superior r10))
   (cheapest (apartment ?x))
   (not (largestGarden (apartment ?x)))
   (cheapest (apartment ?y&~?x))
   (largestGarden (apartment ?y))
 =>
   (not (rent (apartment ?x))))
...
```

Fig. 4. Part of Carlo's requirements in native (CLIPS-like) DR-DEVICE syntax

Rules `r2` and `r7` are shown in Fig. 5 in the RuleML-like syntax of DR-DEVICE. Things to notice here is the expression of the superiority relation as an attribute of the rule label, the expression of complex constraints on the value of a slot based on functions calls and logical operators, and the calculation of the values of the slots in the rule head, through again the use of function calls. Currently, function calls are expressed as unparsed strings, directly in CLIPS-like notation. One of our future goals is to express such function calls directly in RuleML notation, should the initiative support functions.

```
<!DOCTYPE rulebase SYSTEM "http://.../dr-device/defeasible.dtd" [
  <!ENTITY carlo "http://.../dr-device/carlo/carlo.rdf#">
  <!ENTITY carlo_rb "http://.../dr-device/carlo/carlo-rbase.ruleml#">
]>
<rulebase xmlns:carlo_rb="&carlo_rb;" xmlns:carlo="&carlo;"
          rdf_import="&carlo;" rdf_export_classes="acceptable rent"
          rdf_export="http://.../dr-device/carlo/export-carlo.rdf">
  <_rbaselab>
    <ind type="defeasible" href="&carlo_rb;">carlo-rules</ind>
  </_rbaselab>
  ...
  <imp>
    <_rlab superior="r1">
      <ind type="defeasiblerule" href="&carlo_rb;r2">r2</ind>
    </_rlab>
    <_head>
      <neg>
        <atom>  <_opr><rel>acceptable</rel></_opr>
                <_slot name="apartment"><var>x</var></_slot>
        </atom>
      </neg>
    </_head>
    <_body>
      <atom>  <_opr><rel href="carlo:apartment"/></_opr>
              <_slot name="carlo:name"><var>x</var></_slot>
              <_slot name="carlo:bedrooms">
                <_and>
                  <var>y</var>
                  <function_call>(&lt; ?y 2)</function_call>
                </_and>
              </_slot>
      </atom>
    </_body>
  </imp>
  ...
  <imp>
    <_rlab><ind type="defeasiblerule" href="&carlo_rb;r7">r7</ind></_rlab>
    <_head calculations="(bind ?a (+ 300 (* 2 ?z) (* 5 (- ?y 45))))">
      <atom>  <_opr><rel>offer</rel></_opr>
              <_slot name="apartment"><var>x</var></_slot>
              <_slot name="amount"><var>a</var></_slot>
      </atom>
    </_head>
    <_body>
      <atom>
        <_opr><rel href="carlo:apartment"/></_opr>
        <_slot name="carlo:name"><var>x</var></_slot>
        <_slot name="carlo:size">
          <_and><var>y</var><function_call>(>= ?y 45)</function_call></_and>
        </_slot>
        <_slot name="carlo:gardenSize"><var>z</var></_slot>
        <_slot name="carlo:central"><ind>"yes"</ind></_slot>
      </atom>
    </_body>
  </imp>
  ...
</rulebase>
```

Fig. 5. Part of Carlo's requirements in RuleML-like DR-DEVICE syntax

After the rule document in Fig. 5 is loaded into DR-DEVICE, it is transformed into the native DR-DEVICE syntax (Fig. 4). DR-DEVICE rules are further translated into R-DEVICE rules, as presented in the previous section, which in turn are translated into CLIPS production rules. Then the RDF document(s) of Fig. 3 is loaded and transformed into CLIPS (COOL) objects. Finally, the reasoning can begin, which ends up with 3 acceptable apartments and one suggested apartment for renting, according to Carlo's requirements and the available apartments [7]. The results (i.e. objects of derived classes) are exported in an RDF file according to the specifications posed in the RuleML document (Fig. 5). Fig. 6 shows an example of the result exported for class `acceptable` (acceptable or not apartments) and class `rent` (suggestions to rent a house or not). Notice that both the positively and negatively proven (defeasibly or definitely) objects are exported. Objects that cannot be at least defeasibly proven, either negatively or positively, are not exported, although they exist inside DR-DEVICE. Furthermore, the RDF schema of the derived classes is also exported.

```xml
<!DOCTYPE rdf:RDF [
    ...
    <!ENTITY dr-device "http://.../dr-device/export/export-carlo.rdf#">
]>
<rdf:RDF
    ...
    xmlns:dr-device='&dr-device;'>
    <rdfs:Class rdf:about='&dr-device;DefeasibleObject'/>
    <rdfs:Class rdf:about='&dr-device;acceptable'>
        <rdfs:subClassOf rdf:resource='&dr-device;DefeasibleObject'/>
    </rdfs:Class>
    <rdfs:Class rdf:about='&dr-device;rent'>
        <rdfs:subClassOf rdf:resource='&dr-device;DefeasibleObject'/>
    </rdfs:Class>
    <rdf:Property rdf:about='&dr-device;truthStatus'>
        <rdfs:domain rdf:resource='&dr-device;DefeasibleObject'/>
        <rdfs:range  rdf:resource='rdfs:Literal'/>
    </rdf:Property>
    <rdf:Property rdf:about='&dr-device;apartment'>
        <rdfs:domain rdf:resource='&dr-device;acceptable'/>
        <rdfs:range  rdf:resource='rdfs:Literal'/>
    </rdf:Property>
    <rdf:Property rdf:about='&dr-device;apartment'>
        <rdfs:domain rdf:resource='&dr-device;rent'/>
        <rdfs:range  rdf:resource='rdfs:Literal'/>
    </rdf:Property>
...
    <dr-device:acceptable rdf:about="&dr-device;acceptable2">
        <dr-device:apartment>a2</dr-device:apartment>
        <dr-device:truthStatus>defeasibly-not-proven</dr-device:truthStatus>
    </dr-device:acceptable>
...
    <dr-device:acceptable rdf:about="&dr-device;acceptable5">
        <dr-device:apartment>a5</dr-device:apartment>
        <dr-device:truthStatus>defeasibly-proven</dr-device:truthStatus>
    </dr-device:acceptable>
...
    <dr-device:rent rdf:about="&dr-device;rent1">
        <dr-device:apartment>a5</dr-device:apartment>
        <dr-device:truthStatus>defeasibly-proven</dr-device:truthStatus>
    </dr-device:rent>
...
</rdf:RDF>
```

Fig. 6. Results of defeasible reasoning exported as an RDF document

7   Related Work

There exist several previous implementations of defeasible logics. In [19] the historically first implementation, D-Prolog, a Prolog-based implementation is given. It was not declarative in certain aspects (because it did not use a declarative semantic for the not operator), therefore it did not correspond fully to the abstract definition of the logic. Finally it did not provide any means of integration with Semantic Web layers and concepts.

Deimos [30] is a flexible, query processing system based on Haskell. It does not integrate with Semantic Web (for example, there is no way to treat RDF data; nor does it use an XML-based or RDF-based syntax). Thus it is an isolated solution.

Delores [30] is another implementation, which computes all conclusions from a defeasible theory (the only system of its kind known to us). It is very efficient, exhibiting linear computational complexity. However, it does not integrate with other Semantic Web languages and systems.

Another Prolog-based implementation of defeasible logics is in [3], which places emphasis on completeness (covering full defeasible logic) and flexibility (covering all important variants). However, at present it lacks the ability of processing RDF data.

SweetJess [25] is another implementation of a defeasible reasoning system (situated courteous logic programs) based on Jess. It integrates well with RuleML. However, SweetJess rules can only express reasoning over ontologies expressed in DAMLRuleML (a DAML-OIL like syntax of RuleML) and not on arbitrary RDF data, like DR-DEVICE. Furthermore, SweetJess is restricted to simple terms (variables and atoms). This applies to DR-DEVICE to a large extent. However, the basic R-DEVICE language [10] can support a limited form of functions in the following sense: (a) path expressions are allowed in the rule condition, which can be seen as complex functions, where allowed function names are object referencing slots; (b) aggregate and sorting functions are allowed in the conclusion of aggregate rules. Finally, DR-DEVICE can also support conclusions in non-stratified rule programs due to the presence of truth-maintenance rules (section 5.1).

8   Conclusions and Future Work

In this paper we described reasons why conflicts among rules arise naturally on the Semantic Web. To address this problem, we proposed to use defeasible reasoning which is known from the area of knowledge representation. And we reported on the implementation of a system for defeasible reasoning on the Web. It is based on CLIPS production rules, and supports RuleML syntax.

Planned future work includes:

- Adding arithmetic capabilities to the rule language and using appropriate constraint solvers in conjunction with logic programs.
- Implementing load/upload functionality in conjunction with an RDF repository, such as RDF Suite [1] and Sesame [16].
- Study in more detail integration of defeasible reasoning with description logic based ontologies. Starting point of this investigation will be the Horn definable part of OWL [26].
- Applications of defeasible reasoning and the developed implementation for brokering, bargaining, automated agent negotiation, and personalization.

References

[1] Alexaki S., Christophides V., Karvounarakis G., Plexousakis D. and Tolle K., "The ICS-FORTH RDFSuite: Managing Voluminous RDF Description Bases", *Proc. 2nd Int. Workshop on the Semantic Web*, Hong-Kong, 2001.

[2] Antoniou G. and Arief M., "Executable Declarative Business rules and their use in Electronic Commerce", *Proc. ACM Symposium on Applied Computing*, 2002.

[3] Antoniou G., Bikakis A., "A System for Nonmonotonic Rules on the Web", *Submitted*, 2004.

[4] Antoniou G., "Nonmonotonic Rule Systems on Top of Ontology Layers", *Proc. 1st Int. Semantic Web Conference*, Springer, LNCS 2342, pp. 394-398, 2002.

[5] Antoniou G., Billington D. and Maher M.J., "On the analysis of regulations using defeasible rules", *Proc. 32nd Hawaii International Conference on Systems Science*, 1999.

[6] Antoniou G., Billington D., Governatori G. and Maher M.J., "Representation results for defeasible logic", *ACM Trans. on Computational Logic*, 2(2), 2001, pp. 255-287.

[7] Antoniou G., Harmelen F. van, *A Semantic Web Primer*, MIT Press, 2004 (*to appear*).

[8] Antoniou G., Maher M. J., Billington D., "Defeasible Logic versus Logic Programming without Negation as Failure", *Journal of Logic Programming*, 41(1), 2000, pp. 45-57.

[9] Ashri R., Payne T., Marvin D., Surridge M. and Taylor S., "Towards a Semantic Web Security Infrastructure", *Proc. of Semantic Web Services*, 2004 Spring Symposium Series, Stanford University, California, 2004.

[10] Bassiliades N., Vlahavas I., "Capturing RDF Descriptive Semantics in an Object Oriented Knowledge Base System", *Proc. 12th Int. WWW Conf. (WWW2003)*, Budapest, 2003.

[11] Bassiliades N., Vlahavas I., "R-DEVICE: An Object-Oriented Knowledge Base System for RDF Metadata", *Technical Report TR-LPIS-141-03*, LPIS Group, Dept. of Informatics, Aristotle University of Thessaloniki, Greece, 2003.

[12] Bassiliades N., Vlahavas I., Elmagarmid A.K., "E-DEVICE: An extensible active knowledge base system with multiple rule type support", *IEEE TKDE*, 12(5), pp. 824-844, 2000.

[13] Bassiliades N., Vlahavas I., and Sampson D., "Using Logic for Querying XML Data", *Web-Powered Databases*, Ch. 1, pp. 1-35, Idea-Group Publishing, 2003.

[14] Berners-Lee T., Hendler J., and Lassila O., "The Semantic Web", *Scientific American*, 284(5), 2001, pp. 34-43.

[15] Boley H., Tabet S., *The Rule Markup Initiative*, www.ruleml.org/

[16] Broekstra J., Kampman A. and Harmelen F. van, "Sesame: An Architecture for Storing and Querying RDF Data and Schema Information", *Spinning the Semantic Web*, Fensel D., Hendler J. A., Lieberman H. and Wahlster W., (Eds.), MIT Press, pp. 197-222, 2003.

[17] *CLIPS Basic Programming Guide* (v. 6.21), www.ghg.net/clips/CLIPS.html

[18] Connolly D., Harmelen F. van, Horrocks I., McGuinness D.L., Patel-Schneider P.F., Stein L.A., DAML+OIL Reference Description, 2001, www.w3.org/TR/daml+oil-reference

[19] Covington M.A., Nute D., Vellino A., *Prolog Programming in Depth*, 2nd ed., Prentice-Hall, 1997.

[20] Dean M. and Schreiber G., (Eds.), OWL Web Ontology Language Reference, 2004, www.w3.org/TR/2004/REC-owl-ref-20040210/

[21] Gelder A. van, Ross K. and Schlipf J., "The well-founded semantics for general logic programs", *Journal of the ACM*, Vol. 38, 1991, pp. 620-650.

[22] Governatori G., Dumas M., Hofstede A. ter and Oaks P., "A formal approach to legal negotiation", *Proc. ICAIL 2001*, pp. 168-177, 2001.

[23] Grosof B. N. and Poon T. C., "SweetDeal: representing agent contracts with exceptions using XML rules, ontologies, and process descriptions", *Proc. 12th Int. Conf. on World Wide Web.*, ACM Press, pp. 340-349, 2003.

[24] Grosof B. N., "Prioritized conflict handing for logic programs", *Proc. of the 1997 Int. Symposium on Logic Programming*, pp. 197-211, 1997.

[25] Grosof B.N., Gandhe M.D., Finin T.W., "SweetJess: Translating DAMLRuleML to JESS", *Proc. Int. Workshop on Rule Markup Languages for Business Rules on the Semantic Web (RuleML 2002)*.

[26] Grosof B. N., Horrocks I., Volz R. and Decker S., "Description Logic Programs: Combining Logic Programs with Description Logic", *Proc. 12th Intl. Conf. on the World Wide Web (WWW-2003)*, ACM Press, 2003, pp. 48-57.

[27] Hayes P., "RDF Semantics", *W3C Recommendation*, Feb. 2004, www.w3.org/TR/rdf-mt/

[28] Levy A. and Rousset M.-C., "Combining Horn rules and description logics in CARIN", *Artificial Intelligence*, Vol. 104, No. 1-2, 1998, pp. 165-209.

[29] Li N., Grosof B. N. and Feigenbaum J.,"Delegation Logic: A Logic-based Approach to Distributed Authorization", *ACM Trans. on Information Systems Security*, 6(1), 2003.

[30] Maher M.J., Rock A., Antoniou G., Billington D., Miller T., "Efficient Defeasible Reasoning Systems", *Int. Journal of Tools with Artificial Intelligence*, 10(4), 2001, pp. 483-501.

[31] Maher M.J, Governatori G., "A Semantic Decomposition of Defeasible Logics", *Proc. AAAI-99*, Orlando, USA, AAAI/MIT Press, 1999, pp. 299-305.

[32] Maher M.J., "A Model-Theoretic Semantics for Defeasible Logic", *Proc. Workshop on Paraconsistent Computational Logic*, pp. 67-80, 2002.

[33] Marek V.W., Truszczynski M., *Nonmonotonic Logics; Context Dependent Reasoning*, Springer-Verlag, 1993.

[34] McBride B., "Jena: Implementing the RDF Model and Syntax Specification", *Proc. 2nd Int. Workshop on the Semantic Web*, 2001.

[35] Nute D., "Defeasible logic", *Handbook of logic in artificial intelligence and logic programming (vol. 3): nonmonotonic reasoning and uncertain reasoning*, Oxford University Press, 1994.

[36] Seaborne A., and Reggiori A., "RDF Query and Rule languages Use Cases and Examples survey", rdfstore.sourceforge.net/2002/06/24/rdf-query/

[37] *Xalan-Java XSLT processor*, xml.apache.org/xalan-j/

A PDDL Based Tool
for Automatic Web Service Composition

Joachim Peer

Institute for Media and Communications Management
University of St. Gallen, Switzerland

Abstract. One of the motivations for research in semantic web services is to automatically compose web service operations to solve given problems. The idea of using AI planning software to this end has been suggested by several papers. The present paper follows this approach but argues that the diversity of the web service domains is best addressed by a flexible combination of complementary reasoning techniques and planning systems. We present a tool that transforms web service composition problems into AI planning problems and delegates them to the planners most suitable for the particular planning task. The tool uses PDDL, a language supported by a wide range of planning engines, as a transfer format. The present paper describes the tool and its strategies to cope with the problems of incomplete information, various types of web service indeterminism, stateful services and structurally rich goal specifications.

1   Introduction

Web services are a family of distributed software components that can be exposed and invoked over the internet. Commonly, the Web Service Description Language WSDL [1] is used to describe the syntactical interface of a web service and XML based message streams are used to communicate with web services.

Research in *semantic* web services aims to develop methods to explicitly describe the semantic and pragmatic aspects of web services, in addition to the syntactical descriptions provided by WSDL. These additional descriptions should permit the use of computers to reason about the published services. Ultimately, users should be able to describe their needs or goals in a convenient fashion, and software programs should be able to perform the often tedious tasks of identifying and correctly combining web services to achieve the goals specified.

The aim of the work presented in this paper is to provide a practical method of breaking down complex web service composition scenarios to tasks manageable by existing AI planning tools. It does so by decoupling the different concerns like goal description, planning and plan execution from particular planning technologies and implementations, gaining flexibility required to solve a diverse set of web service composition problems.

The paper is organized as follows: First, existing work on the application of planning technology to automatic service composition is discussed and the contribution of the paper is sketched. Thereafter, we give an overview of our

H.J. Ohlbach and S. Schaffert (Eds.): PPSWR 2004, LNCS 3208, pp. 149–163, 2004.
© Springer-Verlag Berlin Heidelberg 2004

tool "WSPlan". In Sect. 3, WSPlan's service markup schema is described. In Sect. 4, we describe WSPlan's planning and execution strategies. In Sect. 5 the implementation, architecture and a user interface of the tool are presented. The paper is concluded by a brief example and a discussion of current limitations and future work.

2   Related Work and Contribution

In the recent years, a number of researchers have been investigating the application of symbolic reasoning and AI planning to the web service composition problem. In a review of existing work, Koehler and Strivastava [2] argue that the ability to deal with complex plans is essential to web service composition, because many of those tasks require conditional selection, iteration and parallel executions of services.

Some of the work presented so far fulfil these properties: in [3], the planning tasks are carried out on top of a GOLOG program which acts as a plan template and may exhibit a rich structure including selection, iteration and parallel execution. In [4], rich plan structures are provided by the specification of HTN (Hierarchical Task Network) methods, which allow to describe selections and iterations. However, the problem of [3] is that the GOLOG programs are difficult to create, hampering the adoption of the technology and the scalability of the underlying calculus is to be questioned. One of the problems with [4] is the lack of parallel execution, a feature frequently needed for efficient web service usage.

In general, it seems not feasible to develop one monolithic (AI-) planning solution that fits *all* the possible requirements of web service composition. Instead, we argue that it is more fruitful to create a flexible non-monolithic framework, which allows to plug in those planners that are best suited for certain planning domains and tasks; this is essential for addressing changing or new requirements of the users. For instance, if resource optimization is required, one could plug in Metric-FF [5] planner; if planning with typed variables and lifted actions are required, one could plug in VHPOP [6]; if durative actions are required, one could plug in LGP [7] (among others).

To our best knowledge, no such integrating framework has been presented to date. However, an important pre-requisite for such a tool does already exist: PDDL, the "Planning Domain Definition Language" [8], is a widely accepted language for expressing planning problems and domains. It allows to describe the technical and epistemological requirements of planning domains and the capabilities of planners in a uniform way. This enables us to effortlessly select the best suited planner for a particular composition task.

3   Semantic Markup

WSDL describes the syntactical interface of a service but it does not capture its semantics, such as preconditions and effects. Hence, pure WSDL based service descriptions can not be used for automatic web service composition; semantic annotation is required. To this end, we introduce a lightweight service description format that enables us to describe the intended semantics of a service. An alternative description format would have been OWL-S, which was not chosen for several reasons: Its current syntax would have led to much larger and less readable descriptions, especially if logical formulae with variables were to be expressed. Furthermore, the incorporation of rule languages to express those logical formulae (e.g. SWRL) into OWL-S is in its early stages yet.

Figure 1 shows relevant parts of the conceptual models of WSDL (on the left side) and PDDL (on the right side) and visualizes how our annotation format (in the middle) is used as a bridge between these two worlds.

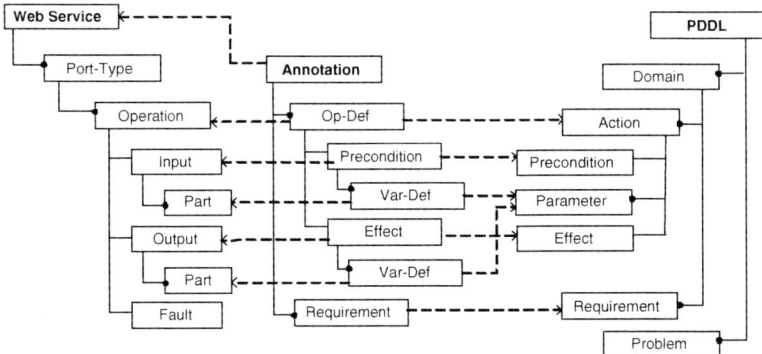

Fig. 1. How annotations connect WSDL and PDDL

Each box in the illustration represents an element of the WSDL 1.2 model, WSPlan's annotation model or the PDDL model, respectively. The solid lines represent concept associations and the dashed lines represent the semantic associations captured by our service annotation concept. In the following paragraphs, this annotation concept is described in greater detail.

3.1   Marking Up Services

Web services are annotated by `service-annotation` elements. The XML fragment below shows the root element of a service annotation, which uses the web service's target namespace and name to uniquely identify the service to be annotated.

```
<service-annotation serviceNamespace="http://my.com/ws" name="MyService">
          <!-- op-def's and var-def's -->
</service-annotation>
```

3.2   Marking Up Operations

Each service operation that should be made available to semantic web agents needs to be marked up, using an `<op-def>` element, referring to the operation's name and its WSDL port-type:

```
<op-def name="register" portType="ShirtService">
```

To describe the preconditions and effects of the service, the elements `<precon dition>`, `<input>`, `<effect>` and `<output>` are provided. Syntax and semantics of these constructs are borrowed from PDDL:

- a precondition is a function free first order logical sentence[1] which must be satisfied in order to meaningfully invoke the specified operation. If a precondition is not fulfilled and an operation is still called, the results are undefined.
- an input is a special kind of precondition. It constrains the objects to be sent to the service.
- an effect is a function free first order logical sentence which may be universally quantified[2]. An agent that calls an operation with a valid precondition may expect that the effect formula will evaluate to true in the world state after the operation is executed, as long as no success condition exists and as long as no error occurs. Both of the latter two cases are discussed in Sect. 3.4.
- an output is used to mark operations that provide information gathering ("sensing") functionality. An output is a special kind of effect; it may return information items but it does not affect the world state when invoked. This concept is similar to the notion of *sensory effects* [9], *learnable terms* [10] or *observations* in NPDDL [11]; however, in WSPlan the output as a whole is assumed learnable; fine grained markup on the level of single terms is not supported by WSPlan.

The predicates and constants used by the formulas may be qualified by namespace prefixes. This is needed to connect the predicates and constants to semantic web ontologies. However, WSPlan does not process ontological information yet (c.f. Sect. 7.2). If no prefix is given, the empty namespace is assumed.

It should also be noted that the truth value of the sentences is generally determined using the closed world assumption (CWA), i.e. formulae that are not true with respect to the agent's knowledge base are considered false. The CWA is partially imposed by the planning systems employed, but a critical review of alternatives justifies our use of CWA: An alternative concept would be the open world assumption, which is problematic because of the problems of sensor abuse and universally quantified knowledge effects [9]. Yet an other alternative would be the use of Local Closed World knowledge (LCW), which differs from CWA by managing an additional database that contains logical formulae which allow the agent to reason about its own knowledge [9]. The main benefit of LCW is that it reduces the problem of excessive sensing. However, this can also be achieved by alternative means; to make use of unknown information, we have to interleave sensing and planning and to update the (closed) world knowledge accordingly

---

[1] The absence of functions helps reducing the intractability problems of pure first order logic.
[2] The absence of existential quantifiers further reduces the computational complexity of the descriptions.

(c.f. Sect. 4). Sensing without sensor abuse can be achieved by keeping book of calls to information gathering operations and filtering out redundant calls.

An illustration of an input (i.e. special class of precondition) and an output (i.e. special class of effect) is shown below. The meaning of the expression on the left side below is "there must exist an object `firstname` in the agent's fact base that has a `personal-data` relation with some other object". In case a fact (`personal-data firstname Susan`) exists in the agent's knowledge base, the input can be constructed.

```
<input>                          <output>
  (personal-data firstname         (forall (?s)
              ?firstname)            (and (in-stock ?s)
</input>                               (property ?s color
                                               ?color)))
                                 </output>
```

An example of an output is given above, on the right side. In outputs, the semantics of the `forall` operator gets an additional – operational – semantics (c.f. Sect. 4) that may be interpreted as an imperative *for each* statement. In the example above, the `forall` clause tells WSPlan that *for each* information piece ?s that may be retrieved, an instance of the conjunction (`and (in-stock ?s) (property ?s color ?color)`) can be obtained and then be added to the knowledge base. The method required to connect variable symbols to concrete pieces of web service inputs and outputs is described in the next section.

3.3   Grounding the Variables

To specify the syntax of the data pieces represented by the variable symbols, an element `var-def` is provided:

```
<var-def var="?username" message="registerResponse"
        part="registerReturn" path="/UserCredentials/login" />
```

The attribute "var" refers to the name of the variable to be described, the attributes "message" and "part" refer to the WSDL message and message part the variable is associated to and the optional attribute "path" may contain an XPATH expression specifying the location of the information piece within the XML structure of the message. This information is needed by WSPlan for properly constructing outgoing messages when invoking the service and for properly interpreting incoming XML messages.

3.4   Describing Indeterministic Results

Currently, WSPlan handles several types of indeterminism (c.f. Sect. 4.2). One type of indeterminism that requires additional markup are conditions on outputs and effects. These conditions are defined by an element "success-condition" inside an effect or output element to be constrained:

```
<success-condition>(eval-JSTL "?result == 'yes'")</success-condition>
```

For developer's convenience, a success-condition can also be written as an attribute of outputs and effects instead as a sub-element. Further, we provide a predicate `eval-JSTL` which evaluates JSTL expressions. JSTL [12] is an expression language inspired by ECMAScript and XPath. It provides support for expressions built of arithmetic, logical and relational operators; it also permits access to software components, a feature that can be used to access an agent's fact base.

It should be distinguished between the concept of success conditions introduced by this paper and the concept of *conditional effects* (also called secondary preconditions) as defined by PDDL: a conditional effect (`when P E`) means that if condition P is true prior to service execution, then E occurs after the action is executed. In contrast, a *success-condition* does not need to be true *before* service execution, but it must be true *after* service execution, to allow the effect to occur.

A single success-condition markup can be used to distinguish between one desired effect and any number of undesired effects (e.g. error messages, out-of-stock notifications). Note that actions that have several different indeterministic but potentially desirable outcomes can not be captured by a single success-condition markup. This can be achieved by defining multiple markups for one operation (each markup specifying a desirable effect).

4   Planning and Execution

WSPlan transforms web service annotation data and information from the agent's knowledge base to PDDL documents. A planner capable of processing PDDL that fits the requirements imposed by the particular domain definitions may process those documents and eventually identify a plan. The resulting plan can be transformed into a flow of web service operations to be invoked. In the following, we will describe the interplay between WSPlan, the AI planners employed and the web services involved in more detail.

4.1   Interleaving Sensing and Planning

One of the challenges of automatic planning is the problem of partial observability of state; a discussion of this problem in the context of automatic web service composition can be found in [13]. The problem refers to the fact that a lack of information impairs an agent's ability to make informed planning decisions.

Therefore, the agent must be given an opportunity to acquire facts about the domain it wants to reason about. The planner must be able to interleave planning and execution [9], i.e. to gather some information, then plan, then gather some additional information and so forth.

Given the size of the web, it will be necessary to constrain this endeavor, i.e. it will be necessary to make sure that the information acquired has at least the *potential* to contribute to the solution of the planning problem (e.g. by closing an open condition). WSPlan achieves this by *relaxing* the output defined: success conditions are ignored and variables do not need to be bound during planning.

```
                                        PDDL:
<output                                 :parameters(?stock)
   success-condition="(eval 'answ=yes')"> ==> :effect(canTrade
   (canTrade broker.com ?stock)                 broker_dot_com
</output>                                        ?stock)
```

The intended semantics of the annotation is: "if the answer is yes, then the relation (`canTrade broker.com ?stock`) holds", where `?stock` is a variable to be defined. The semantics of the relaxed formula however is "this operation will achieve that the formula (`canTrade broker.com ?stock`) is true for all instantiations of `?stock`". This semantic discrepancy will lead the planner to include the action into its plan automatically, if it has unachieved goals that directly or indirectly depend on `canTrade` formulas with unifiable variable bindings. This way, the planner automatically identifies potentially useful information gathering operations and integrates them into its plan.

Based on this heuristic, a replanning strategy has been devised, inspired by on-line planning methods such as agent-centered search [14]. On-line planning methods interleave planning and plan execution, allowing agents to gather information, which reduces the amount of planning performed for unencountered situations and thus allows agents to plan efficiently, even if no complete information is given initially.

The implementation by WSPlan is based on *sensing sub-plans*. A sensing sub-plan is any subset of the steps of a plan that exclusively consists of information retrieval actions. As Fig. 2 illustrates, a sensing sub-plan is extracted from a plan and then executed, which may lead to knowledge acquisition. Equipped with new data, the agent replans from the scratch and generates a new plan. This process continues until either an executable plan is found or no new data can be acquired anymore. The planning process shown in Fig. 2 terminates successfully, i.e. a plan is found that may achieve the goal.

An advantage of this method is that replanning from the scratch in presence of new information often leads to more efficient and shorter plans. Another advantage is that this method can be managed by the external planning and execution framework (WSPlan). Hence, *any* planner capable of solving a problem captured by the given PDDL subset can be used for interleaved planning and execution using the strategy discussed.

A potential disadvantage of this approach is the computational overhead caused by replanning (since domain parsing, construction of data structures for heuristics and other initialization steps have to be repeated at each cycle), but the preliminary tests carried of so far suggest that this overhead is insignificant, especially when compared to the latency of web service calls.

4.2   Dealing with Indeterminism

The two types of indeterminism WSPlan is currently able to handle are opaque decisions and exceptions. To properly handle *opaque decisions*, we introduced the "success condition" markup described in Sect. 3. This information is used to test during service execution time, whether a service call has achieved the

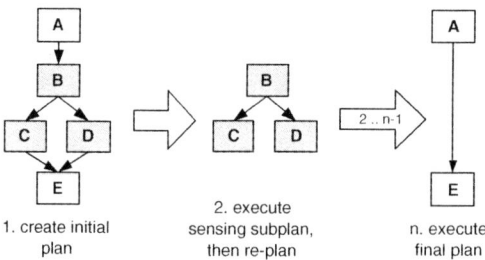

Fig. 2. Sub-plan extraction and replanning

desired effect or failed to do so. In the latter case, WSPlan's service execution component throws an exception, that may be caught by the calling software component, which may have anticipated the possibility of the unwanted result and may provide a fallback solution for that case.

Exceptions may occur at any point of the service execution, even if a fully deterministic method is called. Exceptions may be generated by web services that communicate errors by sending a SOAP message containing the special message part "fault", but they might also come from the underlying network stack or operating system. WSPlan recognizes exceptions, interrupts the execution and signals the exception to the component which had invoked the execution. Similar to success conditions, WSPlan delegates the ultimate responsibility to handle this event to the calling software component which might implement strategies to handle specific types of exceptions (e.g. to retry in case of temporary network problems, or to start replanning in case of permanent or unexplained errors).

4.3   Dealing with Stateful Services

Web services are often stateful, i.e. their operations may behave differently depending on the interactions that have taken place beforehand. Services that depend on a concept of (logical) user sessions, offering login functions or virtual shopping carts, are examples of stateful services. The PDDL model provides good support for handling stateful services: All state dependent information can be stored in relations. Relations to store state information can be thought of following a schema `(predicate-name <state -identifyer> <payload>)`; the predicate has two classes of arguments, those that act as keys to identify a certain state (e.g. a service address qualified by a session-id) and those arguments that make up the payload, i.e. the data items to be stored.

An operation that maintains state information simply needs to provide such a relation as part of its effect. Since the truth values of PDDL formulae persist over time, the stored information will be available during consecutive service calls. To delete the state data, e.g. to terminate a session, a service just has to use an effect that negates the session data sent, e.g. `(not (session-id some.com 39483977))`.

4.4   Dealing with Complex Goal Descriptions

In classical AI planning, goals declaratively describe a particular desired world state (e.g. (on block1 block2) in the well known blocks world domain). As noted in Sect. 2, this notion is rather limiting and is not directly applicable to web service composition, which requires the description of more complex goals, using constructs such as selection, iteration and parallel execution.

Therefore, we need to provide a way to embed the planning tasks into more complex goal structures, similarly to [4] and [3], *without* imposing a particular planning method.

Our currently implemented solution is to expose the components of WSPlan via a Java API to allow developers to incorporate the service composition and execution capabilities of WSPlan into software programs. These programs can be interpreted as (arbitrary complex) goal descriptions. The code fragment below illustrates how the API can be used to create a goal description for planning travel arrangements:

```
protected Plan makeTravelArrangements(Map settings)
  throws PlanningException {
  ExecEnvironment env = ExecEnvironment.getInstance();
  int money = env.getIntValue("have-money", 0);
  if(100 < money < 1000) { /* try to book train */
    String goal = "(and (possess ?t) (TrainTicket ?t)"
               + "(property ?t from "+settings.get("from")+")"
               + "(property ?t to "+settings.get("to")+")"
               + "(property ?t when "+seetings.get("date")+"))";
    return PlanningManager.searchPlan(goal);
  } else if(money >= 1000) { /* try to book flight */
    /* similar to block above  */
  } else output("insufficient financial resources");
}
```

While this approach is straightforward to use, it has a disadvantage: an implicit goal description as shown above does not allow for formal methods of plan verification, reachability analysis or deadlock detection. Therefore, we are working on an alternative way of specifying the high level goal, using activity diagrams and automata, but this work is in early stages yet and is not presented in this paper (c.f. Sect. 7.1).

5   Implementation

5.1   System Architecture

The diagram shown in Fig. 3 gives an overview of the pivotal components of the system.

The diagram reflects the main motivation behind WSPlan: to break down web service composition tasks of some calling component into workloads manageable by AI planning tools.

To start a web service composition task, the caller application invokes a component of type PlanningManager, which coordinates the planning and execution

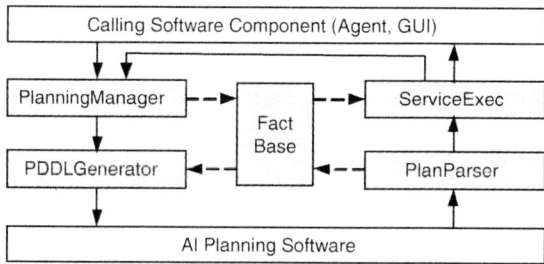

Fig. 3. WSPlan architecture

tasks. The `PlanningManager` will then select the relevant WSDL and annotation files[3], and a PDDL representation of those documents is created by the `PDDLGenerator`. Thereafter, the `PlanningManager` matches the PDDL requirements of the goal and domain description against the available AI planners and determines the most appropriate planning engine and invokes it; the resulting plan (or error message) gets parsed by a `PlanParser` component; depending on the directive of the caller application, the plan may be executed instantly by a `ServiceExec` component, or be forwarded to the caller. In some cases, the `PlanningManager` initiates another round of planning (e.g. to perform sub-plan based replanning). Another central component is the `FactBase`. It serves as information store to hold the user data as well as transactional data received during the process of planning and execution. This data is needed to properly populate outgoing SOAP/XML messages and to evaluate preconditions, conditional effects and success conditions.

5.2   Graphical User Interface

For users who wish to test WSPlan interactively, a GUI has been crafted. Users can define declarative goal descriptions in the text area (top left), and they can access the system's knowledge base (lower left side). After hitting the "find a plan" button, the planning process is started and graphical models of all plans and sub-plans subsequently found are rendered. Users can interactively navigate through these graphical models, which is useful for debugging.

6   A Walk-Through Example

To illustrate how web service composition can be accomplished using AI planners coordinated by WSPlan, two web services published at xmethods.org have been annotated; one service is an e-mail sending gateway that allows clients to send messages over SMTP. Its WSDL file can be retrieved at http://

---

[3] Currently, a predefined list of services is used, no intelligent strategy for pre-selection of possibly relevant web services has been implemented yet.

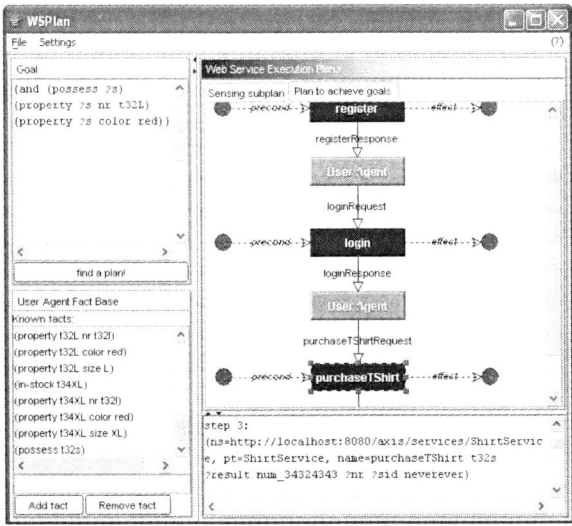

Fig. 4. Graphical User Interface, depicting a plan generated by the tool

webservices.matlus.com/scripts/emailwebservice.dll/wsdl/IEmailService.   This
service offers one operation, `SendMail`, which we annotated as shown below.
Note that the effect has a condition to handle the indeterministic behavior of
the service:

```
<serivce-annotation
serviceNamespace="http://www.borland.com/soapServices/"
name="IEmailServiceservice">
  <op-def name="SendMail" portType="IEmailService">
    <var-def var="?to" message="SendMailRequest" part="ToAddress"/>
    <var-def var="?from" message="SendMailRequest" part="FromAddress"/>
    <var-def var="?subject" message="SendMailRequest" part="ASubject"/>
    <var-def var="?msg" message="SendMailRequest" part="MsgBody"/>
    <var-def var="?result" message="SendMailResponse" part="return"/>
    <input>(have-email ?from)</input>
    <effect success-condition="(eval-JSTL '?result==0')">
      (sent-mail ?to ?subject ?msg)
    </effect>
  </op-def>
</service-annotation>
```

The second service is a geographic information service that offers several
methods to query about geographic entities. Its WSDL file can be found at
http://webservices.instantlogic.com/zipcodes.ils?wsdl. To keep the listing short,
we have annotated only a single method, `ZipCodes`, which takes a U.S. ZIP code
as input and returns information about the referenced location:

```
<service-annotation serviceNamespace="http://www.instantlogic.com/"
name="ZipCodesService">
```

```
<op-def name="ZipCodes" portType="ZipCodesSoap">
  <var-def var="?zip" message="ZipCodesSoapIn" part="Zip"/>
  <var-def var="?city" message="ZipCodesSoapOut" part="CITY" />
  <var-def var="?state" message="ZipCodesSoapOut" part="STATE" />
  <output>
    (and(geo-data ?zip city ?city)(geo-data ?zip state ?state))
  </output>
</op-def>
</service-annotation>
```

A goal that may lead to composition of these two services might be "send the name of the city with ZIP code 30313 to the email address john@some.com". This (slightly artificial) goal may be part of a more complex goal and can be formalized as follows:

```
(and  (geo-data 30313 city ?city-name)
      (sent-mail john@some.com info ?city-name))
```

We feed this specification into WSPlan (using the GUI shown in Sect. 4), and start the planning process. WSPlan constructs a PDDL domain and problem description and determines a planner suitable for the planning task. It does so by comparing the PDDL language requirements imposed by the planning problem with the feature sets of the installed planners. When an appropriate AI planner is found, the PDDL data is fed into it and the planning process is started. The result is a plan consisting of the SendMail and ZipCodes operations. Since ZipCodes is an information retrieval action, it gets extracted from the plan as a sensing sub-plan and is executed. The output of that operation, the ground facts (geo-data 30313 city ATLANTA) and (geo-data 30313 state GA) are then added to the fact base. Thereafter, WSPlan starts replanning and again generates PDDL domain and problem definitions which are shown below. Again, an appropriate AI planner is invoked. This time, the resulting plan only consists of the operation SendMail. Finally, the plan gets executed; if the success condition of SendMail is fulfilled, a mail containing the message "ATLANTA" will arrive at the recipient's mailbox (Atlanta, GA is associated to the ZIP code 30313).

```
;;--- automatically generated by WSPlan ---
(define (domain wsplan)
  (:requirements :strips :typing :equality)
  (:predicates
    (sent-mail ?var1 ?var2 ?var3)
    (geo-data ?var1 ?var2 ?var3)
    (have-email ?var1))
  (:action op_1_1_1                          ;; ZipCodes
   :parameters (?city ?zip ?state)
   :effect (and
     (geo-data ?zip city ?city)
     (geo-data ?zip state ?state)))
```

```
(:action op_2_2_2                        ;; SendMail
 :parameters ( ?to ?from ?result ?subject ?msg)
 :precondition (have-email ?from)
 :effect (sent-mail ?to ?subject ?msg))
(:action achieve-goal                    ;; user's goal
 :parameters ( ?city)
 :precondition (and (geo-data num_30313 city ?city)
                    (sent-mail john_at_some_dot_com hello ?city))
:effect (be-satisfied)))
(define (problem generic_problem1)
  (:domain wsplan)
  (:objects sender_at_foo_dot_com city state john_at_some_dot_com
          ATLANTA GA)
  (:init
    (have-email sender_at_foo_dot_com) (geo-data num_30313 city ATLANTA)
    (geo-data num_30313 state GA))
  (:goal (be-satisfied)))
```

Note that WSPlan has to mask URIs, namespaces, numbers and whitespace, because many planners have rather restrictive syntax rules. Furthermore, the user's goal is implemented as precondition to an action `achieve-goal`; this is necessary because many planners do not support variables in goals but they do support variables in preconditions of actions.

7   Limitations and Future Work

7.1   Complex Goals

In Sect. 2 we discussed the importance of structurally rich complex goals that make use of control constructs such as iteration, selection and parallel execution. In our current prototype, these complex goals are defined as imperative programs; while this appears to be a worthwhile approach that can be utilized by developers who are used to imperative programming, we want to provide a solution that is in the middle-ground between fully declarative descriptions as in classical planning and fully imperative descriptions as currently supported by WSPlan. To this end, we aim to construct goal descriptions as UML activity diagrams and to formalize them as finite automata.

7.2   Heterogenous and Conflicting Information

Another limitation of the current implementation is its inability to deal with heterogenous vocabularies. The system assumes homogeneity with respect to the predicates, types and constants used in the domain and problem descriptions. This is far away from reality and is one of the main challenges of the semantic web as a whole. To partially address the issue in WSPlan, we plan to implement a "pre-processing stage" during which WSPlan will analyze the relations between the predicates, types and constants used and will then try to reduce their heterogeneity (e.g. by substituting synonymous terms, resolving inheritance relationships). Furthermore, as the semantic web is an open media, we have to devise a method to identify conflicting information and to resolve such conflicts.

7.3   Security

Other open issues are security and trust. Currently, service annotations are believed to be correct and facts coming from services are – as long as they are compatible to the WSDL message declaration and annotation – asserted to the agent's fact base without questioning. A malicious service annotation could assert arbitrary facts and even negations to delete facts from the fact base that should not be deleted. Therefore, trust networks and possibly a collection of security relevant predicates have to be established.

8   Summary and Conclusion

We presented a tool for automatic web service composition. The tool takes a novel approach by de-coupling the tasks of composition and execution from particular planning technologies. The web service composition problem is expressed by PDDL specifications which are supported by a wide range of planners. This allows us to dynamically chose the best suited planner for a certain task, providing a degree of flexibility that the existing monolithic approaches for web service composition do not deliver.

We also described the semantic service markup used by the system, its architecture, its strategies to cope with various problems of web service composition, and we walked through a brief example problem. We are looking forward to addressing the limitations discussed above and to presenting our tool's application to more demanding settings.

Acknowledgement

The author would like to thank Jana Koehler for the valuable advise and help, Maja Vukovic for the ongoing productive collaboration, and the anonymous reviewers for their valuable inputs. This research has been funded by the European Commission and by the Swiss Federal Office for Education and Science within the 6th Framework Programme project REWERSE number 506779 and by the Swiss National Science Foundation under contract 200021-104009.

References

1. W3C: Web Service Description Language (WSDL) version 1.2 (2002)
2. Srivastava, B., Koehler, J.: Web Service Composition - Current Solutions and Open Problems. In: Proceedings of ICAPS'03 Workshop on Planning for Web Services, June, Trento, Italy. (2003)
3. McIlraith, S., Son, T.: Adapting Golog for composition of semantic web services. In: Proceedings of the Eighth International Conference on Knowledge Representation and Reasoning (KR2002) Toulouse, France, April 2002. (2002)

4. Hendler, J., Wu, D., Sirin, E., Nau, D., Parsia, B.: Automatic web services composition using SHOP2. In: Proceedings of The Second International Semantic Web Conference (ISWC). (2003)
5. Hoffmann, J., Nebel, B.: The FF planning system: Fast plan generation through heuristic search. Journal of Artificial Intelligence Research (JAIR) (2001)
6. Younes, H.L.S., Simmons, R.G.: VHPOP: Versatile Heuristic Partial Order Planner. Journal of Artificial Intelligence Research (2003)
7. Gerevini, A., Saetti, A., Serina, I.: Planning through stochastic local search and temporal action graphs. (to appear in: Journal of Artificial Intelligence Research (JAIR))
8. Ghallab, M., Howe, A., Knoblock, C., McDermott, D., Ram, A., Veloso, M., Weld, D., Wilkins, D.: PDDL—the planning domain definition language. In: AIPS-98 Planning Committee. (1998)
9. Golden, K.: Planning and knowledge representation for softbots (1997)
10. McDermott, D.: Estimated-regression planning for interactions with web services. In: Proc. of the AI Planning Systems Conference 2002. (2002)
11. Bertoli, P., Cimatti, A., Lago, U.D., Pistore, M.: Extending PDDL to nondeterminism, limited sensing and iterative conditional plans. In: ICAPS'03, Workshop on PDDL. (2003)
12. Sun Microsystems: JavaServer pages standard tag library (2003)
13. Carman, M., Serafini, L.: Planning for web services the hard way. In: Symposium on Applications and the Internet Workshops (SAINT'03 Workshops Orlando, Florida). (2003)
14. Koenig, S.: Agent-centered search. Artificial Intelligence Magazine (2001)

Author Index

Lecture Notes in Computer Science

For information about Vols. 1–3075

please contact your bookseller or Springer